Ethics and Economic Theory

This book takes a multi-disciplinary critique of economics' first principles: the fundamental and inter-related structuring assumptions that underlie the neoclassical paradigm. These assumptions, that economic agents are rational, self-interested individuals, continue to influence the teaching of economics, research agendas and policy analyses. The book argues that both the theoretical understanding of the economy and the actual working of real-world market economies diminish the scope for thinking about the relation between ethics, economics and the economy. It highlights how market economies may 'crowd out' ethical behaviour and our evaluation of them elides ethical reflection.

The book calls for a more pluralistic and richer approach to economic theory, one that allows ample room for ethical considerations. It provides insight into understanding human motivations and human flourishing and how a good economy requires reflection on the ethical relations between the self, world and time.

Khalid Mir is Associate Professor at the Department of Economics at Lahore University of Management Sciences (LUMS). He received his PhD from The University of Essex with a focus on child labour. He has an MSc from The London School of Economics and Political Science. His current interests lie in the relation between ethics, economics and the environment.

Routledge Frontiers of Political Economy

For more information about this series, please visit: www.routledge.com/books/series/SE0345

Ethics and Economic Theory

Khalid Mir

Routledge
Taylor & Francis Group

LONDON AND NEW YORK

First published 2019
by Routledge
2 Park Square, Milton Park, Abingdon, Oxon OX14 4RN

and by Routledge
605 Third Avenue, New York, NY 10017

First issued in paperback 2020

Routledge is an imprint of the Taylor & Francis Group, an informa business

British Library Cataloguing-in-Publication Data
A catalogue record for this book is available from the British Library

Library of Congress Cataloging-in-Publication Data
A catalog record for this book has been requested

ISBN 13: 978-0-367-50435-9 (pbk)
ISBN 13: 978-0-815-39514-0 (hbk)

Typeset in Galliard
by Apex CoVantage, LLC

To my mother and father, because . . .

Contents

Acknowledgements

Any book is the result of a number of relationships and since this book in your hands is also about relationships it is important to acknowledge the great debt I owe to a number of people. My department at The Lahore University of Management Sciences (LUMS) has always given me ample room to explore a rather less than conventional approach to economics. In particular, Ali Cheema persuaded me to teach a course in Philosophy and Economics at LUMS many years ago. I am grateful to him (even though I have lingering doubts as to the wisdom of my response). Other colleagues (Turab Hussain, Mozaffar Qizilbash, and Zahid Ali) have provided me with immense encouragement throughout the writing of the book. I have profited greatly from many stimulating discussions with my dear friend and colleague, Daud Dard. I eagerly await the publication of his own book. Sam Fleischacker, Lisa Hill, and Stefano Zamagni were gracious enough to share some of their work with me. I would like to thank my family, Hajirah, Rasheel and Hamza for (hopefully!) overlooking my many hours of absence. I would also like to express tremendous gratitude to my research assistant, Ali Iftikhar, for his diligence and professionalism. Over and above those qualities I have come to value his keen insights and probing questions. But the life of the mind is perhaps one thing and friendship another. So, I would like to thank him for his friendship more than anything else.

Introduction

The neglect of the social is the neglect of the substantive.

(Milbank and Pabst, 2016, p. 69)

The abstract society rests on learnt rules and not on pursuing perceived desirable common objects; and wanting to do good to known people will not achieve the most for the community, [. . .]

(Hayek cited in Gellner, 1989, p. 26)

Ethics and economics

There is nothing new in this book. What merit it does have resides, I think, in its ability to present the views of many great thinkers – past and living – on the question of the relation between ethics and economics.

The need for rethinking the relation between ethics and economic theory arises from the following observation. The modern world is beset by a number of inter-related contradictions, problems and crises. These include financial and economic crises; some would add that there's a general crisis in education (or more specific ones in the humanities and in economic theory); furthermore, there's the prospect of an ecological crisis on the horizon and the idea that there is a crisis of democracy and of work also looms large in contemporary discourse.[1]

Underlying these manifold crises, I argue, is the diminished importance of relationality or the social.[2] The main thesis of this book is a simple one: economic theory and market economies work in tandem to undermine the social: the way in which we relate to other people, the world around us and to nature.

In the following chapters we will look at the various ways in which this comes about. But before proceeding to that analysis I want to elaborate upon the broader historical context within which economic theory and market economies neglect, undermine or distort the social and the ethical.[3] In doing so I will be arguing for a more pluralistic and richer approach to economic theory, one that allows ample room for ethical considerations. This wider understanding of human motivations and human flourishing will point us to the pressing fact that a good economy requires reflection on the ethical relations between the self, world and time.

The end of liberalism?

Economic theory is perhaps best understood as being located within a broader liberal tradition. The meta-crisis alluded to above might then be explained as a consequence of liberalism imploding – with the result that both economic theory and capitalism (market economies) appear in a state of crisis. In this reading, the contradictions of capitalism stem from the more fundamental contradictions of liberalism.

Liberalism – as a theory and set of practices – rests on a certain 'picture'[4] of what it is to be a human being. Central to that picture is a specific anthropology of the individual, one that implies a particular understanding of relationality, freedom, nature and 'the good'. For example, liberalism is usually understood to be inextricably bound to individualism, negative liberty, property and the primacy of the will (or the right over 'the good').

In the context of this book that picture of the liberal individual is important for many different reasons but I'll stress only two for now. Firstly, the 'atomistic', abstract and disembedded picture of the individual means that social, moral or religious considerations (values and norms) are at best irrelevant to the truth of the individual[5]; at worst they are a severe limitation on his full and free development and must, therefore, be opposed or overcome. It follows that we are, at the most profound level, not social, relational or political beings but, instead, the isolated and perhaps slightly heroic, slightly fear-driven Robinson Crusoe type of individuals that populate our economic textbooks.

Closely following on that is a second implication. Since in the liberal order individual choice is paramount there is less of an emphasis on substantive notions of 'the good', positive liberty, or the ends of human action. A non-teleological approach to human behaviour results in a subjective, private notion of 'the good' and, ultimately, to the belief that human nature/identity is, like everything else, a choice, a mere construct. A liberal order in this reckoning is more concerned about political and social arrangements that foster procedural fairness in relation to individual goods than in supporting an overarching, comprehensive and substantive notion of the good life.

But what's wrong with this picture and why should it entail a contradiction or a crisis of liberalism? The short answer is that because we are in essence relational beings this false picture of the liberal individual, and policies built around it, end up 'crowding-out' social life. The contradiction arises, therefore, because a liberal regime undermines the social but is also simultaneously dependent on it for it to be viable.[6]

If we think of sociality as a culture grounded in experience, history and place (Deneen, 2017), an education oriented to transmission and the virtues, and practices that embody substantive notions of 'the good' then we can think of the social as a necessary pre-requisite for the thriving of any system. Without the social we are left, according to Milbank and Pabst (2016) with fearful, greedy, competitive and violent individuals. And no political-economic order can, in the long-run, do well if based on such foundations. A constitution for knaves based on the law and monetary incentives can never be a substitute for culture, education, social relationships, trust, generosity and goodwill.[7]

Both the liberalisms of the right and the left (the market and the state) view the individual in abstract terms, and as governed by abstract, impersonal mechanisms (by markets and/or bureaucracy). And for both, individual choice and the pursuit of individual interests are paramount. But if sociality – gift-giving, sympathy, trust, benevolence and the intermediary institutions and associations that give expression to them – are central to our humanity then liberalism can only be seen as being inimical to our social relationships.

If liberalism is predicated on a number of separations (between ethics and economics, the material and the symbolic, the private and the public, faith and reason)[8] then, it is argued, we're left with a shallow and isolated individual interested only in abstract wealth (or utility) rather than human flourishing and substantive common goods. This liberal subject, shorn of any attachments, associations and any deep-rooted habits or inclinations bar those stemming from his biological reality, is a man without any qualities, someone who has become an amalgamation of the "*purely* animal and the *purely* and arbitrarily artificial" (Milbank and Pabst, 2016, p. 51).[9] Such an individual, far from being genuinely autonomous, is highly susceptible to technical and managerial control.[10]

The end of capitalism?

For some thinkers we are coming to the end of a long and drawn-out historical process in which impersonal rules and abstract reason replaced reciprocity and sociability (Gellner, 1989).[11] In this section, however, I want to ignore the questions framed within that longer-time horizon (which starts with the first stirrings of an agriculture-based civilization) and focus instead on the possible demise of capitalism.[12]

There is now a growing chorus of voices ranged against the idea that the survival of capitalism is somehow inevitable. For some thinkers the system is threatened by a number of inter-related phenomena: low levels of innovation and growth (Gordon, 2012); inequality; erosion of the public realm; corruption and indebtedness (Streeck, 2014a, 2014b).

For others, there are a series of interlocking contradictions of capitalism: the dominance of commodification, private property, exchange values, concentrations of power, the conflict between production and realization (Harvey, 2015) as well as the tension between the reproduction of capital and what is called 'social reproduction' (Fraser, 2016).

I think underlying this notion of contradictions we can detect a more central problem at work. Following Polanyi (2014), it could be argued that for both market economies and market societies to flourish they themselves require the continued existence of particular non-economic attitudes, values, principles and approaches to life, the world and other people (or what I've labeled 'the social' for short). The problem arises from the fact that market economies erode or distort the social. As with our broader discussion of liberalism, it could be argued that they do this by emphasizing forms of separateness and the absence of social relationships. For example, in market societies we're encouraged to think of ourselves as utterly distinct from nature which is mere dead matter, a resource or an 'input'. Similarly, we think of radical distinctions between: the body and the true self (Radin, 1987); contract and gift; a value-neutral economy and traditions of mutuality, fraternity and solidarity; individual states of mind and substantive notions of 'the good'[13]; and the symbolic and the material.

Both market economies and the foundations of economic theory rely on a picture of economic agents as rational, self-interested individuals. Both, that is, envisage a limited scope for gratuity, charity and reciprocity in the constitution of our being and in our interactions. Given what was said above about the dangers of such a picture, the urgent task before us is to reimagine economic theory by giving due consideration to the fact that we are in fact relational beings in both our thinking and in our practices.

Such a 'metaphysical reconstruction of economics' (McCarraher, 2011) would require of us to radically rethink what we mean by scarcity, work, wealth and the environment; it would involve us in a discussion about both the ethical limits to commodification and the problems that arise from obscene levels of income and wealth inequality; more than anything, it would lead us to think more carefully about the difference between the person and the individual, and the type of common goods that are deeply intertwined with the former concept.

Outline of the book

This book is an attempt at rethinking all of those things, and is nothing more than my second thoughts about first principles. The structure of the book is as follows:

> In the first chapter I look at scarcity, a concept that is foundational to economic theory. Both classical (Perelman, 2000) and modern day economists ignore the fact that for most of human history societies were organized around a subsistence ethic since solidarity and social relationships were considered more important than economic efficiency and growth.

Economic theory and capitalist economies would barely be imaginable without the primitive accumulation that expropriated social wealth. Since household and subsistence economies controlled their own means of production they were hardly conducive to the creation of a wage class and the perpetuation of an endless process of capital accumulation.[14] Scarcity, in other words, had to be instituted (and economic theory played – and continues to play – its part in that process).

To think of abundance and grace – or at least freedom (Etzioni, 2004) – rather than of scarcity and optimization necessarily draws us to the meaning of rationality in economic theory.

In chapter 2 I look at rationality, the first of the three structuring assumptions behind the idea of *homo economicus*. I try to show that the view of rationality in economic theory is typically a very constricted one and that a large part of that narrowness stems from the fact that theory presumes we always think alone, and never together.

Instrumental rationality usually involves us in an optimal choice of commodities. In the third chapter I turn to how the expansion of markets (commodification) alters both the way in which we understand ourselves and the way in which we relate to other people, things and nature. Given that, I ask if there are any ethical limits to that expansion. One such limit, it is argued, follows from the way in which commodification distorts how we think about personhood.

Chapter 4 sees us turning to the second of the main structuring assumptions: individualism. Here I try and sketch the transition from the wider concept of relational 'persons' to the atomistic individual that we find in economic theory. That depiction of the disembedded individual is usually supplemented by the economist's belief that economic actors are exclusively driven by the pursuit of their own interests.

In chapter 5, therefore, I turn to the second structuring assumption: the notion that we are *self-interested* individuals. By restricting all of our concerns within the narrow ambit of the self we seem to be declining the relational characteristics that are so central to what it means to be a human being. If economic theory is to be more realistic and more humane it has to, therefore, acknowledge a more pluralistic account of human motivation. In other words, for economic theory to become more relational it has to consider concepts such as sympathy,[15] altruism and commitment.

An exclusive focus on our own interests can lead to the possible 'crowding-out' of other-regarding and relational perspectives (such as sympathy and commitment). It can also result in us ignoring the crucial issue of inequality, which is the subject matter of chapter 6. The central argument here is that when we talk about equality we are not simply referring to a distributive concept; in addition we are concerned about the relational idea of social equality.[16] Inequality can, therefore, distort the way in which we relate to one another in both economic and political realms.

One key way in which an over-emphasis on self-interest can be detrimental to the flourishing of society is the way in which it crowds out intrinsic motivation in the public sector. That is something I look at in chapter 7. I then show that one specific example of that crowding-out is the eclipse of older ways of thinking about education in an era that is dominated by the rise of the neoliberal university.

In chapter 8 I look at the problem of climate change, possibly the most important issue discussed in the book. At the heart of the problem is the fact that market economies and economic theory encourage us to incorrectly think of our relation to nature and future generations in a detached and abstract way. The problem of climate change, then, revolves around a series of separations and exclusions – both in our thinking and in our practices (Patel and Moore, 2017).

A large part of the climate change problem derives from how we think about time: whether our own lives have a narrative structure to them; the relation of those lives to both past and future generations as well as to the flourishing of the lives of non-human beings over time; and the importance we give to the perpetuation of value over time.

In chapter 9, therefore, I take a broad look at how both market economies and economic theory may be altering our self-understanding in relation to time before focusing on climate change. The main argument is that both economic theory and practices may be making it more difficult to take up a much needed long-term and relational approach to climate change.

In the last chapter, chapter 10, I continue the argument that because economic theory ignores the importance of sociality it represents a limited and partial understanding of human behaviour. Those limitations stem from both an insufficiently rich view of the individual (and her motivations) as well as a particularly narrow conception of the 'ends'[17] of economic activity (abstract wealth or abstract utility). In this chapter I briefly outline an alternative approach – the civil economy approach – that addresses those shortcomings.

For analytical convenience I have broken down the analysis of the relation between ethics and economics into separate chapters. But that should not mislead us since in reality the ideas presented in each separate chapter are closely related to one another. As with ecological thinking, it might be more accurate to say that in reality we are dealing with a system of inter-related systems. If that is true we may not be able to say 'first things first'. But we must begin somewhere.

Notes

1 With all these crises at hand it might be proffered that we face a crisis in crisis theory!

2 Throughout the book I will be using these two terms interchangeably. The social, while manifested in associations, practices, norms and institutions is fundamentally the conceptualization of a way of being in the world that is dependent on both genuine relationships *and* a substantive notion of 'the good'. Thus 'the social' (which includes inter-personal relationships and our relationship to objects, places and nature) is to be differentiated from both false notions of relationality as well as pernicious forms of sociality. In the former case we can think of envy as paradigmatic; in the latter, the impersonal and domineering bureaucratic state, or the aspiration to dominate or exclude by mafias, cartels and tribal groups. Not all forms of the social are ethical/good.

3 Once again, I will be simplifying by conflating the ethical with the social. The innermost core of the social/ethical is a primitive recognition of other human beings. The ethical is not, in this reading, the same thing as a universal, impartial and abstract rule; but even though it can involve attachments to specific people, places and things it isn't necessarily reducible to group loyalties either (Wiggins, 2009). I also use the word 'ethical' in a more inclusive sense so that the traditional distinction between moral obligations ('morality') and considerations of a good life ('ethics') are subsumed to it. This more expansive notion of ethics allows us to potentially move beyond standard welfare analysis ('well-being') and concentrate on human flourishing and the *common* good.

4 A 'picture' can be descriptive or normative. It includes notions of our fundamental motivations, conceptions of 'the good', as well as the relation of the self to the world, nature, other human beings and time. *Homo Economicus*, for example, is one such picture.

5 It is worth noting that the erasure of the social and the disparaging of the communities, associations and intermediate institutions that embody it, has not necessarily led to greater autonomy. In fact, it could be argued that in practical terms our lives remain to a large degree ordered by the state (law, regulation and surveillance), cultural norms and the market (the structure of wage labour in organizations, for example).

6 We will see the same kind of argument throughout this book in respect to capitalism. In order to flourish market economies require non-economic realms (values), but they simultaneously work to undermine them, thus leading to an unresolvable contradiction.

7 See Bowles (2017).

8 Since "faith gives a direction to our whole being" (Taylor, 2013, p. 16), it can help the intellect feel its way forward to know what it already dimly knows via imagination and *eros*. That reason/philosophy can be opened up to new paths/directions is also stressed by Macintyre (2007). Iqbal (2013) puts it slightly differently: "Faith, like the bird, sees its trackless way unattended by intellect" (p. 1).

9 In chapter 4, I will suggest that the picture of the person as a fundamentally relational being is in the process of being erased – and that this is in no small part due to influence of economic theory and real-world markets. In his stead is the pure animal with his or her bodily desires or the artificial robotic individuals of economic theory with their artificial intelligence. The question then becomes: are we living in a virtual rather than a virtuous reality?

10 Market economies foster a mode of governance that can be called 'the biopolitical'. It is made possible by the restriction of our understanding of equality and freedom to the mere formal sense of those concepts; the substitution of pleasure for 'the good'; the liberation of individual choice from the bonds of responsibility; and the "economizing of the entire social field" (Milbank, 2011, p. 35).

11 Those writing from an ecological perspective claim that part of the reason why we're in a catastrophic situation is precisely this lack of relationality or connectedness (Morton, 2018). We have come to believe that an abstract and universal reason places us above and outside nature, thereby facilitating progress by helping us to both tame chance and adopt a long-term perspective.

12 Capitalism (real-world market economies) may differ from the market economy that economic theory typically studies. In the latter we typically assume a timeless world in which small-scale transactions take place under conditions of perfect information, complete contracts, and limited institutional specification. One upshot of thinking about economic transactions in that way is that questions relating to power (class conflict, hierarchy within firms, the influence of corporate power, and debt) are minimized. However, the picture of economic man in both theory and real-world markets rests on the shared assumptions that economic agents are rational, self-interested individuals. The lack of sociality in capitalist markets, economic theory and in other academic disciplines (Milbank and Pabst, 2016) is reflected in the belief that the self is separate, rational and in control.

13 It could be that in our relentless desire to maximize wealth (or utility/well-being) we have lost sight of the relation between economic activity and the good life (Skidelsky, 2009). In a similar vein, Amartya Sen has vociferously and consistently questioned economists' exclusive reliance on utility information in the assessment of what makes for a good life.

14 Perelman (2000) rightly argues that primitive accumulation is not simply a phenomenon that occurs *prior* to the extension of the markets. In fact, the current emphasis on the importance of cultural, social, cognitive and human capital to economic growth suggests that the extraction of 'social wealth' is very much part of the dynamic of contemporary capitalist expansion.

15 On the idea that sympathy binds together the cosmos, the body and human society, see Milbank (2013). Interestingly, Milbank argues that it may be feelings (rather than reason) that "*truly* discloses us to the real" (p. 120).
16 On the relation between distribution and social equality see Wolff (2015).
17 Milbank (2014) persuasively argues that absent the notion of teleologically given ends our desires become infinite. The idea that there are substantive common goods is, therefore, critically connected to the notion of scarcity discussed in chapter 1.

Bibliography

Bowles, S. (2017). *The Moral Economy: Why Good Incentives Are No Substitute for Good Citizens*. New Haven, CT: Yale University Press.

Deneen, P. J. (2017). The Tragedy of Liberalism. *The Hedgehog Review, 19*(3). Retrieved from http://iasc-culture.org/THR/THR_article_2017_Fall_Deneen.php

Etzioni, A. (2004). The Post Affluent Society. *Review of Social Economy, 62*(3), 407–420. Retrieved from www.jstor.org/stable/29770270

Fraser, N. (2016). Contradictions of Capital and Care. *New Left Review, 100*. Retrieved from https://newleftreview.org/II/100/nancy-fraser-contradictions-of-capital-and-care

Gellner, E. (1989). *Plough, Sword and Book: The Structure of Human History*. Chicago, IL: University of Chicago Press.

Gordon, R. J. (2012). *Is U.S. Economic Growth Over? Faltering Innovation Confronts the Six Headwinds*. Working Paper No. 18315, NBER, Cambridge, MA.

Harvey, D. (2015). *Seventeen Contradictions and the End of Capitalism*. Oxford: Oxford University Press.

Iqbal, M. (2013). *The Reconstruction of Religious Thought in Islam*. Stanford, CA: Stanford University Press.

MacIntyre, A. C. (2007). *The Tasks of Philosophy: Volume 1: Selected Essays*. Cambridge: Cambridge University Press.

McCarraher, E. (2011). We Communists of the Old School. In A. Pabst (Ed.), *The Crisis of Global Capitalism: Pope Benedict XVI's Social Encyclical and the Future of Political Economy*. Eugene, OR: Cascade Books.

Milbank, J. (2011). The Real Third Way for a New Metanarrative of Capital and the Associationist Alternative. In A. Pabst (Ed.), *The Crisis of Global Capitalism: Pope Benedict XVI's Social Encyclical and the Future of Political Economy*. Eugene, OR: Cascade Books.

Milbank, J. (2013). Hume Versus Kant: Faith, Reason, and Feeling. In S. Coakley (Ed.), *Faith, Rationality and the Passions*. Malden, MA: Wiley.

Milbank, J. (2014, October 24). Can the Market Be Moral? Peace and Prosperity Depends on a Reimagined Socialism. *ABC Religion and Ethics*. Retrieved from www.abc.net.au/religion/articles/2014/10/24/4114040.htm

Milbank, J., and Pabst, A. (2016). *The Politics of Virtue: Post-Liberalism and the Human Future*. Lanham, MD: Rowman & Littlefield International.

Morton, T. (2018). *Being Ecological*. UK: Pelican.

Patel, R., and Moore, J. W. (2017). *A History of the World in Seven Cheap Things: A Guide to Capitalism, Nature, and the Future of the Planet*. Oakland, CA: University of California Press.

Perelman, M. (2000). *The Invention of Capitalism: Classical Political Economy and the Secret History of Primitive Accumulation*. Durham, NC: Duke University Press.

Polanyi, K. (2014). *The Great Transformation: The Political and Economic Origins of Our Time*. Boston, MA: Beacon Press.

Radin, M. J. (1987). Market-Inalienability. *Harvard Law Review, 100*(8), 1849–1937. doi:10.2307/1341192

Skidelsky, R. (2009). *Keynes: The Return of the Master*. New York, NY: Public Affairs.

Streeck, W. (2014a). How Will Capitalism End? *New Left Review, 87*. Retrieved from https://newleftreview.org/II/87/wolfgang-streeck-how-will-capitalism-end

Streeck, W. (2014b). Taking Crisis Seriously: Capitalism on Its Way Out. *Stato E Mercato, 1*, 45–68.

Taylor, C. (2013). Reason, Faith, and Meaning. In S. Coakley (Ed.), *Faith, Rationality and the Passions*. Malden, MA: Wiley.

Wiggins, D. (2009). Solidarity and the Root of the Ethical. *Tijdschrift Voor Filosofie, 71*(2), 239–269. Retrieved from www.jstor.org/stable/40890480

Wolff, J. (2015). Social Equality, Relative Poverty and Marginalized Groups. In G. Hull (Ed.), *The Equal Society: Essays on Equality in Theory and Practice*. Lanham, MD: Lexington Books.

1   Needs and scarcity

Scarcity means that society has limited resources and therefore cannot produce all the goods and services people wish to have.

(Mankiw and Taylor, 2011, p. 2)

The real world has its limits; the imaginary one is infinite.

(Rousseau cited in Nazar, 2018, The Eyes of Others:
Rousseau and Adam Smith on Judgment and Autonomy)

Hell hath no limits.

(as cited in Berry, 2008)

1.0   Introduction

The bedrock of economic theory rests on three assumptions: economic agents are rational, self-interested individuals. In later chapters I will critique each of those three inter-related and structuring assumptions. One of the central premises of this book is that we often ignore, at our own peril, the fact that assumptions used in an academic discipline originate in a particular historical context and that our assumptions about human behaviour (motivations and 'ends') may not, therefore, have universal validity. The deployment of "universal categories without reference to time, place or context" (Milonakis and Fine, 2009, p. 3) is itself a historical phenomenon that calls for an explanation of both the trajectory of society and, parallel to it, the development of economic theory.

A second and related theme that runs throughout the book is the idea that the picture we form of ourselves (in this case: *homo economicus*) can have a profound influence on both our sense of identity and our relation to other people, time and the natural habitat. And because we can grow into the picture we form of ourselves we may fail to acknowledge how a picture of reality can *change* the way in which we relate to both other people and the world. Our structuring assumptions then go unquestioned because our behaviour has *become* consistent with them.

In this chapter I examine the idea of scarcity because it is profoundly inter-twined with the idea that we are rational, self-interested individuals. Scarcity is so central to our understanding of the economics discipline that it stands to define the economic point of view itself.

In the following section (1.1) I ask how it came to be that traditional societies, which were historically oriented to maintaining subsistence levels of economic well-being, were transformed into ones where scarcity became the prevailing idea. In the second section I briefly summarize the history of economic thought to explain how scarcity as a concept came to be foundational to economic theory.

One of the main reasons why scarcity has seemed so important to our way of thinking is undoubtedly the belief that it would be an impetus to economic growth. But does that imply that with the achievement of high income levels, such as we see in the modern world, scarcity is no longer a relevant concept? That question forms the basis of our discussion in section 3.

Another way of addressing the latter question is to think about the idea of limits (section 4). Although scarcity is about limitations it holds within it the promise of future abundance, a time of utopian possibility in which limits are surpassed or no longer meaningful. As we shall see, the idea of scarcity is a deeply ambivalent one. In this section, therefore, I want to ask if there is a way of accommodating ourselves to the fact that human life is in some sense always limited and, if so, whether the desire to overcome or eradicate those limits is always something to be sought.[1] We have to seriously question, again, whether there are limits to growth. That is not so much a question about the progress of technology or the existence of ecological constraints – although it is informed by them – as it is a question of the *moral* worth of a way of living that is related to subsistence, 'dwelling', human needs and the household economy.[2]

The question of the relation between ethics and economics, then, is intimately related to the question of limits and scarcity. The paradox for economic thought remains that without any ethical limits on the economy, or an ethical ordering of desires, we have come to think of ourselves as having infinite desires. But, being the creatures we are, we recognize that they can never be fulfilled, that we will always be found wanting.

1.1 From subsistence to scarcity

In this section I ask how the idea of the supposed universality of scarcity can be reconciled with the fact that for large swathes of time human beings did not think that their desires were infinitely extendable but that, on the contrary, they were limited by a subsistence ethic.

In an influential book Marshal Sahlins (1974) claimed that pre-modern societies were in fact the original, affluent societies since they could meet their limited needs or desires. Limitations (low levels of production and accumulation) may, then, have been the result of design rather than circumstance. In addition, the common view that non-modern people led impoverished lives has also been challenged (Brody, 2001) since pre-agrarian societies may actually have been organized in a less hierarchical[3] way (Zerzan, 2008).

Although there may have been periods of dearth scarcity is not a universal phenomenon; nor is it an essential feature of the human condition. It is reasonable to maintain, therefore, that if societies existed at low levels of development over vast stretches of time then that was because they consciously chose to adopt a subsistence ethic. Of course, it could be that low levels of technological development and high incidences of disease meant that the subsistence ethic itself was a reflection of limited opportunities in the sense that people's preferences and cultural outlook adapted to those constricted circumstances. But that does beg the crucial question of why, if human beings are inherently transgressive[4] and dynamic creatures, impelled forward by scarcity, so few societies throughout human history have actually managed to break out of the stasis – and that too, only very recently.

And stasis there was. It appears that even with the advent of agriculture and the production of surpluses most societies were caught in a Malthusian trap (Clark, 2007) such that output per head remained remarkably stable at a very low level (Haldane, 2015). In fact, it has only been in the last 200 years that a small number of countries have made significant progress in what some economists call 'the great divergence' from the normal human lot (Acemoglu, Johnson and Robinson, 2005). But if that is true then we have to consider the existence of a subsistence ethic as the human norm – whether it was a cause or a result of low growth.

So, for most of recorded history subsistence peasant/household economies were actually the norm. In that sense, Finley (1999) is correct to say that for the ancients actual market economies were very thin, with limited trading, small amounts of production for the market, and a social organization of land, labour and credit arrangements that was distinct from the market order. Exchanges typically took place within a dense network of social relations, a habitus.[5] This, then, was a world of "self-sufficiency, autarky and a self-contained life" (Braudel, 1992, p. 55). And if that is true it is highly questionable whether an economic theory whose assumptions bear the trace of their foundations in a capitalist economy can actually explain very much about non-capitalist economies or the reality of peasant societies. Georgescu-Roegen (1966) is correct, therefore, to say "what particular reality is described by a given theory can be ascertained only from the latter's axiomatic foundation" (p. 361).

Since market economies are characterized by acquisitiveness and competitiveness these traits can hardly be said to fully or adequately represent human nature given that markets are not a universal[6] phenomenon but, as Gellner (1989) writes, a "very specific historical constellation" (p. 186) of ideas, practices and outlooks. Egoism, contract and a particular understanding of individualism only come together to help give shape to a mentality and set of practices that we associate with market economies at a specific point in time. It follows that scarcity and economizing[7] are not universal features of the human condition.

The systems of organizing relations in various arenas of social life (land, labour and capital) continues to diverge significantly from the assumptions underlying economic theory and the practices associated with the market system (Polanyi, 2014). This holds particularly for developing economies.[8] It would be inaccurate to portray economic agents in these societies as being essentially similar to the disembedded, rational[9] individuals described by economic theory and found in advanced market economies. Instead of arrangements between people governed by the notion of contract – a kind of relation which is free of non-economic religious, political and social influence – it would be more accurate to say that 'contacts', social capital (Durlauf and Fafchamps, 2005), community networks (Munshi, 2014) and compacts play a leading role in governing relations.[10]

The disembeddedness of the economy in general, and the emancipation of the economizing attitude from political, social and religious constraints in particular, could not have taken place without a weakening of the hold of a particular religious tradition – and the endorsement by another (Tawney, 1926). More speculatively, the decline in religious sensibilities in the 19th century and the gradual loss of the sense of immortality (Jonas, 2001), may have played a part in accentuating the idea that we are essentially finite creatures and that scarcity is, therefore, natural to our state. If that is true then Robbins' (1935) comment, "We have neither eternal life nor unlimited means of gratification" (p. 15) coupled with the idea that we have infinite desires suggests limitation and scarcity is a deeply rooted feature of our modern lives.

The actual development of markets (and market mentalities) from the 18th century onwards has also been crucial to lending material and intellectual support to the notion of scarcity. Markets promote the proliferation of individual desires, shape them in commodity form and advance an intense competition over commodities. In that respect, scarcity is a specific 'invention' of modernity and not a trans-historical feature of all societies. If needs are associated with a relatively stable, determinate view of the human person and a substantive notion of 'the good', desires and wants are, in contrast, taken to be socially and culturally determined.[11] And because society and culture are supposedly constantly advancing in the modern period there is no question of our desires being static. To say this is to recognize the pivotal role that luxury (Hobsbawm, 2000) and fashion (Simmel, 1957) have played in the history of capitalistic development, for both encourage the idea that our desire for novelty knows no bounds.

It is also worth remarking that the invention of scarcity would hardly have been possible without the atrophying of social bonds (Dumouchel, 2014) and the dominance of individualism as an orienting political and cultural outlook in modernity. Scarcity, then, "is the social construct of a particular web of human relationships" (Tijmes and Luijf, 1995, p. 329). It is easier to imagine needs as being common to if not our shared metaphysical identity then at least to our shared biological inheritance. But desires and wants, because postulated as referring to individuals' internal psychological states, unmoored from any necessary connection to a structure of meaning, cease to be bound by either a common human nature or by *traditional* social, ethical and cultural norms. Scarcity, in this reading, is both cause and effect of the disintegration of a genuine sociality.[12]

Scarcity and individuation, then, are inextricably linked to one another. It is intriguing to think that we usually associate abundance – whether it occurs at the beginning or end of history – as a time of equality and community rather than as one of differentiation and individualism. On the other hand, the now dominant picture of the human being, inherited from liberalism, is that of a solitary and isolated individual making choices without a background picture of values and realities that transcend him.[13] Iris Murdoch (1961) is correct to suggest, there-fore, that Liberal theory has struggled to see Man as "free and separate and related to a rich and complicated world from which, as a *moral* being, he has much to learn" (p. 18).

One consequence of both the 'desiring self' (Minogue, 2001) and the 'libera-tion' of our appetites becoming so central to modern consciousness is that the very notion of restraint becomes increasingly difficult to imagine or justify. We can see this in economic theory where questions pertaining to the determination (and therefore possible limitation) of desires are elided. Preferences (or desires) are typically self-regarding, shorn of ethical content and not subject to critical scrutiny. In addition, in the neoclassical framework the historical and social forma-tion of those preferences is usually disregarded. How individuals form, modify, evaluate and order their desires/preferences is generally left unexplained.

The underlying view that is expressed by Iris Murdoch's (2001) question – "Should we want many goods in the shop or just 'the right goods'?" (p. 8) – is antithetical to the perspective of scarcity[14] since the notion of 'right goods' sug-gests a judgement over our preferences. Economists, taking preferences as simply 'given', are reluctant to venture into the murky waters of judging what constitutes our 'true' preferences.[15]

1.2   From wealth to scarcity

It is often commented upon that the core interest of economics as a discipline, at least in its early stages of its development, was bound up with an examination of the causes of the wealth of nations. At its most rudimentary level 'wealth' was conceived of in materialistic terms (commodities and income) but the notion could very well be expanded in a humanistic direction to take on the form of a wide and more encompassing idea of 'prosperity'. For Ruskin (1967), for exam-ple, a sound economy depended on the *appropriate* production, preservation and distribution of meaningful and pleasurable things. If 'all wealth is life' then it was clear to him that 'life' was not pure animal existence or a life of accumulating riches ("getting and spending", Wordsworth, 1807). Wealth and value (*valorem*) in this richer vein of thought were not quantifiable and their importance quite clearly depended on the kind of life they made possible. It is hard to imagine Ruskin thinking that wealth could really mean much if it wasn't accompanied by justice, the virtues and a proper use of objects.

In this wider and richer view wealth, like property, is not thought of as simply being a moveable, fungible and measurable asset that generates *economic* value. Property and the ownership of things, for example, could be thought of as anchors in a rapidly changing world, connected to a way of life that embodied a set of durable and dense relations – both with other particular people and a specific place or locale. Property, in that sense, is closely aligned to a whole host of *use* values,[16] ranging from the protection and the nurturing of privacy and intimacy (Warnock,

2015), to the development of the capacity to *tend to* something and care for it. Property can establish a sense of identity and belonging, can help foster both a sense of independent choice and responsibility; it can also lead to an appreciation of aesthetic values and to a heightened awareness of the deep continuities in life.

It should also be noted that the idea of what constitutes wealth has sometimes been thought of in more constricted sense, namely: the meeting of basic needs or subsistence. A discussion of needs is closely linked to Ruskin's idea of *appropriate* production and distribution rather than the unbounded desire for more and more commodities that underpins the idea of scarcity in economic theory.

It is also the case that this old sense of wealth/property has important political connotations. James C. Scott (2014) argues that it was precisely the artisans and small property-holders that, up until the end of the 19th century, were the main bulwark against the advancement of a nascent capitalism (Calhoun, 2012). The life of a small property owner may certainly have been a limited one in many respects but it also offered, through its communitarian traditions, ample scope for relatively egalitarian practices and the formation of a sense of local cohesiveness. Property ownership, then, afforded a space for creativity and for the freedom that stood opposed to the regulation and control imposed by state and market alike.

Property and interests might, then, conceivably be thought of as conducive to a good life. Seen in this light, the problem with consumer societies is not their worldliness, but precisely the opposite (Arendt, 1998). Scarcity, as a fundamental principle that cannot be overcome, ends up devouring any attachments (to all that is solid) in the relentless pursuit of ever more goods/happiness/income. Iris Murdoch (1993) is right to pronounce in contrast that "the quality of our attachments is the quality of our understanding" (p. 295).

I will presently argue that economic theory has in some sense moved beyond the idea that the proper 'object' of economic study is the accumulation of wealth. But it is quite clear that that is not the full story.[17] In fact, it remains questionable whether the discipline has ever truly escaped its materialist foundations. The emphasis on commodification in actual market societies (see chapter 3) as well as the importance of commodities in generating welfare, means that both as a discipline and as a set of practices economic theory and the economy remain wedded to the materialism and individualism of the 19th century. Even to the extent that economic theory does take into account a broader set of considerations (culture, nature, services) it does so by treating them *as if* they were commodities.

It is fair to say that in the classical period of the 19th century there were significant differences in the way in which people thought about political economy according to the varying "visions of the nature of markets, society and human beings" (Satz, 2009, p. 676). According to Kirzner (2009) there was shift in late 19th century vision of the economy such that wealth and commodities were increasingly seen not as ends in themselves but as means to 'inner goods' such as health, knowledge, happiness or well-being. This greater emphasis on the subjective side – the relation between commodities and human beings, between commodities and goodness – potentially[18] opened up the space for critical reflection and a more humanistic discipline.

By the early 20th century there is a further change as economic theory progressively becomes less interested in which specific 'objects' or 'ends' are to be pursued (wealth, welfare, etc.). Economics in the early part of the century turns its attention, according to Kirzner, to an *economic aspect* of all behaviour, namely: economizing.

This shift in focus in economic thought is closely connected to changes in the understanding of what is meant by 'utility' (Broome, 1999). According to the older view, utility was thought to be synonymous with happiness or pleasure. In the new understanding, however, utility is not an 'end', a goal that someone aims for. To say that economic agents are economizing only means that they try to maximally satisfy their preferences given their constraints. Constrained optimization does not imply that agents try to maximize their 'satisfaction' or 'utility' – as if these were substantive concepts. Axiomatic utility theory makes no such demands.

Following from that, it could be argued that Man is the measure of things and that something is good *because* it is desired, rather than the converse. Economic theory takes this shift to the subjective side one step further and posits that utility is only a representation of one's preferences and not 'the good'. Under this thin concept of utility economic actors still maximally satisfy their preferences. Whether doing so necessarily leads to goodness or well-being is debatable.[19]

From the beginning of the last century, then, economic theory becomes more subjective since the aim of 'getting more for less', a supposed universal feature of human nature, doesn't need to make any kind of distinction between objectively 'higher' and 'lower' desires ("pushpin is as good as poetry", Bentham famously said). This erasure of distinctions helps ward off the traditional criticism that economics is only concerned about human beings' lower impulses (acquiring money, greed) since now, potentially, any activity and any preference – even altruistic ones – can be thought of as having an 'economic' dimension to them. Constrained optimization (economizing) is a feature of our relation to any kind of preference, self-interested or altruistic.

In positing an abstract urge to further one's own purposes we can see the strong relation between scarcity and the picture of human beings as isolated, rational individuals. Economic theory, in its modern guise, suggests economic activity is neither restricted to a specific area of social life nor determined by a specific 'end' (wealth, happiness, or well-being). Furthermore, the theory eschews a 'thick' or contextualized conception of the self, one that is enmeshed in relations with other people and ethical obligations. Instead, scarcity entails a *positive* description of human choices under constraints such that one rationally optimizes one's *own* means to achieving certain goals, irrespective of whether the latter can be morally or reasonably defended or not. This, along with the absence of a *telos* of Man, makes the argument that the pursuit of those 'ends' might be restricted by individual or political reason, by moral or religious prohibition, all the more difficult to sustain.[20]

In the establishment of a purely formal relation between means and ends, a relation that has the added advantage of being amenable to mathematization, it is perhaps right to see Lionel Robbins[21] as one of the pivotal figure in this story. It is worth stressing at this point that scarcity, the key grounding assumption of the discipline, was not based (or meant to be based) on historical facts and could not be overturned by its simple lack of empirical validity. Barbara Wootton (2013) is right to criticize the deductive approach taken by economics when she writes of the mistaken belief that "important truths can be discovered by merely thinking, without the aid of observation" (p. 118).

In any case, it was usually taken for granted that the human condition was bound up with some kind of deficiency in one area of life or the other. For example, scarcity could be thought of in terms of people lacking basic necessities (food, shelter, etc.) or in other, religious, terms (Arendt, 2005). In the latter case not only were we by definition time-ridden, limited creatures, always dependent on something beyond us, but we were often unaware of what we *really* needed[22] and could, therefore, quite easily pursue the wrong kind of 'goods', mistaking them for our ultimate good (*summum bonum*). It follows that either the human condition spoke of ineradicable insufficiency or that human nature itself was incomplete, somehow unfinished.

There is something intuitively plausible about the idea that we are, by definition, creatures that lack something or the other, and that we are always found wanting. And some of our oldest myths suggest that with some initial fall from grace an absence of unity and repose entered our lives, throwing us off balance, turning our hand to seek redress. Perhaps absence and limitation, in fact, structure and give force to our very desiring, as well as to our sense of freedom? The erotic – in the sense of the reaching for 'the good' beyond our grasp or full comprehension – has, I suspect, always been an important way of thinking about the human condition and its entanglement with our forward-dreaming to a 'north of the future' (Steiner, 2002). As Augustine would say, it is "yearning that makes the heart grow deep" (as cited in Brown, 1969, p. 156).

Whether non-satiation and scarcity are actually universal features of the human condition or ones that has been instituted by society remains, however, a controversial question. As we have seen above, the move away from discussions of objective notions of our 'ends' and purposes (such as wealth or happiness) led to an emphasis on subjective experiences. But it is easier to argue that our subjective desires (rather than objective 'ends') are boundless[23] and that scarcity is, therefore, an irredeemable feature of human life.

Also, since money replaces use values in a market economy and since the desire for money is potentially limitless, there will always be scarcity. More broadly, it is not hard for us to imagine that we will *always* lack something in our lives – commodities, time, money or social relationships.

In the economizing view, as we have seen, desire is boundless but also abstract or 'empty':[24] the desire for more – no matter what that 'more' is – has come to defines us. The frustration and disappointment that accompanies the notion of scarcity is, far from being an indication of our tragic situation, now something that is normalized. In that sense it is not the promise of satiation, the enjoyment of luxury or the utopian possibility of abundance and fullness that keeps us going. There is no specific end of action, following from a substantive notion of human flourishing, that keeps us going; instead, there is only an abstract will, an empty freedom and an infinity of desires.

The desire for social distinction, refinement and variety – whether natural tendencies or socially constructed by cultural expectations, the media and advertising companies – might be leading us to want what we don't really need. But to phrase it like that is to miss the point since any idea of our 'real' needs only makes sense against both a particular picture of what it is to be a human being and against an objective notion of 'the good'. There is little room for either in current economic thinking. Also, as Adam Smith saw all those years ago, even though our desire for 'trinkets and baubles may in fact be a form of deception (Manent, 2000), it is emulative desire and vanity that keep the 'industry of mankind' in motion.

In modern political thought life may have been conceived to be initially radically insufficient, as being nasty, brutish and short, but it was not inevitable that it had to continue to be so. In fact, if scarcity induced growth then the constant struggle over material necessities might be transcended. Scarcity and insufficiency would eventually be vanquished by abundance. Such a view was, however, bound to lead to a fundamental problem: what happens if growth ceases to be a means to an end (the abolition of scarcity) and becomes an end in itself? We are living in the shadow of that problem, the paradoxical situation where scarcity exists in the very midst of affluence.

1.3   Growth and the ambivalence of scarcity

In a remarkable paper Keynes (1932) predicted that sustained productivity growth over time would result in higher living standards and a reduction in the number of hours voluntarily[25] worked. For Keynes's grandchildren the economic problem – the struggle over subsistence – would have effectively been solved once and for all. Although he recognized that there was a class of relative and insatiable needs his optimism rested on the belief that there was also a class of 'absolute needs'. Once those latter needs had been met, he thought, we could "devote our further energies to non-economic purposes" (Keynes, 1932, Economic Possibilities for our Grandchildren).

Keynes's prediction resonates with the main story of this chapter: the idea that we are driven by a love of money and greed, what he called a 'disgusting morbidity' (Skidelsky, 2009); that both inclinations have been part of our psychological make-up for a significant periods of time; and that far from being simply a vice to be frowned upon by moral philosophers, both tendencies should be seen as a *necessary* evil. Greed, scarcity and envy are, in this reading, a spur to innovation, growth and the eventual overcoming of scarcity. Private vices might, after all, lead to the public good.

The idea that scarcity acts as a spur to economic growth can also be understood to be a political argument for scarcity. Built into the growth narrative is the normative claim that economic growth would result in better living standards, higher levels of welfare, social progress and enlightenment.[26] In addition, economic growth is the surest way to minimize the chances of violence and bring about peace, social order. But why is that?

Firstly, it has to do with the fact that markets promote freedom, formal equality, rationality and individuality. If violence is the result of collective acts of unthinking behaviour aimed at domination then it is obvious the positive role markets can have in this regard. Economizing behaviour in a market setting offers a model of how we can channel our energies to productive activities (as opposed to the destructiveness of war). It also indicates that conflict can be resolved through peaceful means (the model of exchange and bargaining).

Secondly, scarcity promotes economic growth. This means that individuals now have a lot more to lose if they resort to violence (of course, they also potentially have a lot more to gain by resorting to cheating, appropriation or violence). However, it is not just that growth reduces the *incentive* to act violently. The case for the importance of scarcity can also be made in a slightly different way. Scarcity results in growth and the ultimate transcending of scarcity. In those conditions of abundance, it is argued, everyone can get what they want and need, and so envy and competitive striving lose their sting. If violence is a product of the scramble for scarce resources then growth and abundance undermine the very *possibility* of violence (and not just the *incentive* to commit violence).

Thirdly, scarcity promotes self-interested behaviour and an indifference to the welfare of others. Alternatively, one could say that scarcity is only made possible by the prior dissolution of social bonds and obligations. Either way, the key point is that violence is a result of contagion (Dumouchel, 2014). The weakening of social relations has the effect of mitigating the power of violence to spread since economic actors would not have to rely on the benevolence of others in their time of need. The presence of calculating, asocial individuals in the market may, then, acts as a bulwark against the perpetuation of violence.

Putting these arguments together, it is not hard to see how the market economy and economizing behaviour could act as a model for the political[27]. In other words, contract, individualism and autonomy come to be seen as important in *both* the economic and the political realm.

We should pause here, though and re-iterate that scarcity is a profoundly ambivalent concept. If scarcity refers to absolute needs and if scarcity acts as a spur to growth then it is indeed plausible that with technological and productivity gains scarcity would eventually be abolished. We could then, as Keynes conjectured, use our freed-up leisure time and energies to pursue *higher* ideals (which included friendship and aesthetic pursuits). This, essentially, was also the political argument made above. Abundance would provide the conditions under which violence and competitiveness finds no footing. But if scarcity refers to our open-ended *relative* needs/wants and if scarcity is a universal aspect of the human condition (as understood by economic theory) then there is a problem. Scarcity, it is claimed, is the cause of violence but because it is the foundation of growth and both political and social order it is also the best mechanism of escaping that violence.

Keynes failed to recognize, or give sufficient consideration to this point. It seems that he was simply following a long line of thinkers who thought that labour, perhaps because traditionally associated with materiality and the body, was essentially a burden. Once we could free ourselves from its yoke we could devote more leisure[28] time to our true, and higher calling.

Of course, Keynes also, acutely, remarked on how difficult it would be to manage this shift in sensibilities given that the outlook of humans had been shaped by a prolonged battle with necessity. Would we be able to give direction to our lives[29] in an age of abundance when so much of our thinking and so many of our habits were formed in times of scarcity and the preponderance of limits?

It is also telling that Keynes's implicit assumption that work only represented a disutility, something to be overcome so that eventually our true proclivities could shine through, now sounds somewhat antiquated. For large parts of the 20th century and beyond people have identified themselves with their working lives and have believed or been persuaded to believe that meaningfulness and fulfillment cannot be separated from work. So much so that the lack of employment brings with it not only the terrible social stigmas of failure, a lack of autonomy, and laziness (now elevated to a cardinal sin) but it also raises the spectre of our lives becoming unstructured and devoid of a coherent narrative without it.[30]

Also, it should be added that leisure is now not something that stands orthogonal to the economy, a realm that affords the possibility, as Keynes seems to have envisage, of pursuing higher ideals. Instead, as a result of commodification, leisure[31] and culture are themselves subject to the same techniques of production, marketization and passive consumption that we see when it comes to ordinary commodities in the economy. The proliferation of commodity and leisure 'choices' may also, in some sense, work to undermine the *quality* of the experience of leisure. It is worth remembering, in this vein, Russell's (2004) pointed observation that the very "capacity for light-heartedness and play" (p. 11) may be inhibited by an exaggerated focus on efficiency.

Summarizing, we can say that Keynes failed to take into account the possibility that even though needs may in some sense be absolute, our desires are not. Instead, in a market economy desires are historical and relative to both the prevailing consumption norms of the time in which we live as well as to other peoples' consumption levels.[32] These relativities, coupled with an increasing emphasis on novelty have helped create the perfect storm in which scarcity is perpetuated at the very heart of abundance.

What Keynes did not foresee – and perhaps *could not* foresee – is the startling way in which capitalist economies and cultures would be transformed over the century. If half of modernity is about the transient, the fleeting and the contingent, it is fair to say that we are now riveted to just those aspects of it, having forgotten what is permanent, durable and grounded (which was the other half of modernity). By tying material goods to our non-material desires, capitalist economies have sacrificed satisfaction and contentment at the altar of permanent scarcity and progress. We have more commodities and greater income but are we necessarily happier or better off? Could it be that from both an ecological and a well-being perspective we are irrationally choosing excessive amounts of consumption and work (Stiglitz, 2010)?

Both economic theory and market economies hardly refer to the *needs* of people. Instead, their focus is on desires, which are both infinitely extendable[33] and not distinguishable along the lines of being 'higher' or 'lower' desires. How, then, do we think about limits again? Especially given the declining force of traditional social, cultural and moral constraints on consumption.

1.4 The importance of limits

In the analysis above it was suggested that there is an 'internal critique' or limit to growth because it is questionable, beyond a certain level, what purpose it serves. Growth, it seems, has become an end in itself. An alternative critique suggests that capitalist economies may simply not be *able* to grow at the rates previously witnessed over the last century. Part of this growth – pessimism stems from concerns about the ecological sustainability of continued growth – especially if China and India aspire to and attain the levels of affluence seen in the West. Beyond that, however, there is in addition the feeling that financial instability, inequality, the attenuation of political democracies and regulatory institutions (Streeck, 2014), spell trouble ahead. Also, debt, speculative and unproductive investments, the lack of technological innovation (Gordon, 2012) and the escalating costs of providing health, education and care for the elderly in greying populations (Balakrishnan, 2009) leave us with the prospect of low growth for the foreseeable future.

What this pessimistic line of reasoning suggests is that the high growth trajectory we have witnessed over the last two centuries may have been no more than a blip in the more normal long-term pattern of very low growth. In fact, concerns about the ability of the capitalist system to generate ceaseless growth are not too dissimilar to previous bouts of pessimism in the history of economic thought (Wrigley, 1988).

For the classical economists growth would eventually be limited because of the lack of opportunities for productive investment, the fixed supply of land or demographic pressures. For more contemporary thinkers the question revolves around whether we can imagine prosperity without growth (Jackson, 2009) and a return to a subsistence ethic, an idea of the good life that was consistent with human flourishing within certain limitations. Such a notion of flourishing does not necessarily entail the denial of a material basis to social life, but it does induce a profound scepticism towards both our current obsession with limitless growth and with our fixation on connecting prosperity to the possession of commodities.

Crucially, a return to a subsistence ethic would result in the overturning of the idea of scarcity and require of us to think more seriously about what we really *need* to lead a good life. It would imply that we start to ask what growth is *for*, what we mean by wealth and what work is *for* (Morris, 2008).

Part of the difficulty in answering those questions is that we take self-interest, envy and unbounded desire to be central to the self-conception we have of ourselves. It follows that the idea of an individual life that is circumscribed by needs and/or a subsistence ethic cannot but be viewed in a negative fashion. I think we need to contest this negative portrayal of such a life even as we recognize that self-interest and envy are *a part* of our fundamental make-up. To do so depends on the ability to correct our understanding of scarcity and needs in the following way.

Firstly, we should put to one side the association of needs with basic needs. According to that view the meeting of our basic needs ensures our survival but little else. Real progress only emerges once the realm of necessity is transcended and the subsequent transition from the language of needs and rights to the language of markets and preferences (or desires) has taken place. The necessity of such a transition sits at odds with the notion that a quiet, limited and in some ways small life is not always an impoverished and meaningless way of being in the world.[34] We need, therefore, to recalibrate our understanding of needs so that the human good and human flourishing can be consistent with vulnerability and the continued existence of some level of limitation (and therefore need).

Secondly, because the discussion of basic needs usually supposes they are absolute or objective, the inclusion of subjective desires into a concept of human flourishing seems to be barely admissible. A wider notion of needs, however, can accommodate desires – up to a point. This more capacious concept of needs is favourable because even though it depends on a non-relative notion of 'the good' (Nussbaum, 1988) it can both accommodate pluralism (at some level) as well give due weight to the importance of desire-satisfaction. What it stands radically at odds with, however, is not just the idea that 'the good' is vague, subjective or arbitrary; in addition, it refutes the claim that desires are infinite.

Restrictions on the pursuit of uninformed, subjective desires would require a role for both individual and – more controversially – *social* judgement as well as for customary expectations. Some have argued, however, that that constitutes a restriction on our individual freedoms. A reflective, informed-desire[35] account of what constitutes a good life can, it is argued, at once be objective and at the same time make room for the freedom to pursue one's own individual understanding of 'the good' (Griffin, 1986). Although there is much to be said in favour of that argument, the informed-desire account potentially opens the door to an endless pursuit of (informed) desires and therefore re-introduces the idea of scarcity through the back door.

Thirdly, if the good life is achievable right here, and right now, then the notion of scarcity loses a lot of its validity. According to this view, strange though it may sound, human history has been characterized by excess[36] rather than scarcity. It is not just that what is excessive has always fascinated us (Phillips, 2010); it is that much of what we value in human endeavour exceeds what is, strictly speaking, useful or necessary: art, beauty, the pursuit of 'useless knowledge' (Russell, 2004), heroic displays of courage, extreme piety, and sporting prowess. All of these indicate the importance we have always assigned to non-utilitarian pursuits.

The difference, then, between older, archaic societies and modern ones rests, perhaps, in the emphasis in the latter on material/commodity forms of excess and their lack of shared, symbolic meaning. However, another possible difference results from the fact that excess was previously a ritualized exception that re-established and justified the social order; modern excess[37] on the other hand, argues Bauman (2001), has in some sense become the norm, however paradoxical that sounds.

The first view I mentioned (above) stresses that we might learn to accept, up to a point, that life will always be limited and imperfect in some way or the other. That means that even though scarcity exists it is no longer a pressing concern. Furthermore, the frenetic attempt to escape all forms of scarcity through *economic* growth and technological change brings with it its own problems (disappointment, anxiety, restlessness, ecological damage and a constant forward-dreaming (Clark, 2012) at the expense of present enjoyment).

Alternatively, the third view mentioned above posits the non-existence of scarcity because we, Keynes's grandchildren, already have close at hand what we need for a good life.

Instead of focusing on needs (as above) we might turn to an alternative, relational approach that requires of us a more reflective ordering of our desires according to particular evaluative standards – whether these be dependent on ethical, aesthetic or spiritual perspectives or otherwise.[38] However, the problem with any change in our mode of thinking is, as Keynes rightly perceived, explaining how such attitudes and values might actually come about after so much of our time, and so much of our energy, has being guided by the pursuit of naked self-interest and money.

In addition, it is not at all clear what kind of institutional set-up would be required to support these changes in orientation since they would be "in opposition to the structures and values that dominate society" (Jackson, 2009, p. 151). For example, the kind of educational institutions that would have to be established might be significantly different from our current ones.[39] Scitovsky (1992), was right to alert us to the possibility that the dominance of economic forces, science and technology could lead to an emphasis on quantifiable productive skills at the expense of the "crowding-out of a liberal, humanistic education" (p. 229).

More generally, his view that as market economies become more complex it is often non-market 'goods' and satisfactions – determined by non-market institutions (custom, tradition, law, family and the public sector) – that really engage us is well worth attending to. I will return to that key issue later on, but the sceptical point to note here is whether, given the dominance of market rhetoric and mentalities in our day and age, a significant and autonomous role for those non-market institutions (or non-commoditized sectors) can be envisaged.

It may appear, then, that we've come to an impasse but if we return to Keynes' views it is possible to read him as saying that the necessary material conditions for living a more meaningful life – a life lived wisely, well – have actually been achieved. This means that in a post-capitalist 'stationary state' (Mulgan, 2015) we can start to think seriously about the moral, and not just the ecological limits to economic growth. And *that* would entail a return to what Mill (1848) would call an opening up to 'higher' pursuits, so that our "minds ceased to be engrossed by the art of getting on" (p. 317). Marx, too, would write about recovering our 'true humanity' and sense of authentic needs (Xenos, 1989) when work is abolished (Weil, 2006).

But what is our 'true humanity' and what resources, if any, do we have at our disposal to reclaim a more realistic and humane notion of ourselves? Whether we think of the relation between ethics and economics in terms of needs or of an ethical ordering of desires one thing is for certain: we will have to reject the narrow image of human personality that economists have inherited from 19th-century liberalism. The picture of human beings as self-interested, self-aggrandizing individuals choosing under conditions of scarcity hardly seems tenable any more – and doubts persist as to whether it ever did.

1.5   Conclusion

In this chapter I have been arguing for a return to subsistence and to the idea of needs. A wider notion of needs moves us beyond the biological and, therefore, asks of us what makes for a meaningful and good life (Miller, 2003). The old Greek idea that unlimited wants produced hubris, instability in the human soul and community (Xenos, 1989) coupled with our modern understanding of the ecological unsustainability of endless growth suggests we ought to think seriously about ethical limits to market transactions. The question is, therefore: can we think of progress[40] and development without equating them with a revolt against needs, forms of necessity (Illich, 1978a)?

We may not be able to completely return to the self-sufficiency of the household and the local economy, but there is some merit in re-instating the idea of needs in place of permanent scarcity. Such a notion does not have to be a sparse one. It can rightfully be seen as drawing an older understanding of 'austerity' (Illich, 1990) in which not all enjoyment is excluded. Only desires that are distracting or inimical to 'the good' and to social relationships are ruled out.

The re-instatement of the central importance of this broader notion of needs would go hand-in-hand with both a re-evaluation of leisure and also a shift in our relation to time. If Simone Weil (2003) was correct to state that there is a particular relation to time that suits thinking beings then 'idleness' (Russell, 2004) and 'slowness' (Solnit, 2007) may be ways of breaking the hold of the work ethic and the organization of time under the capitalist system.[41]

Such a move would also entail radically questioning the notions of rationality and individuality that lie at the heart of the picture we form of economic agents in economic theory. Focusing on needs (or satisficing preferences)[42] entails moving away from the ideas of perfect knowledge and rational (maximizing) behaviour in standard economic theory. And the latter, as we shall see in the next chapter, is often intimately related to a narrow, and therefore questionable, conception of individuality.

It is a curious feature of modern societies that scarcity – which implies the endless *pursuit* of our desires – may actually be reducing our freedoms, as we become both more enthralled to passive consumption and less able to resist addictive, compulsive, excessive and distracting[43] behaviours. A return to self-subsistence or a 'vernacular mode of being' (Illich, 1981; Scott, 1998) could actually lead to an increase in *substantive* freedom since it would decrease our dependency on commodities (things we do not produce or design ourselves and that are also sometimes inimical to the development of social relationships). Austerity or a reasonable frugality might allow us to live more autonomously and creatively, so as to "design and craft one's own distinctive [way of] dwelling" (Illich, 1978b, p. 10) and to form attachments to specific things, places and people (Cohen, 2013). 'Voluntary simplicity', as Etzioni (2004) calls it, also has profound implications for ecological sustainability (chapter 9) and inequality (chapter 6).

It remains a remarkable fact that for all the fanfare about individual freedom and self-determination our lives are in reality determined by vast, impersonal market and state systems. As a consequence of their dominance we may have, irretrievably, lost the habits of mutuality – or what in this book I call relationality – that constituted an older mode of experience.

Standardization and homogenization – of our workplaces, language, architectural and cultural forms, cities, economic and political systems and approaches to education – bode ill for the co-existence of plural perspectives and ways of living. Furthermore, if autonomy, choice, responsibility and a deep sense of relationality depend on the survival of those localized perspectives, they could be undermined by the expansion of market subjectivities. It is hard to now imagine our lives unstructured by the nexus of modern management systems (schools, hospitals, the workplace etc.) and the legal, cultural and political institutions that go up to determine the tenor of them.[44]

A critique of scarcity, then, could renew a deeper sense of how we relate to other people and to the world, opening up avenues for genuine sociality and a richer, less materialistic culture (Kugelmann, 2002). Freedom in market societies and political liberalism is usually conceived of as being 'free from' rather than the deliberate maintenance of connections (Berry, 2008). In a similar vein, economic theory posits that we reason alone. It is to that topic that I now turn.

Notes

1 "Man has a responsibility to find himself where he is, in his own proper time and place, in the history to which he belongs" (Merton, 2008, p. iv). Nussbaum (2009) also writes that we can recognize an attachment to human transcendence and at the very same time choose and value mortal life.

2 On the latter, see chapter 10.

3 A fundamental theme running throughout this book is that a proper recognition of non-hierarchical relationality is vital if we want to think about the possibility of an ethical economy. On the importance of a 'society of equals', see chapter 6.

4 On the centrality of transgression in modern times see Rieff (2006).

5 The term 'habitus' refers to a "lived environment comprised of practices, inherited expectations, rules which both determined limits to usages and disclosed possibilities, norms and sanctions both of law and neighbourhood pressures" (Thompson, 1993, p. 102).

6 If the constellation of rules, values, norms, motivations, property relation and cultural/ethical constraints specific to market economies are historically relative then older modes of social organization are very different from markets (Boldizzoni, 2011). Of course, the distinction isn't that clear in practice since even in advanced market economies it could be argued that trust, goodwill and honesty

play some role in economic transactions. Also, there may be satisficing behaviour (Camerer, Babcock, Loewenstein and Thaler, 1997) in market economies.

7 It appears that traditional institutions – especially when it comes to the distribution of food – were more concerned about countering idiosyncratic risks and the maintenance of fairness and community solidarity through redistribution and reciprocity rather than promoting efficiency and growth.

8 Land, labour, credit and insurance are typically organized around socially embedded informal institutions (Ray, 1998; Banerjee and Duflo, 2007). This is not wholly surprising given the costs of establishing and maintaining formal institutions (Herbst, 2000; Greif, 1993) may be high and the benefits from non-localized exchanges and trades low.

9 Recent work by Mullainathan (2004) suggests that the poorest (in rural areas) may not always be rational maximizers; self-interest is often bounded by social obligations (Platteau, 1991) and moral norms (Thompson, 1993).

10 From the economic point of view these informal institutions and solidarity networks (Platteau, 2006) must themselves be a product of individuals' choices and/or a response to imperfect market conditions. Mutual insurance, for example, can be explained as a result of rational self-interested behaviour in an infinitely repeated game (Coate and Ravallion, 1993); the social norms that allowed long-distance trades to take place were themselves sustained because it was in everyone's interest to abide by the rules (Greif, 1993); and a society's institutions can be seen as the result of optimal *choices* (Acemoglu, Johnson and Robinson, 2005).

11 Of course, in mainstream economic theory desires and preferences are not usually thought to be socially determined (or endogenous to the system) but, instead, as originating with the autonomous individual. The key point is that whether we think of desires as stemming from the individual herself or as being socially/culturally determined in neither case do we envisage them being bounded. Older customs and traditional modes of social organization may have limited our aspirations but modern societies seem to ignore the old saying, "hell hath no limits" (as cited in Berry, 2008).

12 To say that an individual's preferences are either relative to other people's consumption or to societal norms means that they can be 'socially determined' without reflecting *genuine* sociality (or relationality) as we understand it. Sociality, closely related to the common good (see chapter 10), embodies an *ethical* relation. Societal norms, on the other hand, can actually be ethically pernicious and so 'norms' do not always necessarily refer to a normative ethical standard.

13 In chapter 2 we will see that rational choice, which is the practical solution to scarcity, is an instrumental form of reasoning that typically involves little discussion about our ultimate values or, indeed, the values of other people.

14 In his book, *The Origin of Wealth*, Beinhocker (2006) states that if we think of wealth not in terms of income but as the *variety* of goods available then New York would be more than a hundred million times 'wealthier' than a typical hunter-gatherer tribe. This is a startling example of the deficiencies in thinking produced by an excessive focus on the quantity of goods available. There is no mention of the quality of the commodities, how they relate to happiness or the good life, or the ethical and ecological implications of the production of so many goods. More is always better!

15 To do so might compromise the sovereignty of individuals and also reintroduce ethical notions into what is supposed to be a positive science. Also, the idea that some desires might be ruled out by ethical considerations wouldn't bode well for capitalistic expansion.

16 According to de Soto (2000) the surplus value from a house is released via a conversion process that transforms it from being a unique home to collateral (a functioning asset) that has exchange value. This 'emancipatory' process, often celebrated, pays scant attention to the possible loss of the use values. That a home

can help orient our lives by being a locus of our memories, a provider of security, refuge, repose and stability, and a crucible in which some of our most important traits are forged – sociality, human warmth, the distinction between 'inner' and 'outer' (Bachelard, 2013) – is simply glossed over.

17　Despite criticism of the limitations of GDP (Stiglitz, Sen and Fitoussi, 2009) the idea remains at the heart of much of economic policy. Perhaps not unsurprisingly so given the belief that economic growth and political stability are deeply intertwined. For the history of 'GDP' see Lepenies (2016).

18　I say 'potentially' because both a richer picture of human beings and a substantive notion of 'the good' require cultural, intellectual and institutional support.

19　In reality most academic economists continue to assume that economic agents are perfectly rational *and* that they have self-interested preferences. Under those circumstances preference satisfaction does indeed enhance welfare. More recently, however, some economists have argued that agents in the real world may not have perfect information and/or may choose out of impulse or habit rather than their 'true' self-interest. This fact introduces the possibility of manipulation (Akerlof and Shiller, 2016) and also implies that the pursuit of one's interests doesn't necessarily maximize an individual's well-being.

20　It is worth noting the close association of the economic point of view with political liberalism. In both the emphasis is on private choice and individually determined 'ends'.

21　Over seven decades ago he defined economics as a science that studies "human behaviour as a relationship between ends and scarce means that have alternative uses" (Robbins, 1935, p. 16).

22　See Ignatieff's (1994) The Needs of Strangers (chapter 2) for a fascinating account of the problem that we may be unaware of our real needs. Market freedom, under those circumstances, cannot but appear to be a strangely empty concept.

23　Such an understanding garners support from the widely accepted idea that progress is a never-ending process. Scarcity follows because we can always imagine ourselves having (and *needing*) more. In addition, there will always be scarcity because we worry there will inevitably be other people who have more than us (Claassen, 2009). Scarcity, in that sense, is result of us imagining ourselves to be essentially competitive beings, driven by envy and rivalry. In our modern, non-hierarchical societies such competitive pressures may have intensified. Since there are no longer any fixed notions of status to limit one's desires our ambitions (and expectations) know no bounds.

24　We have moved from a picture of ourselves as constantly seeking happiness machines to simply constantly seeking machines.

25　A lot of our current concerns are that there will be an involuntary displacement of human labour by machines (Mokyr, Vickers and Ziebarth, 2015).

26　Given the rise of inequalities and the problem of climate change we are now less sanguine about some of these claims. Whether growth and the expansion of choices lead to greater happiness/welfare has been questioned by Easterlin (1974) and Schwartz (2004). Worse still, the relentless pursuit of growth may be counterproductive (Dupuy, 2013).

27　Alternatively, it could be argued that abundance signals the end of the political if the latter is considered to be the answer to the question of what binds individuals with conflicting interests to one another.

28　Perhaps this is in essence another version of the old Baconian idea that knowledge and power would release us from the bonds of necessity and misery (Jonas, 2001). An older tradition would maintain that the freedom from work for some could be purchased only at the cost of enslaving others.

29　As has often been remarked, there's something boring about a utopia of abundance (Clark, 2002) since it represents a dreamlike, conflict-free mode of existence where choice and responsibility are drained of their potency. Would we really want to opt for more leisure over consumption and work? This question assumes the existence of real choice in the matter. The reality of our limited choices over the quality *and* quantity of work (and leisure) is brilliantly explored by Fleming (2015, 2017).

30 This assertion has to be tempered given the changes over the last 30 years in technology and the global economy. Coupled with the preponderance of low-paid flexible labour and, more generally, wage stagnation, it could be that people are now less likely to find work a source of happiness, meaning or identity. The pressure to work and the "creation of artificial needs ensures workers' loyalty to the work ethic" (Skidelsky and Skidelsky, 2012, p. 33).

31 The commodification of leisure means that we 'consume' it because of the pleasure/ utility we derive from it. This stands in stark contrast to the older religio-philosophical idea that leisure is a vehicle for contemplation (Pieper, 1998).

32 Since emulation, rivalry and competitiveness are central ingredients of a market economy all that happens as we enter an age of abundance is that those tendencies get transposed into social scarcities of positional goods (Hirsch, 2010) and symbolic markers of social stratification. It is sometimes taken for granted that envy is a basic human propensity, one that finds expression in every human society (Foster et al., 1972). In traditional societies the dangers posed to social and political cohesion by envy or mimetic desire were clearly recognized, as was the need to dampen their effects with the aid of both cognitive outlooks as well as cultural and institutional forms of control (sharing, redistribution mechanisms). In contrast, in modern, opulent societies envy, emulation and competitiveness are something to be harnessed as a mechanism of promoting growth.

33 A basic assumption of economic theory, 'non-satiation', posits that more is always better than less. Desire is boundless because greater production itself might stimulate us. Markets, in this more realistic view, do not simply aim to satisfy *given* preferences/desires; instead, through innovation, novelty, advertising and marketing they aim to generate new desires and alter our preference ordering. Individuals' preferences for commodities (over leisure) may then be endogenous to the economic system (Stiglitz, 2010).

34 Merton (2005) writings of humility should "help us to lead quite ordinary lives, peacefully earning our bread and working from day to day in a world that will pass away" (p. 119).

35 A lot rests on the term 'informed-desire'. This is not, in my opinion, a value-neutral term and depends on moral understanding, social norms and social relationships.

36 'Abundance', rather than excess, is probably a better word. On the conquest of abundance by scientific and economic outlooks (abstractions and the exchange of abstract values, that is), see Feyerabend (2001). The variety of languages, specific ways of being in the world and non-human species are all increasingly becoming scarce.

37 How we navigate our way through the glut of information, commodities and flickering images that go up to make the "open-ended inventory of modern life, a series without a final term" (Hughes, 2016) is a difficult question and not one that is likely to be broached by an economics discipline which studiously avoids questions of ethical limitations.

38 The discussion here is similar but not identical to what I described as the 'second view' above.

39 In chapter 7 I argue that with the rise of the neoliberal university, older ways of thinking about a humanistic education might be difficult to sustain.

40 The compatibility of growth or progress with limitations can be thought along the lines of aesthetic appreciation of limited forms, or in terms of friendship. In

neither is more necessarily better! In case of the former, I am reminded of Casals, the great cellist, who writes that after 80 years of playing Bach "The music is never the same, never" (Casals and Kahn, 1970, p. 17).

41 See chapter 9 for a fuller discussion.

42 Satisficing may be an adequate description of rational behaviour given our cognitive constraints. But for our purposes it is the normative dimension that is of note. To be content with what is good enough is to adopt an 'inherently' satisficing perspective such that our desires are-reordered or transformed (Slote, 2004).

43 On distraction see Crawford's (2015) invaluable book, *The World Beyond Your Head*. More generally, see Offer (2006).

44 Graeber (2015) is right, therefore, to highlight the fact that in a free-market era the tentacles of bureaucratic management and control have actually spread.

Bibliography

Acemoglu, D., Johnson, S., and Robinson, J. A. (2005). Institutions as the Fundamental Cause of Long-Run Growth. In P. Aghion and S. Durlauf (Eds.), *Handbook of Economic Growth*, 1A. Amsterdam: Elsevier North-Holland. Available at https://doi.org/10.106/S1574-0684(05)01006-3

Akerlof, G. A., and Shiller, R. J. (2016). *Phishing for Phools: The Economics of Manipulation and Deception*. Princeton, NJ: Princeton University Press.

Arendt, H. (1998). *The Human Condition*. Chicago, IL: University of Chicago Press.

Arendt, H. (2005). Love as Caring: The Anticipated Future. In J. C. Stark and J. V. Scott (Eds.), *Love and Saint Augustine*. Chicago, IL: University of Chicago Press.

Bachelard, G. (2013). *The Poetics of Space* (M. Jolas, Trans.). Boston, MA: Beacon Press.

Balakrishnan, G. (2009). Speculations on Stationary State. *New Left Review, 59*. Retrieved from https://newleftreview.org/II/59/gopal-balakrishnan-speculations-on-the-stationary-state

Banerjee, A. V., and Duflo, E. (2007). The Economic Lives of the Poor. *Journal of Economic Perspectives, 21*(1), 141–167. doi:10.1257/jep.21.1.141

Bauman, Z. (2001). Excess: An Obituary. *Parallax, 7*(1), 85–91. doi:10.1080/13534640010015962

Beinhocker, E. D. (2006). *The Origin of Wealth: Evolution, Complexity, and the Radical Remaking of Economics*. Boston, MA: Harvard Business School Press.

Berry, W. (2008, May). Faustian Economics: Hell Hath No Limits. *Harper's Magazine*.

Boldizzoni, F. (2011). *The Poverty of Clio: Resurrecting Economic History*. Princeton, NJ: Princeton University Press.

Bowles, S. (1998). Endogenous Preferences: The Cultural Consequences of Markets and Other Economic Institutions. *Journal of Economic Literature, 36*(1), 75–111. Retrieved from http://citeseerx.ist.psu.edu/viewdoc/download?doi=10.1.1.335.7577&rep=rep1&type=pdf

Braudel, F. (1992). *Civilization and Capitalism, 15th–18th Century, Volume II: The Wheels of Commerce* (S. Reynolds, Trans.). Berkeley, CA: University of California Press.

Brody, H. (2001). *The Other Side of Eden: Hunters, Farmers, and the Shaping of the World*. San Francisco, CA: North Point Press.

Broome, J. (1999). *Ethics Out of Economics*. Cambridge: Cambridge University Press.

Brown, P. (1969). *Augustine of Hippo: A Biography*. Berkeley, CA: University of California Press.

Calhoun, C. J. (2012). *The Roots of Radicalism: Tradition, the Public Sphere, and Early Nineteenth-Century Social Movements*. Chicago, IL: University of Chicago Press.

Camerer, C., Babcock, L., Loewenstein, G., and Thaler, R. (1997). Labor Supply of New York City Cabdrivers: One Day at a Time. *The Quarterly Journal of Economics, 112*(2), 407–441. doi:10.1162/003355397555244

Casals, P., and Kahn, A. E. (1970). *Joys and Sorrows: Reflections.* New York, NY: Simon & Schuster.

Claassen, R. (2009). Scarcity. In J. Peil and I. V. Staveren (Eds.), *Handbook of Economics and Ethics.* Cheltenham: Edward Elgar Publishing.

Clark, G. (2007). *A Farewell to Alms: A Brief Economic History of the World.* Princeton, NJ: Princeton University Press.

Clark, T. J. (2002, April 17–19). *Painting at Ground Level.* Lecture presented at The Tanner Lectures on Human Values in Princeton University, Princeton, NJ.

Clark, T. J. (2012). For a Left With No Future. *New Left Review, 74.* Retrieved from https://newleftreview.org/II/74/t-j-clark-for-a-left-with-no-future

Coate, S., and Ravallion, M. (1993). Reciprocity Without Commitment: Characterization and Performance of Informal Insurance Arrangements. *Journal of Development Economics, 40*(1), 1–24. doi:10.1016/0304-3878(93)90102-s

Cohen, G. A. (2013). Rescuing Conservatism: A Defense of Existing Value. In M. Otsuka (Ed.), *Finding Oneself in the Other.* Princeton, NJ: Princeton University Press.

Crawford, M. B. (2015). *The World Beyond Your Head: On Becoming an Individual in an Age of Distraction.* London: Penguin Books.

De Soto, H. (2000). *The Mystery of Capital: Why Capitalism Triumphs in the West and Fails Everywhere Else.* New York, NY: Basic Books.

Dumouchel, P. (1988). *Violence and Truth: On the Work of René Girard.* London: Athlone.

Dumouchel, P. (2014). *The Ambivalence of Scarcity and Other Essays.* East Lansing, MI: Michigan State University Press.

Dupuy, J. (2013). *The Mark of the Sacred* (M. B. DeBevoise, Trans.). Stanford, CA: Stanford University Press.

Durlauf, S., and Fafchamps, M. (2005). Social Capital. *Handbook of Economic Growth, 1*(1), 1639–1699. doi:10.3386/w10485

Easterlin, R. A. (1974). Does Economic Growth Improve the Human Lot? Some Empirical Evidence. *Nations and Households in Economic Growth,* 89–125. doi:10.1016/b978-0-12-205050-3.50008-7

Etzioni, A. (2004). The Post Affluent Society. *Review of Social Economy, 62*(3), 407–420. doi:10.1080/0034676042000253990

Feyerabend, P. K. (2001). *Conquest of Abundance: A Tale of Abstraction Versus the Richness of Being.* Chicago, IL: University of Chicago Press.

Finley, M. I. (1999). *The Ancient Economy.* Berkeley, CA: University of California Press.

Fleming, P. (2015). *Resisting Work: The Corporatization of Life and Its Discontents.* Philadelphia, PA: Temple University Press.

Fleming, P. (2017). *The Death of Homo Economicus: Work, Debt and the Myth of Endless Accumulation.* London: Pluto Press.

Foster, G., Apthorpe, R., Bernard, H., Bock, B., Brogger, J., Brown, J., . . . Whiting, B. (1972). The Anatomy of Envy: A Study in Symbolic Behavior [and Comments and Reply]. *Current Anthropology, 13*(2), 165–202. Retrieved from www.jstor.org/stable/2740970

Gellner, E. (1989). *Plough, Sword and Book: The Structure of Human History.* Chicago, IL: University of Chicago Press.

Georgescu-Roegen, N. (1966). *Analytical Economics.* Cambridge, MA: Harvard University Press.

Gordon, R. J. (2012). *Is U.S. Economic Growth Over? Faltering Innovation Confronts the Six Headwinds.* Working Paper No. 18315, NBER, Cambridge, MA.

Graeber, D. (2015). *The Utopia of Rules: On Technology, Stupidity, and the Secret Joys of Bureaucracy.* Brooklyn, NY: Melville House.

Greif, A. (1993). Contract Enforceability and Economic Institutions in Early Trade: The Maghribi Traders' Coalition. *The American Economic Review, 83*(3), 525–548. Retrieved from www.jstor.org/stable/2117532

Griffin, J. (1986). *Well-being: Its Meaning, Measurement and Moral Importance.* Oxford: Clarendon Press.

Haldane, A. (2015, February 17). *Growing, Fast and Slow.* Speech presented in University of East Anglia, Norwich.

Herbst, J. I. (2000). *States and Power in Africa: Comparative Lessons in Authority and Control.* Princeton, NJ: Princeton University Press.

Hirsch, F. (2010). *Social Limits to Growth.* New York, NY: ToExcel.

Hobsbawm, E. J. (2000). *The Age of Revolution, 1789–1848.* London: Phoenix.

Hughes, R. (2016, January 14). Art Notes: My Friend Robert Rauschenberg By Robert Hughes. *The Talbot Spy.* Retrieved from http://talbotspy.org/art-notes-my-friend-robert-rauschenberg-by-robert-hughes/

Ignatieff, M. (1994). *The Needs of Strangers.* London: Vintage.

Illich, I. (1978a). *Toward a History of Needs.* New York, NY: Pantheon Books.

Illich, I. (1978b). *The Right to Useful Unemployment and Its Professional Enemies.* London: Marion Boyars.

Illich, I. (1981). The War Against Subsistence. In *Shadow Work.* Boston, MA: Marion Boyers.

Illich, I. (1990). *Tools for Conviviality.* London: Boyars.

Jackson, T. (2009). *Prosperity Without Growth: Economics for a Finite Planet.* London: Earthscan.

Jonas, H. (2001). *The Phenomenon of Life: Toward a Philosophical Biology.* Evanston, IL: Northwestern University Press.

Keynes, J. M. (1932). Economic Possibilities for Our Grandchildren. In *Essays in Persuasion* (pp. 358–373). New York, NY: Harcourt, Brace & Company.

Kirzner, I. M. (2009). *The Economic Point of View.* Indianapolis, IN: Liberty Fund.

Kugelmann, R. (2002). Economy, Subsistence, and Psychological Inquiry. In L. Hoinacki and C. Mitcham (Eds.), *The Challenges of Ivan Illich: A Collective Reflection.* New York, NY: State University of New York Press.

Lepenies, P. (2016). *The Power of a Single Number: A Political History of GDP.* New York, NY: Columbia University Press.

Manent, P. (2000). *The City of Man.* Princeton, NJ: Princeton University Press.

Mankiw, N. G., and Taylor, M. P. (2011). *Microeconomics.* Australia: South-Western Cengage Learning.

Merton, T. (2005). *No Man Is an Island.* Boston, MA: Shambhala.

Merton, T. (2008). *Choosing to Love the World: On Contemplation: Easyread Large Bold Edition* (p. IV). Retrieved from ReadHowYouWant.com.

Mill, J. S. (1848). *Principles of Political Economy: With Some of Their Applications to Social Philosophy.* Boston, MA: C.C. Little & J. Brown.

Miller, D. L. (2003). *Principles of Social Justice.* Harvard, MA: Harvard University Press.

Milonakis, D., and Fine, B. (2009). *From Political Economy to Economics: Method, the Social and the Historical in the Evolution of Economic Theory*. New York, NY: Routledge.

Minogue, K. (2001). *The Liberal Mind*. Indianapolis, IN: Liberty Fund.

Mokyr, J., Vickers, C., and Ziebarth, N. L. (2015). The History of Technological Anxiety and the Future of Economic Growth: Is This Time Different? *Journal of Economic Perspectives, 29*(3), 31–50. doi:10.1257/jep.29.3.31

Morris, W. (2008). *Useful Work Versus Useless Toil*. London: Penguin Books.

Mulgan, G. (2015). *The Locust and the Bee: Predators and Creators in Capitalism's Future*. Princeton, NJ: Princeton University Press.

Mullainathan, S. (2004). *Development Economics Through the Lens of Psychology*. Working Paper No. 28974, Vol. 1, The World Bank. Retrieved from http:// documents.worldbank.org/curated/en/415731468779687162/Development-economics-through-the-lens-of-psychology

Munshi, K. (2014). Community Networks and the Process of Development. *Journal of Economic Perspectives, 28*(4), 49–76. doi:10.1257/jep.28.4.49

Murdoch, I. (1961, January). Against Dryness. *Encounter*, 16–21.

Murdoch, I. (1993). *Metaphysics as a Guide for Morals*. London: Penguin Books.

Murdoch, I. (2001). *The Sovereignty of Good*. London: Routledge.

Nazar, H. (2018). The Eyes of Others: Rousseau and Adam Smith on Judgment and Autonomy. In V. Soni and T. Pfau (Eds.), *Judgment and Action: Fragments Toward a History*. Evanston, IL: Northwestern University Press.

Nussbaum, M. C. (1988). Non-Relative Virtues: An Aristotelian Approach. *Midwest Studies in Philosophy, 13*(1), 32–53. doi:10.1111/j.1475-4975.1988.tb00111.x

Nussbaum, M. C. (2009). *Love's Knowledge: Essays on Philosophy and Literature*. New York, NY: Oxford University Press.

Offer, A. (2006). *The Challenge of Affluence: Self-Control and Well-Being in the United States and Britain Since 1950*. New York, NY: Oxford University Press.

Phillips, A. (2010). *On Balance*. New York, NY: Farrar, Straus and Giroux.

Pieper, J. (1998). *Leisure: The Basis of Culture*. South Bend, IN: St. Augustines Press.

Platteau, J. (1991). Traditional Systems of Social Security and Hunger Insurance: Past Achievements and Modern Challenges. *Social Security in Developing Countries*, 112–170. doi:10.1093/acprof:oso/9780198233008.003.0004

Platteau, J. (2006). Solidarity Norms and Institutions in Village Societies: Static and Dynamic Considerations. In S. Kolm and J. M. Ythier (Eds.), *Handbook of the Economics of Giving, Altruism and Reciprocity* (Vol. 1). Amsterdam: Elsevier.

Polanyi, K. (2014). *The Great Transformation: The Political and Economic Origins of Our Time*. Boston, MA: Beacon Press.

Ray, D. (1998). *Development Economics*. Princeton, NJ: Princeton University Press.

Rieff, P. (2006). *My Life Among the Deathworks: Illustrations of the Aesthetics of Authority*(K. S. Piver, Ed.). Charlottesville, VA: University of Virginia Press.

Robbins, L. (1935). *An Essay on the Nature and Significance of Economic Science*. London: MacMillan and Company.

Ruskin, J. (1967). *"Unto This Last": Four Essays on the First Principles of Political Economy*. Lincoln, NE: University of Nebraska Press.

Russell, B. (2004). *In Praise of Idleness and Other Essays*. London: Routledge.

Sahlins, M. D. (1974). *Stone Age Economics*. New York, NY: Routledge.

Satz, D. (2009). Nineteenth-Century Political Economy. *Cambridge History of Philosophy in the Nineteenth Century (1790–1870)*, 676–698. doi:10.1017/cho9780511975257.031

Schwartz, B. (2004). The Tyranny of Choice. *Scientific American, 290*(4), 70–75. doi:10.1038/scientificamerican0404-70

Scitovsky, T. (1992). *The Joyless Economy: The Psychology of Human Satisfaction.* New York, NY: Oxford University Press.

Scott, J. C. (1998). Thin Simplifications and Practical Knowledge: Metis. In *Seeing Like a State: How Certain Schemes to Improve the Human Condition Have Failed.* New Haven, CT: Yale University Press.

Scott, J. C. (2014). *Two Cheers for Anarchism: Six Easy Pieces on Autonomy, Dignity and Meaningful Work and Play.* Princeton, NJ: Princeton University Press.

Simmel, G. (1957). Fashion. *American Journal of Sociology, 62*(6), 541–558. Retrieved from www.jstor.org/stable/2773129

Skidelsky, R. J. (2009). *Keynes: The Return of the Master.* New York, NY: Public Affairs.

Skidelsky, R. J., and Skidelsky, E. (2012). *How Much Is Enough?: Money and the Good Life.* London: Allen Lane.

Slote, M. (2004). Two Views of Satisficing. In M. Byron (Ed.), *Satisficing and Maximizing: Moral Theorists on Practical Reason.* Cambridge: Cambridge University Press.

Solnit, R. (2007, September 1). Finding Time. *Orion Magazine.*

Steiner, G. (2002). *Grammars of Creation.* New Haven, CT: Yale University Press.

Stiglitz, J. E. (2010). Toward a General Theory of Consumerism: Reflections on Keynes's Economic Possibilities for Our Grandchildren. In L. Pecchi and G. Piga (Eds.), *Revisiting Keynes: Economic Possibilities for Our Grandchildren* (pp. 41–86). Cambridge, MA: MIT Press.

Stiglitz, J. E., Sen, A. K., and Fitoussi, J. (2009). *The Measurement of Economic Performance and Social Progress Revisited: Reflections and Overview* (Working paper No. 2009-33). Centre de Recherche en Economic de Sciences Po. Retrieved from https://www.ofce.sciences-po.fr/pdf/dtravail/WP2009-33.pdf

Streeck, W. (2014). How Will Capitalism End? *New Left Review, 87.* Retrieved from https://newleftreview.org/II/87/wolfgang-streeck-how-will-capitalism-end

Tawney, R. H. (1926). *Religion and the Rise of Capitalism.* New York, NY: Harcourt, Brace & Company.

Thompson, E. P. (1971). The Moral Economy of the English Crowd in the Eighteenth Century. *Past & Present, 50*, 76–136. Retrieved from www.jstor.org/stable/650244

Thompson, E. P. (1993). *Customs in Common.* London: Penguin Books.

Tijmes, P., and Luijf, R. (1995). The Sustainability of Our Common Future: An Inquiry Into the Foundations of an Ideology. *Technology in Society, 17*(3), 327–336. doi:10.1016/0160-791x(95)00012-g

Warnock, M. (2015). *Critical Reflections on Ownership.* Cheltenham: Edward Elgar Publishing.

Weil, S. (2003). *The Need for Roots: Prelude to a Declaration of Duties Towards Mankind.* New York, NY: Routledge.

Weil, S. (2006). *Oppression and Liberty.* New York, NY: Routledge.

Wootton, B. (2013). *Lament for Economics.* New York, NY: Routledge.

Wordsworth, W. (1807). *The World Is Too Much With Us.* Retrieved from www.poetryfoundation.org/poems/45564/the-world-is-too-much-with-us

Wrigley, E. (1988). The Limits to Growth: Malthus and the Classical Economists. *Population and Development Review, 14*, 30–48. doi:10.2307/2808089

Xenos, N. (1989). *Scarcity and Modernity.* London: Routledge.

Zerzan, J. (2008). *Twilight of the Machines.* Los Angeles, CA: Feral House.

2 Rationality and economic theory

He who sees only ratio sees only himself.

(Blake cited in Damon, 2013, p. 341)

It is important to reclaim for humanity the ground that has been taken from it by variously arbitrarily narrow formulations of the demands of rationality.

(Sen, 2004, p. 51)

I have in mind another human being who will understand me. I count on this. Not on perfect understanding, which is Cartesian, but on approximate understanding, which is Jewish. And on a meeting of sympathies, which is human.

(Bellow cited in Harper, 1994, p. 67)

2.0 Introduction

In this chapter I turn my attention to rationality, one of the three structuring assumptions in economic theory. A chief difficulty in doing so arises partly from the fact that analysis of rational choice theory (RCT) typically ignores the wider historical context from which it emerges. There have, after all, been other ways of thinking about the form and content of reason; and the importance we assign to reason in explaining or predicting behaviour, the scope of its applicability to different areas of social life, has also greatly varied over time.

Our problems are compounded if we consider that rationality is intimately related to how we understand other concepts, such as utility, self-interest, freedom, power and individuality. Things are not made any easier by the fact that even *within* economic theory there hasn't always been a consensus on what is meant by rationality.

It is impossible to do justice to these complexities within the framework of a single chapter. So, although I will touch on a number of these issues the main thrust of this chapter is to emphasize only one point: that the narrowness of RCT, which stems in large part from it being closely aligned with individualism, drastically alters the way in which we think about our relation to other people, places, time and objects of value. In short, because we think alone,[1] we often think only of our own individual interests.

The structure of the chapter is as follows. In the next section I briefly outline how, seen against a broader historical context, economic reason is only one way in which we might understand what is meant by reason, and only one way of explaining human behaviour. In particular, I argue, we cannot understand the profound importance of economic rationality – and economic theory itself – to modernity if we decouple it from a discussion of how, from a historical perspective, it has been implicated with individualism.

Rationality in economic theory is only, therefore, one way of thinking about reason and understanding. In that sense it is limited. In section 2, I want to elaborate on that theme by looking at the idea of 'bounded rationality'. The best way to do that is, I think, to briefly explain the various ways of understanding rationality in economic theory.

Before concluding I return in the third section to the connection between rationality and individualism in economic theory. Is there an alternative way of conceptualizing reason, a way that would involve acknowledging our social nature? In other words, if we want to take ethics and relationality seriously then we have to think about the possibility of 'thinking together'. This in itself is of profound importance but it is also intimately linked with many of the themes in the rest of the book. Thinking from the perspective of a plural subject is crucial if we are to think seriously about inequality, exclusion, a public spirit ethos, common goods, and climate change and our shared responsibility to both non-human beings and future generations.

2.1 History and reason

For a very long time now we have tended to think of reason as the distinguishing feature of what it is to be a human being. Theoretical, abstract reasoning – and contemplation – (Arendt, 1998) may appear to some to be the highest human faculty, god-like even, because of its alleged ability to strike upon universal truths and avoid the messiness of the real world,[2] time, and other people. But *theoria*, as a knowledge of 'higher things' (Jonas, 2001) can lead to an "unreasonable disregard for the practical problems of living" (Graves, 1960, p. 600).

It can also support a number of other important exclusions.[3] Women[4] (Gilligan and Richards, 2009) and colonial subjects (Brody, 2001), seen against the benchmark of reason, have often been considered to be less than fully rational (and therefore subject to domination). Not unrelatedly, emotions, intuition, imagination, religion and morality have often been thought of as being detrimental to the full flowering of reason and to the ordering of society.

The latter point raises the question of the relation between reason and politics.[5] I'll come back to that in the conclusion but for now it is worth noting the dominant role rationality and planning play in the structuring[6] of many aspects of our current lives (work, education, public policies and political decisions). But when did that process begin?

It has been argued that by the 17th century the new reason of mathematics and experimental science was gaining ground over older, scholastic definitions

(Hill, 1969). This 'colder' form of rationality (Willey, 1972) might have envisioned the mind as a *tabula rasa* (and thus free from the past). More importantly from our perspective, it signaled a questioning of Revelation, authority and the social. From now on we could – and should – think alone.[7] It is not hard to see how this would become a central theme of the Enlightenment (Foucault, 1984) and the counter-Enlightenment resistance to it.

As with our discussion on the rise of rationalism in Greece (see footnote 2), it appears that the counter-Enlightenment points us to a fundamental clash in approaches to the nature of, and our understanding of, reality (Gellner, 1999). Reason (science and mathematics) might help us explain the physical world but can the same methods be applied to the understanding of the social world and human behaviour? At stake here is the question of whether we can understand behaviour 'externally' (objectively, logically, mathematically) without any notion of social context and an 'inner' and sympathetic insight that draws on references to goals, purposes and values?[8] If the social world is inherently unpredictable, dynamic and social[9] (rather than probabilistic, static and atomistic) then it seems that those methods are of limited use (Bronk, 2011a, 2011b).

In other words, if the social world is actually a 'dappled world' (Cartwright, 1999) then "reality is not a unified, timeless, immutable structure of which a logically perfect language could give a direct transcription" (Hausheer, 2013, p. lvi).

How does all of this tie in with the emergence of *economic* reason in the classical period? First, it helped foster the idea of mechanical rationality such that human (and economic) action could be explained in a functional form without recourse to introspection or subjective states of the mind (Maas, 2005). Second, this meant that reason was essentially a method, an instrumental tool to achieve ends that, since they are determined by the passions, are not themselves subject to rational scrutiny (Sugden, 1991). Third, as this notion of instrumental rationality extends its hold into areas of our personal, political and social lives "it 'colonizes', reifies, and mutilates[10] the very relational fabric on which social integration, education and individual socialization depend" (Gorz, 2011, p. 107).

From all of this it follows that economic reasoning, as a set of mechanical decision procedures, weakens our relationship to lived experience, to the world and to other people. We might even go so far as to ask whether under this notion of rationality the individual still exists – or whether he has been replaced by the 'substanceless subjectivity' of the perpetually desiring machine?[11]

In recent years it has been argued that the immense success of RCT in economics departments[12] in the latter half of the last century was partly a legacy of its association with individualism during the Cold War period. S.M. Amadae (2003) argues that in mid-century America the development of a formal, axiomatic, logical and universal method of reasoning (in the social sciences, decision theory, and public policy analysis) was part of a larger attempt to defend capitalist democracy and Enlightenment values (liberalism). Crucially, it is the criteria that define what is meant by rationality (rather than the result that Arrow establishes, 'The Impossibility Theorem') that connect individuality with rationality.

Since only subjective desires ('wantability') matter and only individual preferences count, the scope for 'the social' (in the formation of preferences or the ordering of them) is drastically curtailed. Because sovereign individuals are held to make rational decisions there is no allowance for social class or identity[13] in the determination of choices. As McCumber (2016) points out, the human mind (the reasoning process and knowledge itself) is conceived of as being independent of culture, history, emotions and genuine sociality. And rationality doesn't so much as rule out ethics as ignore it or incorporate it into the perspective of desire/preference, thereby undermining its substantive import.

2.2 The limitations of RCT

A standard interpretation of RCT is that we select means to maximally satisfy our preferences/ends. Economic theory doesn't commit us one way or the other on the actual substantive nature of those preferences but economists typically tend to narrow them down to self-interested ones. So let's start with this version of RCT.

Do economic agents always rationally maximize utility?[14] Should they? This notion of rationality has been criticized along several distinct lines. One strand of criticism emphasizes that the theory is 'inadequate' (Elster, 1993) because in reality people do not always behave according to what the theory predicts. This may be because of the complexity of the decision, our limited time, information and/or cognitive capacities. Secondly, and more realistically, our decisions may be swayed or constrained by normative and affective considerations (Etzioni, 1990; Elster, 1996). Why should we not include in our understanding of rationality certain 'means' or processes of choice that are based on ethical considerations; and why should the pursuit of non-self-interested, ethical goals be considered beyond rational consideration?

The first of these limitations of the standard approach, taken up by behavioural economics and neuroeconomics (Schüll and Zaloom, 2011), suggest that in contrast to RCT's predictions actual behaviour is anomalous (or sometimes predictably irrational). We can and often do make mistakes[15]; we can be driven by envy, myopia, influenced by 'framing effects' or suffer from weakness of will. Our preferences might not be complete or stable.[16]

We are not, in summary, disengaged thinkers who always know and automatically (and exclusively) maximize our interests without regard to the history of our choices, our identity and our relation to other people. And we can and do reflectively evaluate the worthiness or reasonableness of our preferences, guided sometimes by social and moral norms (Walsh, 2007). Self-interest maximization is, therefore, a narrow conceptualization of reason and the rich array of decision-making behaviour.

It is often argued that because this version of RCT proposes a minimal notion of psychology (maximizing happiness/pleasure/utility) there is still some bare notion of the individual and its relation to the world (Giocoli, 2003). But this notion of rationality (and utility) has been under pressure since the beginning of the 20th century (Bruni and Sugden, 2007). It seems that the dominant trend has been an increase in formalization such that the axiomatic approach to rationality only requires the maximization of all-things-considered preferences. The substantive content of the latter is now irrelevant to RCT as long as they are formally[17] rational (well-ordered: reflexive, transitive and complete). Formalization, it could be argued, has therefore been part of a 'de-subjectivization process' (Hands, 2006) that removes the mind and subjective sensations from human behaviour in favour of acting algorithmically.

It is questionable, therefore, whether this sparse and allegedly scientific and rigorous version of RCT actually explains *human* behaviour. Shorn of any account of an individuals' beliefs, desires, mental states and distinct human purposes, and how those relate to her institutional and social context – a view from nowhere – are we even talking about individuals, interpretation and human agency at all[18] (Hands, 2008)? Furthermore, it could be questioned whether this thin version of RCT *explains* behaviour at all since if we are by definition utility maximizers then it's not an empirically falsifiable theory (Hodgson, 2013).

It is against this background that Amartya Sen (2004) has tried to argue for a more capacious notion of reason, one that allows for plural reasons of choice. Under this wider understanding of reason we do not have to think of individual choices taking place at a particular moment of time, independent of context, circumstances, the history of my previous decisions, my purposes and goals or my relations with other people.[19]

This notion of rationality, importantly, relates reasoning to freedom[20] both because we have plural reasons to value things and because we can subject our goals to rational scrutiny. The latter point means that at least a part of reason entails moving beyond the relentless pursuit of my own goals (self-interested or otherwise). The point to emphasize here is that not only does reason require a pause in our thinking: slowness, deliberation, the exercise of judgement and learning over time; it can also accommodate taking into account the goals of other people (without subsuming them in an instrumental fashion to my own goals). Reason, then, is inextricably bound to sociality. As we shall see below, the reasoning process itself is dialogic, depending on other people and social evaluations: in addition, at least some of our goals are social in nature insofar as they relate to the pursuit of the common good.

2.3   Thinking together

In the analysis above we have seen that one of the chief drawbacks of RCT is that it assumes that all thinking is individualistic in nature: we reason alone. With its presumption of being a universal method it also ignores specific social contexts: we reason in the void. RCT, then, elides the concept of the social, since social relationships, socially inflected evaluative standards/norms and social contexts typically play little role in the description of rational choice.

In contrast to this formal, austere and private form of reasoning I want to suggest that we adopt a "latitudinarian tolerance for a great miscellany of forms of reasoning" (Baier, 1997, p. 12). A more pluralistic approach to reason would take into account our embodied natures,[21] our 'situatedness', as well as the understanding that reason is not necessarily independent of wit, humour, pleasure (Cooper, 1999) and emotional intelligence.[22] There is, therefore, no single, universal method of reasoning because our lives and experiences are irreducibly diverse (Sen, 2011).

A more open-ended and inclusive notion of reason would also entail two fundamental ideas. Firstly, both a recognition and a grateful acceptance of the fact that we are dependent on other people (teachers, loved ones) for initiating us into the reasoning process. In other words, to become an individual reasoner is an acquired *social* skill that we learn over time. We are not, as economic theory seems to assume, these automatically autonomous and fully-formed thinkers. A better description of how we reason would be to draw an analogy with the learning of a foreign language, a craft, or how to play a musical instrument. In the latter case, for example, being competent depends on an instrument that was crafted and designed by someone else; a musical score or 'script' that I didn't compose myself; and live (or recorded) performances in front of other people (an audience). Innovation or individual interpretation only comes from years of being immersed in an ongoing tradition.

This first fundamental idea might be slightly misleading, though, since it seems to suggest that although initially dependent on 'the social', we eventually develop into independent and individual thinking beings. I want to temper that with the second fundamental idea, namely that not only is reasoning inherently dialogic or conversational; in addition 'the good' that I pursue is social or common. To learn to be an independent thinker is not, therefore, to escape into a realm of autonomy or self-sufficiency.

Before explaining how social relationships and the virtues (of acknowledged dependence) are necessary for both the formation and sustaining of independent practical reasoners, it is important to distinguish Macintyre's notion of 'reasons for action' and that found in economic theory. In economic theory, since we have wanton preferences which are taken as 'given', desire or the passions – and not reason – determine my *individual* goals. Reason, under this view, is merely instrumental, leading me to maximally satisfy my individual preferences. For MacIntyre (2017) (and the older tradition he represents) a reason to act is only comprehensible insofar as it promotes goodness and the latter itself is only intelligible against a background notion of human flourishing or human nature. Unlike in economic theory and in what Griffin (2003) calls 'the taste model' the maximal satisfaction of desire – any desire – can in and of itself not be a sufficient reason to act.[23]

To become an independent reasoner, then, depends on the development of certain skills, capacities, virtues and – as we shall see – social relationships. I must be able to stand back from my present desires and evaluate them. This itself requires a reliance on memory and imagination – how have my desires made me what I currently am, and how might I think about future goods? Furthermore, I should be able to structure my desires since I need to be able to form a judgement as to which of the possible reasons to act is the best reason. The key point is that reasoning is not simply an exercise of individual capacities or the deepening of self-knowledge. Instead, both depend on a prior and continued presence of the social.

For MacIntyre (2001) reasons for action are intelligible to ourselves (and others) within a context of ongoing social relationships and the practical knowledge and cultural discourses bound up with them.[24] The ability to distance[25] myself from my desires and recognize 'the good', to imagine other future forms of 'the good', and to evaluate, modify, order and reject reasons for action, do not simply follow from individual qualities of the mind and a person's character; each is sustained by my social interactions and the history of those interactions. But 'the social' enters our discussion in a second way as well.

As was said above, the second fundamental aspect of a wider notion of reason is tied up with the idea that it is a virtue to acknowledge my dependence on others for my flourishing. Furthermore, I cannot form an adequate conception of that flourishing "apart from and independently of the flourishing of that whole set of relationships in which we have found our place" (MacIntyre, 2001, p. 108). To become an independent reasoner, then, requires not merely an acknowledgement of our debts[26] to others but a commitment to promoting common goods. Just as others cared about my good so, too, I must care[27] about the good of others. Reason would not be reason, it is argued, if it didn't prompt us to further the goods of other people and the community. Reason in that sense is inherently social and to think of rationality as the economist understands it is to see, as William Blake pointed out, only oneself.

So far I have set out the idea that reasoning itself is a dialogical or conversational process. We can add a level of depth to that discussion by briefly noting some of the salient points associated with the idea of 'team reasoning'.

In Tomasello's (2014) fascinating book it is claimed that we can break the act of thinking/reasoning down into three pre-cultural and pre-linguistic components: cognitive representation, simulation and inference, and self-monitoring/ evaluation. Cognitive representation implies an ability to represent to ourselves situations of our environment such that a being[28] can direct its attention to the achievement of its goals (rather than simply instinctively respond to stimuli). Simulation and inference refers to the ability to causally connect those representations. Evaluation refers to behavioural and cognitive self-monitoring.

The fundamental point made by Tomasello is that since most animals are competitive 'individuals' there is only individual intentionality/thinking. Because human beings are fundamentally cooperative and social beings each of the components of reasoning was transformed under ecological pressures (the need to coordinate foraging activities between small bands of humans). We develop, that is, new, or rather socially inflected and modified modes of reasoning: perspectival and symbolic representations; socially recursive inferences; and social and normative standards of evaluating behaviour.

What distinguishes humans from other animals, then, is not so much the existence of reason in one and the lack of it in another; instead, it is the *social* nature of reasoning in humans. Human beings, under the selective pressure to survive, became more cooperative and interdependent. As a result they first developed what Tomasello calls 'joint intentionality':[29] joint goals and joint intentions. Reasoning, then, is an inter-subjective phenomenon that takes place in a shared world and is directed towards the common good.[30]

In this framework there is an understanding that over time we become plural subjects (a 'we')[31] interested[32] in achieving and sustaining the common good. Sharing, a recognition of the common ground we have with others, a grateful acknowledgement of our dependence on others, mutuality, sympathy and imaginative insight are not simply optional add-ons but, instead, fundamental to understanding what it is to be human.

2.4　Conclusion

I have hinted that it is best not to think of the rise of a deeply individualistic notion of rationality in economic thought in isolation from its support for capitalist democracy in the post-war period. Looking through a wider historical lens, it would be more accurate to place economic rationality within the context of political liberalism and the Enlightenment, since both are inextricably tied to an abstract, 'disembedded' notion of the individual and to a hollowing out of any substantive notion of 'the good'.

The organization of work, education, culture, agricultural and industrial economic activity along rationalistic lines – individualistic and maximizing mentalities and practices – is, therefore, profoundly related to both a particular (liberal) understanding of the political and to the reduction of the concept freedom to 'negative liberty'.[33]

We should not, I suggest, continue to think of rationality being important to capitalist democracy simply because it introduces order, discipline and an individualistic outlook to specific institutions (schools, factories, governments). In our current condition we have to think, in addition, as to how reason and governance are implicated in the liberation of desire in our late capitalistic 'control societies' (Deleuze, 1992).

It seems, then, that we are moving into a new 'rationality of desire' (Beistegui, 2016), a capitalist regime that aims to proliferate and stimulate desires. This bipolitical regime's primary focus is, then, on facilitating the emergence of the supposedly 'natural' infinity of desires. In some sense all this is closely linked to economic theory. First, theory also maintains that desires are infinite ('non-satiation').

Second, what moves us to act is the "brave and naked will" (Murdoch, 1999, p. 290) of the sovereign individual and not 'the good' and/or any regard for the community. The question is only one of living, and not of *living well*.[34] As we have seen with regard to RCT, the individual is moved to maximally satisfy his or her desires/preferences – no matter what they might be. In that sense we have moved to a post-utilitarian scenario since what counts is pure enjoyment (*jouissance*) rather than 'satisfaction' or 'utility'.

The latter point introduces a potential difficulty since if the freedom of the will is paramount, something that escapes reason, then in reality any *theory* of individual decision-making must be a very thin one. Are, for example, the theoretical restrictions we impose on desire (such as claiming the structure of preferences must be rational) a limitation of our freedom?

If that is the case then why not do away with economic theory's stable representations altogether – especially if individuals in practice do not choose rationally but make mistakes?[35] The problem of thinking about freedom in this way, unconstrained by goals, purposes, structure, or the concerns of other people is that it ends up as a pointless or hollow series of negations and transgressions (Eagleton, 2005). If we ask why we should want more and more commodities – a topic to which I presently turn – the economist may reply, 'there is no why here'.[36] That seems like an empty and lonely kind of freedom!

Notes

1   In contrast, Knight (1940) suggests that all thinking is social or dialogic (intercommunicative). I return to this in section 3.

2   For Feyerabend (2002), the rise of rationalism in Greece was the discovery of a situation-independent and therefore universal *method* of knowing. Not only did this entail a devaluing of plural and local ways of approaching reality (through poetry, myths, religion); it also opened up the possibility of the centralization of power and a growth in the authority of experts. The separation of knowledge from life, the 'ancient quarrel' between philosophy and poetry, is a question that is very relevant to academics and their engagement in the so-called 'life of the mind'. On the scientific reduction of experience in more modern times see Gadamer (1996).

3   On the exclusion of the mad from society see Foucault (2006).

4   In a stunning essay, Midgley (n.d.) asks whether there is a relation between, on the one hand, the fact that so many influential philosophers were bachelors and, on the other hand, the style of thought/reason, the type of questions they were interested in. Instead of thinking as isolated individuals, instead of reasoning being a closed system – and holding those up to be the ideal – how would we reason if, alternatively, we recognized that we are, fundamentally, "animals that go in pairs"? (p. 2).

5   On the importance of reason and rational self-interest for political order see Foucault (1979), Hirschman (1997) and Scott (2008).

6   Ivan Illich was acutely aware of how that top-down structuring could impose limitations on our ability to live genuinely autonomous lives. Instead of a reflective age full of representations (and misrepresentations) he would advocate that "we enjoy an unorganized earth, and one that cannot be organized within a future" (Farias, 2002, p. 61).

7   The idea that from the 17th century onwards experience and our knowledge of it resided purely in the mind, in each *individual* mind, is explored by Reed (1996). The loss of primary experience and its replacement by representations is, of course, related to the development of capitalism: the devaluation of craft skills (Crawford, 2015), the divorce between knowledge and life in our schools, and in late capitalism the growth of mediated knowledge and leisure 'activities' through a screen culture.

8   This point is central to Sen's (2004) criticism of the 'internal consistency' view of RCT. He argues that it is a 'bizarre' notion. Consistent choice is only comprehensible if we consider reasons that are 'external' to the choice sets themselves. In any case, it has often be queried whether consistency isn't really a virtue of small minds.

9   Lawson's (2009) apt summary is "social reality, then, is a relational totality in motion" (p. 765).

10 The crowding-out of solidarity, genuine autonomy, and relationality is a recurring theme in this book. Gorz (2011) sees this, along with the liberation of desires ('non-satiation') and the elimination of reflection on our needs and our rational 'ends' as necessary for continued capitalist expansion. Economic rationality, in that sense, goes hand in hand with capitalist rationality. If economic rationality emphasizes maximization and calculation it is inimical to what in the last chapter I called a 'subsistence ethic'.

11 On the fascination with this abstract individuation see Mirowski (2001). If all knowledge is algorithmic are economic agents (and markets) just information processing systems?

12 It is worth noting the growing importance of rationality across disciplines as it becomes a normative theory rather than a mere description of behaviour in the limited empirical context of markets. In the latter half of the century we see the growth of the law and economics movement, rational expectations (macro), rational strategies (game theory), rational self-interested actors in political philosophy (Rawls) and in public policy analysis (Buchanan).

13 Since economic theory is founded on methodological individualism, the private self, it generally eschews analysis of identity issues because that opens the door to an emphasis on 'the social'. For recent exceptions see Akerlof and Kranton (2010). On the role of identity in both shaping our understanding of the world (the 'perceptual function' of community) and influencing our ethical evaluations (of actions, states of affairs), see Sen (1999). It does not follow, Sen is keen to point out, that we can only reason from within a particular community/identity.

14 See Varoufakis (2005). He questions whether it is justifiable to say that agents act 'as if' they were self-interested maximizers.

15 In the presence of poor informational environments and discrete (rather than continuous) choices, we may be slow learners; some people may make fewer mistakes than others, depending on the context (Thaler, 2000).

16 Some have argued that it follows that to prevent rationality from being falsified it should be normative rather than a theory that explains or predicts actual behaviour (Hands, 2015). Alternatively, perhaps theorizing is itself redundant.

17 It is not surprising that Broome (1999) could state that we should only be concerned about the structure of 'the good' and not its substance.

18 I return to this idea of the disappearance of the individual in chapter 4. It is a strange state of affairs in which the narrower the theory of rationality becomes the more it is believed to be universal! Reason may claim to explain a large range of actions but it does not explain them in a large way (Chesterton, 2008).

19 The lack of 'ontological fit' between the logical/deductive approach of the atomistic RCT and the social realm which is open, meaningful and relationally constituted is brilliantly described by Lawson (2003). Similarly, it seems Keynes also argued that if social reality was inherently organic (complex, interdependent and non-deterministic) then individual rationality on its own would not in all circumstances determine our decisions; instead, we would have to rely on conventional judgement (tradition, customary expectations or reference points). In other words: *social* norms. (Dow, 2013).

20 In a remarkable passage Murdoch (1999) questions whether we should always think about freedom in terms of the unconstrained will and the expansion of possibilities: "The ideal situation, on the contrary, is rather to be represented as a kind of 'necessity'. This is something of which saints speak and which any artist will readily understand. The idea of a patient, loving regard, directed upon a person, a thing, a situation, presents the will not as unimpeded movement but as something very much like 'obedience'" (p. 331).

21 The disembodied version holds that we are calm and collected observers of the world (or, rather, representations of it). It might be more accurate to say that "the

world is known to us because we live and act in it" (Crawford, 2015, p. 50). The importance of taking into account our bodily and animal nature, is at the heart of Macintyre (2001) and is best summarized by Aquinas's words, "my soul is not I" (as cited in MacIntyre, 2001, p. 6).

22 On the important idea that we may not just come to understand someone accurately, but justly and lovingly, is brilliantly described by Murdoch (2001).

23 This is another way of saying that 'the good' cannot be reduced to desire; 'the good' itself is desirable, or elicits desire, but it does not follow that whatever we desire is good. The same holds true for pleasure.

24 Thus, for example, sympathy should not be seen – as it typically is in economic theory – as simply an individual reason for action. An action based on sympathy is not an optional 'choice' faced by an autonomous individual. Rather, sympathy is constitutive of the ethical and social dimension of a form of human life.

25 Sen (1977) calls this the ability to form 'meta preferences'. In a similar vein, Frankfurt (1971) claims that our ability to form second-order preferences is what distinguishes us as persons from other animals.

26 This concept of debt may be inimical to the economic way of thinking since it suggests that an element of 'givenness' is woven into our very being. The voluntary transactions of the ideal economic agent, on the other hand, assumes that we can always start from scratch.

27 To invoke the concept of care is really to highlight the idea that reason, as understood as the promotion of common goods, fundamentally ties together the social and the ethical. This is another way of saying that we need to think of ourselves as belonging to a 'continuous moral community' (Baier, 2012) if we are to reimagine an ethical economy and a solution to some of our fiercest challenges, such as climate change (see chapter 9).

28 Two points stand out here. As with MacIntyre (2001), a goal/good can be associated with the notion of a being's flourishing rather than as an automatic response to a desire. Also, I use the word 'being' because it appears that animals, to a varying degree, have this capacity. In that sense we might want to think of animals as being 'weakly cognitive' (a point also emphasized by MacIntyre) and reason as existing on a continuous scale throughout animal life.

29 Only later on, under pressure to generalize joint intentionality across larger number of groups did 'collective intentionality', conventions and culture develop.

30 This understanding of reason is the complete opposite of how we characterize rationality in economic theory! In the latter reasoning takes place in an individual's mind and is directed towards his own private good.

31 We can think of walking together as a paradigm of 'we-reasoning' in the sense that there is a mutual understanding that each participant in the joint activity is expressing a commitment to becoming a plural subject with a single goal: 'we want to walk *together*' (Gilbert, 1990). As with Macintyre's analysis it is important to remember that there is always a role for the individual practical reasoner within this 'we' perspective. The individual is not subsumed under the collective but thinks: "what should I do as a group member" (Hakli, Miller and Tuomela, 2010, p. 293). Given that, it is perhaps better to adopt Etzioni's (1990) terminology and think about an 'I-we' perspective.

32 That we care about 'the good' of other people and the common good suggests a very different notion of the self to that found in economic theory. Instead of the self-sufficient, pathologically isolated and 'bounded self' of the economic agent we should picture ourselves as being open to "actual relationships between embodied persons" (Held, 1990, p. 330).

33 I do not consider what kind of educational, cultural or political institutions would be needed to make the idea of pluralistic reason that I have been advocating a viable one. One possibility, with its similar emphasis on tradition, memory and mutuality (Benda et al., 1988) is the civil economy tradition (see chapter 10).

34 It is not surprising, then, that there is so much focus on the body and bodily desires in academic literature (see chapter 4).

35 This does, indeed, seem to be part of the impetus behind the empirical turn which includes behavioural economics, neuroeconomics as well as the emphasis on 'Big Data' and the endless flow of uncritical, real-time information (Davies, 2015a). This sets up a disturbing possibility in a post-crisis world whereby individual choice is 'nudged' to the appropriate behaviour by corporation and the state. This new form of government rationality is built upon the knowledge of patterns and connections that spontaneously emerge (Davies, 2015b). The point here is that the connections, relations and networks offer a false notion of 'the social' because they are ultimately only data points deprived of any normative content or ongoing social relationships. And the 'neocommunitarians' (Davies, 2012) are really just policy technocrats – architects, designers, academics and scientists – trying to influence behaviour through the creation of 'social' environments and 'smart cities'. Where, we might ask again, is the individual in late capitalism?

36 This response, taken from a very different context, comes from Levi's (1996) haunting *Survival in Auschwitz*.

Bibliography

Akerlof, G. A., and Kranton, R. (2010). *Identity Economics: How Our Identities Shape Our Work, Wages, and Well-Being*. Princeton, NJ, Woodstock, Oxfordshire: Princeton University Press. Retrieved from www.jstor.org/stable/j.ctt7rqsp

Amadae, S. M. (2003). *Rationalizing Capitalist Democracy: The Cold War Origins of Rational Choice Liberalism*. Chicago, IL: University of Chicago Press.

Arendt, H. (1998). *The Human Condition*. Chicago, IL: University of Chicago Press.

Baier, A. C. (1997). *The Commons of the Mind*. Chicago, IL: Open Court.

Baier, A. C. (2012). *Reflections on How We Live*. Oxford: Oxford University Press.

Beistegui, M. D. (2016). The Government of Desire: A Genealogical Perspective. *Journal of the British Society for Phenomenology*, *47*(2), 190–203. doi:10.1080/00071773.2016.1139928

Benda, V., Šimečka, M., Jirous, I., Dienstbier, J., Havel, V., Hejdánek, L., . . . Wilson, P. (1988). Parallel Polis, or An Independent Society in Central and Eastern Europe: An Inquiry. *Social Research*, *55*(1 and 2), 211–246. Retrieved from www.jstor.org/stable/40970497

Brody, H. (2001). *The Other Side of Eden: Hunters, Farmers, and the Shaping of the World*. San Francisco, CA: North Point Press.

Bronk, R. (2011a). Uncertainty, Modelling Monocultures and the Financial Crisis. *Business Economist*, *42*(2), 5–18.

Bronk, R. (2011b). *Epistemological Difficulties With Neoclassical Economics*. Working Paper, Southern Economic Association, Washington, DC, USA, pp. 19–21.

Broome, J. (1999). *Ethics Out of Economics*. Cambridge: Cambridge University Press.

Bruni, L., and Sugden, R. (2007). The Road Not Taken: How Psychology Was Removed From Economics, and How It Might Be Brought Back. *The Economic Journal*, *117*(516), 146–173. doi:10.1111/j.1468-0297.2007.02005.x

Cartwright, N. (1999). *The Dappled World: A Study of the Boundaries of Science*. New York, NY: Cambridge University Press.

Chesterton, G. K. (2008). *Orthodoxy*. West Valley City, UT: Waking Lion Press.

Cooper, A. A., Earl of Shaftesbury (1999). Sensus Communis, an Essay on the Freedom of Wit and Humour. In L. E. Klein (Ed.), *Characteristics of Men, Manners, Opinions, Times*. Cambridge: Cambridge University Press.

Crawford, M. B. (2015). *The World Beyond Your Head: On Becoming an Individual in an Age of Distraction*. London: Penguin Books.

Damon, S. F. (2013). *A Blake Dictionary: The Ideas and Symbols of William Blake*. Hanover, NH: Dartmouth College Press.

Davies, W. (2012). The Emerging Neocommunitarianism. *The Political Quarterly*, *83*(4), 767–776. doi:10.1111/j.1467-923x.2012.02354.x

Davies, W. (2015a). The Chronic Social: Relations of Control Within and Without Neoliberalism. *New Formations: A Journal of Culture/Theory/Politics*, *84*, 40–57.

Davies, W. (2015b). The Return of Social Government. *European Journal of Social Theory*, *18*(4), 431–450. doi:10.1177/1368431015578044

Deleuze, G. (1992). Postscript on the Societies of Control. *October*, *59*, 3–7. Retrieved from www.jstor.org/stable/778828

Dow, S. (2013). Keynes, Knowledge, Expectations and Rationality. In R. Frydman and E. S. Phelps (Eds.), *Rethinking Expectations: The Way Forward for Macroeconomics*. Princeton, NJ: Princeton University Press.

Eagleton, T. (2005). *Holy Terror*. Oxford: Oxford University Press.

Elster, J. (1993). Some Unresolved Problems in the Theory of Rational Behavior. *Acta Sociologica*, *36*(3), 179–189. Retrieved from www.jstor.org/stable/4200854

Elster, J. (1996). Rationality and the Emotions. *The Economic Journal*, *106*(438), 1386–1397. doi:10.2307/2235530

Etzioni, A. (1990). *Moral Dimension: Toward a New Economics*. New York, NY: Free Press.

Farias, D. (2002). *The Challenges of Ivan Illich: A Collective Reflection* (L. Hoinacki and C. Mitcham, Eds.). Albany, NY: State University of New York Press.

Feyerabend, P. (2002). *Farewell to Reason*. London: Verso.

Foucault, M. (1979, October 10 and 16). *Omnes et Singulatim: Towards a Criticism of 'Political Reason'*. Lecture presented at The Tanner Lectures on Human Values in Stanford University, Stanford, CA. Retrieved from https://tannerlectures.utah.edu/_documents/a-to-z/f/foucault81.pdf

Foucault, M. (1984). *The Foucault Reader* (P. Rabinow, Ed.). New York, NY: Pantheon Books.

Foucault, M. (2006). *Madness and Civilization: A History of Insanity in the Age of Reason* (R. Howard, Trans.). New York, NY: Vintage Books.

Frankfurt, H. (1971). Freedom of the Will and the Concept of a Person. *The Journal of Philosophy*, *68*(1), 5–20. doi:10.2307/2024717

Gadamer, H. G. (1996). *The Enigma of Health: The Art of Healing in a Scientific Age*. Stanford, CA: Stanford University Press.

Gellner, E. (1999). *Language and Solitude: Wittgenstein, Malinowski and the Habsburg Dilemma*. Cambridge: Cambridge University Press.

Gilbert, M. (1990). Walking Together: A Paradigmatic Social Phenomenon. *Midwest Studies In Philosophy*, *15*(1), 1–14. doi:10.1111/j.1475-4975.1990.tb00202.x

Gilligan, C., and Richards, D. A. (2009). *The Deepening Darkness: Patriarchy, Resistance, and Democracy's Future*. Cambridge: Cambridge University Press.

Giocoli, N. (2003). *Modeling Rational Agents: From Interwar Economics to Early Modern Game Theory*. Northampton, MA: Edward Elgar Publishing.

Gorz, A. (2011). *Critique of Economic Reason*. London: Verso.

Graves, R. (1960). The Case for Xanthippe. *The Kenyon Review*, *22*(4), 597–605. Retrieved from www.jstor.org/stable/4334072

Griffin, J. (2003). *Value Judgement: Improving Our Ethical Beliefs.* Oxford: Clarendon Press.

Hakli, R., Miller, K., and Tuomela, R. (2010). Two Kinds of We-Reasoning. *Economics and Philosophy, 26*(3), 291–320. doi:10.1017/s0266267110000386

Hands, D. W. (2006). Individual Psychology, Rational Choice, and Demand: Some Remarks on Three Recent Studies. *Revue de Philosophie Economique, 13*, 3–48.

Hands, D. W. (2008). Introspection, Revealed Preference and Neoclassical Economics: A Critical Response to Don Ross on the Robbins-Samuelson Argument Pattern. *Journal of the History of Economic Thought, 30*(4), 453–478.

Hands, D. W. (2015). *Normative Rational Choice Theory: Past, Present, and Future* (Working paper). Research Paper Series, SSRN. Available at: https://papers.ssrn.com/sol3/papers.efm?abstract_id=1738671 or http://dx.doi.org/10.2139/ssrn.1738671

Harper, G. L. (1994). *Conversations With Saul Bellow* (G. L. Cronin and B. Siegel, Eds.). Jackson, MS: University Press of Mississippi.

Hausheer, R. (2013). Introduction. In I. Berlin (Author) *Against the Current: Essays in the History of Ideas* (2nd ed.). Princeton, NJ: Princeton University Press.

Held, V. (1990). Feminist Transformations of Moral Theory. *Philosophy and Phenomenological Research, 50*, 321–344. doi:10.2307/2108046

Hill, C. (1969). 'Reason' and 'Reasonableness' in Seventeenth-Century England. *The British Journal of Sociology, 20*(3), 235–252. doi:10.2307/588950

Hirschman, A. O. (1997). *The Passions and the Interests: Political Arguments for Capitalism Before Its Triumph.* Princeton, NJ: Princeton University Press.

Hodgson, G. M. (2013). *From Pleasure Machines to Moral Communities: An Evolutionary Economics Without Homo Economicus.* Chicago, IL: University of Chicago Press.

Jonas, H. (2001). *The Phenomenon of Life: Toward a Philosophical Biology.* Evanston, IL: Northwestern University Press.

Knight, F. (1940). 'What is Truth' in Economics? *Journal of Political Economy, 48*(1), 1–32. Retrieved from www.jstor.org/stable/1825908

Lawson, T. (2003). *Reorienting Economics.* London: Routledge.

Lawson, T. (2009). The Current Economic Crisis: Its Nature and the Course of Academic Economics. *Cambridge Journal of Economics, 33*(4), 759–777. doi:10.1093/cje/bep035

Levi, P. (1996). *Survival in Auschwitz.* New York, NY: A Touchstone Book.

Maas, H. (2005). Jevons, Mill and The Private Laboratory of the Mind. *The Manchester School, 73*(5), 620–649. doi:10.1111/j.1467-9957.2005.00468.x

MacIntyre, A. C. (2001). *Dependent Rational Animals: Why Human Beings Need the Virtues.* Chicago, IL: Open Court.

MacIntyre, A. C. (2017). *Ethics in the Conflicts of Modernity: An Essay on Desire, Practical Reasoning, and Narrative.* New York, NY: Cambridge University Press.

McCumber, J. (2016). *The Philosophy Scare: The Politics of Reason in the Early Cold War.* Chicago, IL: University of Chicago Press.

Midgley, M. (n.d.). *Rings and Books.* Essay. Retrieved from www.womeninparenthesis.co.uk/wp-content/uploads/2016/05/rings-and-books.pdf

Mirowski, P. (2001). Economists Encounter Cyborgs. In C. Gerschlager (Ed.), *Expanding the Economic Concept of Exchange: Deception, Self-Deception and Illusions.* Boston, MA: Kluwer Academic.

Murdoch, I. (1999). *Existentialists and Mystics: Writings on Philosophy and Literature.* New York, NY: Penguin Books.

Murdoch, I. (2001). *The Sovereignty of Good.* London: Routledge.

Reed, E. S. (1996). *The Necessity of Experience.* New Haven, CT: Yale University Press.

Schüll, N. D., and Zaloom, C. (2011). The Shortsighted Brain: Neuroeconomics and the Governance of Choice in Time. *Social Studies of Science, 41*(4), 515–538. doi:10.1177/0306312710397689

Scott, J. C. (2008). *Seeing Like a State: How Certain Schemes to Improve the Human Condition Have Failed.* New Haven, CT: Yale University Press.

Sen, A. K. (1977). Rational Fools: A Critique of the Behavioral Foundations of Economic Theory. *Philosophy & Public Affairs, 6*(4), 317–344. Retrieved from www.jstor.org/stable/2264946

Sen, A. K. (1999). *Reason Before Identity.* Oxford: Oxford University Press.

Sen, A. K. (2004). *Rationality and Freedom.* Cambridge, MA: Belknap Press of Harvard University Press.

Sen, A. K. (2011). *The Idea of Justice.* Cambridge, MA: Belknap Press of Harvard University Press.

Sugden, R. (1991). Rational Choice: A Survey of Contributions From Economics and Philosophy. *The Economic Journal, 101*(407), 751–785. doi:10.2307/2233854

Thaler, R. H. (2000). From Homo Economicus to Homo Sapiens. *Journal of Economic Perspectives, 14*(1), 133–141. doi:10.1257/jep.14.1.133

Tomasello, M. (2014). *A Natural History of Human Thinking.* Cambridge, MA: Harvard University Press.

Varoufakis, Y. (2005). *Foundations of Economics: A Beginner's Companion.* London: Routledge.

Walsh, V. (2007). Amartya Sen on Rationality and Freedom. *Science & Society, 71*(1), 59–83. Retrieved from www.jstor.org/stable/40404363

Willey, B. (1972). *The Seventeenth-Century Background: Studies in the Thought of the Age in Relation to Poetry and Religion.* Harmondsworth: Penguin Books.

3 The ethical limits of markets

Epstein's world is one of quiet individuality. 'It is about the pursuit of pleasure before pleasure was commodified', he says. 'Now everything is so packaged'. People drink, dance, hold hands and gaze out to sea, independent of the frantically consumerised world growing up around them like a jungle that gradually blocks out all the light.

(Roux, 2005)

3.0 Introduction

In the pursuit of a clearer understanding of the relation between ethics and economics, I want to broach the question of whether there are ethical limits to commodification (market expansion). Market expansion can be conceived as an extension in the exchange of commodities across different countries and regions (globalization). It can also be thought of as a *deepening* process with the result that items, activities or 'goods' that were once produced and exchanged via non-market institutions are now brought within the ambit of the market mechanism. Essential to the deepening process is not just privatization, outsourcing and the penetration of markets into ever-increasing areas of natural, social and political life; in addition it involves a change in human subjectivities: our attitudes, values, character and self-perceptions. The fact that commodification negatively modifies our relationships[1] (to other people, nature and things of value) is one facet of what I have called 'the main thesis' of this book.

In section 1 I outline, in contrast, why for economists expansion is thought to be a good thing. I do so by briefly reflecting on the historical dimension of the process. However, the main aim of this chapter is to explain the moral case for the limitation of market expansion. I contextualize the discussion of limits against a broader look at the idea of limits in economic theory and markets themselves (section 2) before examining various conceptual frameworks that might delimit and justify[2] the boundaries of market transactions (section 3).

Any discussion of commodification is bound to be a complex one since examining its history is essentially equivalent to analysing the history of capitalism. The process has proceeded at different speeds (in different countries and for different commodities), making any general theoretical understanding of the process problematic. For example, commodification at an early stage of capitalism primarily involves the production and exchange of physical items, while at a later stage it increasingly invades the lifeworld, as human subjectivity, social relations, and culture (representations and sign-value) become commodities. I look at this in section 4.

Commodification is a multi-faceted process that is related to technology, legal institutions, power relations, culture, property relations, agency and contract. In that sense commodification is not simply an *economic* process but a wide-ranging socio-political and historical one. Given the increasing commodification of a wide range of activities and areas of everyday life it is important to fine tune our understanding of that process and relate it to our earlier discussion in the chapter. I do so in section 5 before concluding.

Commodification is profoundly related to many other of the themes I explore in this book. Inequality, for example, can in an important sense be thought of as a question of who possesses commodities and who doesn't; at the heart of climate change is our obsession with commodities and the attempt to think of nature as nothing but a commodity; in the public realm market-led policy reforms are based on the idea that we should think of education, health and care as private goods (commodities); And as we saw in the last chapter, rationality is bound up with the idea of the rational organization of commodity production.

3.1   Market expansion, freedom, efficiency and growth

In justifying commodification (market expansion) economists have typically focused either on the narrow economic argument that markets promote efficiency, welfare and income growth, or on the more specific policy agenda of privatization to counter the alleged[3] economic inefficiencies of the public sector and state bureaucracies (Le Grand, 2013).

In addition to that strictly economic argument is the idea that markets promote not just opportunity freedoms but agency or process freedoms as well (Sen, 1993). There is, therefore, a wider social and political argument that decentralized markets foster innovation and dynamism, are the best mechanism of satisfying people's preferences, and that they help promote individualism, freedom[4] and pluralism.

The debate over how far market relations, rhetoric and ideology should penetrate social relations is not a new one (Thompson, 1993; Calhoun, 2012). The extension of markets, however, hasn't always been seen in a wholly negative light. Market interactions, it has been claimed, could foster desirable character traits (Hirschman, 1982; McCloskey, 2007). Hirschman (1997), for example, articulates the political argument that modern societies could not be organized on the basis of passions or moral sentiments alone since these were too divergent, unreliable and too fiercely contested. Instead, a society based on each person rationally pursuing his or her own interests (or private good) through market interactions is more likely to lead to a predictable and orderly arrangement.

Charles Taylor (2007) is right to suggest, therefore, that the market has, over time, come to be understood as a key plank in the construction of our modern 'social imaginary' because it serves as a metaphor for the peaceful and orderly resolution of conflicts.[5]

Before the left succeeded in linking together the idea of the bourgeois with superficiality, shallowness and materialism in the popular imagination, it was possible to think of the solid, sober and restrained world of the bourgeois in a positive light. In fact, in a world of rapidly shifting technologies, complexity and ambiguity it may be that we *now* look back at the old, solid world of inherited small pleasures (Hughes, 2005), ownership and possession, settled convictions and stable habits with if not quite nostalgia, then at least with a sense of something of value having been lost.

Of course, to suggest that objects may help provide a sense of continuity to our lives is not to endorse commodification *per se*, but merely to point out, along with Jim Ede, that "a continuing way of life in which objects, stones, glass, pictures, sculpture in light and in space . . . make manifest the underlying stability which more and more we need to recognize if we are not to be swamped by all that is rapidly opening up before us" (Fuller, 1985, p. 149).

In the mid-19th century Ruskin (1967) suggested that not everything should be for sale. In thinking about the judiciary, the army, the priesthood or teachers we are reluctant, he rightly pointed out, to think that their specific actions and judgements should be determined exclusively by monetary considerations. That is, we place certain aspects of our social life – as well as moral and civic 'goods' beyond the logic of the market and typically argue that they shouldn't be thought of in market terms, let alone actually be incorporated into market provision.

From a historical perspective it has often[6] been argued that commoditization and a commercial society undermine republican virtues and civic 'goods'. Markets have, of course, often been seen as harbingers of change, as importantly reducing the hold of authoritative traditions, customs and norms on people's lives. But if markets reflect and encourage individual, voluntary choice it is not surprising that many thinkers also viewed them as being, at some level, in conflict with the political. The latter's emphasis on obligations, a long-term perspective and on collective aspirations stands in stark contrast to the pursuit of short-term, individual interests in market settings.

There has been significant concern, then, that the expansion of the market hollows out citizenship, tarnishes republican virtues, and hinders the efficacy of the public sector (and with them, the plausibility of social democracy).

Commodification can be understood as shift from the production and use of items whose meaning and value are embedded within an overall framework of cultural, religious and social norms to a system of production for the market. This shift, from use-values to exchange values, is sometimes represented abstractly as a move from (C-M-C) to a capitalist system (M-C-M'). In reality the process involves a lot of sociological changes and couldn't have taken place without the growing role of quantification, impersonalization, money and contracts in society.

Historically, criticisms of market expansion have therefore been expressed in terms of how commoditization alters or corrupts our social and contextual understanding of labour, land[7] and human subjectivity (Polanyi, 2014) and how the process dissolves the human bonds – a sense of obligation and commitment – that are necessary to orient us in the world we live. To paraphrase Simmel, money[8] (and contracts) released individuals from institutions and obligations that included the entire person (Slater and Tonkiss, 2004).

An enduring historical criticism of commodification has centred on the idea that the process generates the development of a false consciousness. We mistakenly come to believe that commodities are the secret to well-being[9] and happiness, and this encourages us to esteem the formal freedoms to buy and sell whatever we want, ignoring the deeper, structural inequalities of class and power.

Furthermore, our very understanding of happiness, 'needs', pleasure and human flourishing may change as these things are sought and expressed in commodity form. Ultimately, we may need to ask not just who produces wealth and how it is distributed but also return to an older political economy tradition and ask, along with Ruskin, what is meant by 'wealth'. The answer to *that* question profoundly influences how we think about inequality, fairness, the public good and sustainability.

3.2   The idea of limits

There is no single theoretical framework to explain or justify why market transactions should be limited. Within the liberal tradition universal commodification can perhaps[10] be resisted if we recall that social reality can (and should be) fairly neatly parceled into various 'spheres', distinct realms subject to their own standards of excellence, definitions of appropriate behaviour, norms governing motivations and accepted ways of transacting within them.

In what Radin (1987) calls a 'domino effect' this clear demarcation of distinct areas of life can be undermined by the complete dominance of the principles and evaluative standards pertaining to one 'sphere'. For example, from a liberal point of view we are deeply disturbed by the intrusion of politics into our private lives or, conversely, of the emergence of family-type networks in the political realm. Seen in this light the ethical criticism of markets is not a critique of markets *per se*; instead it is an attempt to uphold a version of pluralism, one that recognizes the incommensurability of the principles, motivations and evaluative standards in the different realms of our lives.

For earlier thinkers (Polanyi, 2014) land, labour and capital would always be 'fictitious commodities' since they were not produced by or for the market. Building on Polanyi's idea it is reasonable to think that knowledge, culture and the natural habitat can also never really be fully commoditized without leading us to either perish from social dislocation or environmental collapse. This line of thinking suggests that there are some human and non-human natural or inherent limits to commodification. Seen in this light, the non-commoditized aspects of our lives, family relations, national and religious identities, culture, social networks and politics (state regulation, for example) are a bulwark against the ravages of unfettered markets, offering us social protection from the dissolution of social bonds at the hands of market forces.

Both the liberal idea of distinct sources of value and Polanyi's notion of fictitious commodities point to the belief that the erasure of limits (universal commodification) will have profound social and political repercussions. In addition, commoditization can also contribute to the weakening of the market itself. This is another way of saying that for market economies to flourish the price mechanism cannot be infinitely extended. At the very least the framework (contracts, rule of law, regulation) within which market transactions take place must itself be immune from self-interested and competitive market principles. Not everything can be for sale.

On the other hand, it has often been thought that large parts of modernity (the economy and culture) are driven by the need to break down or surpass limits (Rieff, 2006). In art and fiction it has been maintained that modernity is intimately associated with novelty (Hughes, 2012) and the discarding of not just older forms but the very idea of conventions or standards themselves. The counter-cultural notion of the 'boundless self', globalization (and the expansionary logic of capitalism), the spread of information technologies and the emphasis on innovation all help to make the idea of limits hard to sustain.[11]

How do we reconcile these two tendencies, the relentless logic of expansion and the simultaneous need for limits?

In contrast to Polanyi, Nancy Fraser (2014) does not see land, labour and nature in ahistorical terms, as if they existed as social formations offering 'refuge' from, because separate from, capitalistic development. Instead, she sees the existence of limits *within* the framework of a crisis or contradiction in capitalism. The crisis stems from a 'double movement': on the one hand a logic of greater commodification (in the relentless search for profits) and on the other hand the realization that non-commoditized spheres of social existence are required as a 'structural condition' for the possibility of commodification. Society *cannot* be commoditized all the way down in this reading because it would result in an unsustainable ecology and the withering away of the capacity for social reproduction.[12]

The argument made by Fraser allows for the possibility that non-commoditized sectors or non-market institutions are not inherently valuable and something to be preserved at all costs from market forces. Indeed, echoing Adam Smith, non-capitalist land, labour and money relations can be based on hierarchies, exclusion and dominance, while markets, with their emphasis on formal equality, can be liberating.

But there is another point made by Fraser and others (Mitropoulos, 2012) that should be emphasized. For Fraser, capitalism is a transgressive force that simultaneously needs and erodes the non-commoditized sectors (what she calls 'background conditions') necessary for ecological, social and economic sustainability. The limits to commodification – which are often thought to arise from institutions (the state), social values (ethics and culture), or notions of a natural realm existing outside the market – are not actually *external* to the capitalist system, but at the heart of its very foundations.

Seen in this light, it is easier to understand the existence and proliferation of 'borders' and limits in a supposedly globalized world. Commodity production, then, actually *requires* non-commoditized social, ecological and political zones. For example, commodification does not just depend on labour becoming a commodity itself; it also structurally depends on what can be called 'semi-proletarianized' households (non-market domestic and affective labour, typically provided by women). Similarly, market expansion depends on non-commodity consumption (in 'the periphery') and a non-market, infinite supply of natural 'resources'. And since market exchanges depend on the state guaranteeing property rights, contracts and the legal order are underwritten, ultimately, by violence and/or the threat of violence. Restrictions on the movement of people, border controls, detention centres, prisons (Gopnik, 2012), surveillance, gated communities that isolate the rich from the poor, an increase in bureaucratic control (Graeber, 2015), austerity, expulsions (Sassen, 2014) and debt – which limits the future possibilities of debtors – can all be thought of as limits that co-exist within, and that are imbricated with, the capitalist system.

For the remaining part of this chapter, I will largely ignore this more complicated understanding of limits and focus on the arguments against market expansion.

3.3   The grounds for ethical limits to markets

In the current literature on the commodification process there are distinct but related arguments in favour of ethical limits to markets and market expansion (Satz, 2012). The first relates to the distribution of wealth, opportunities and power in society. The concern raised here is that markets exacerbate already existing inequalities in society and, furthermore, that they may help create new ones. There are two ways of thinking about this critique. First, it is argued that if in actual, real-world market societies market principles dominate then those who lack access to markets will inevitably be in an inferior position vis-à-vis other members of society. This is to be contrasted, it is suggested, with societies in which allocation is determined on normative principles that stress individuals' rights, needs, equality or solidarity irrespective of wealth.[13] In this vein of thinking, a second-best world of missing or imperfect markets coupled with the absence of institutions of solidarity result in some members of society being 'rationed out' (Ray, 1998) of the economy. The lives of those people are, therefore, severely curtailed.

But a second view also to be noted is that even if markets are perfect there will still be people who lack opportunities because of: a relative lack of skills/assets, differences in inherited wealth or just because of bad luck. Whether markets are perfect or imperfect, some people may not have access to commodities and the well-being they afford.

Another criticism of markets, however, points out that even those who do have access to commodities may do so on fundamentally unequal terms. Not only are markets at fault for the way in which they generate inequalities in wealth and power in a society, but the actual *process* of market exchange itself is ethically questionable since it rests on and is only made possible by fundamental inequalities.

At least some of our transactions, then, take place against background situations of asymmetrical power relations and unequal bargaining positions.[14] This dominance is most blatant when we think of exchanges that are tainted by gender, religious, ethnic or race discrimination.

According to this view markets are ethically blameworthy because the actual *process* of market exchange is unfair. In such cases the criticism of market transactions are grounded on the idea of exploitation, 'coercion' (Sandel, 2013) and the reduction of the autonomy of market participants. Unfair or highly asymmetric initial conditions – inequalities in market and non-market power – mean that the idea of voluntary[15] transactions, a central tenet of free markets, becomes highly questionable.

If market participants engage in a transaction out of necessity, dependency, vulnerability or a sense of desperation then that opens up the possibility that those transactions should be blocked. Satz (2010) suggests that the blocking of an economic exchange may actually *further* a person's autonomy (and welfare), a point also made by Titmuss (1997) in the context of his arguments against a market for blood.

To state the case negatively, a market in child labour, for example, would restrict a person's *effective* freedom and in addition have the consequence of reinforcing the power structure that entrenches subservience (Satz, 2007). The continuation of the structure of domination has important ramifications not just for the quality of human lives and labour market interactions but for political equality in society more generally. It is difficult to envisage how political democracy can effectively function if it co-exists with such a stark lack of economic freedom (Ambedkar, 2001).

It should be noted that I am not highlighting the lack of autonomy in markets *per se* but, rather, its absence or severe limitation is *specific* markets. It stands to reason that in reality there will be many cases in which market participants transact with one another starting out from very different initial conditions. This raises a number of difficult questions: at what point do those unequal conditions translate into exploitation or desperate exchanges? The question of a lack of real autonomy will be overlooked if we focus – as markets and market theorists tend to do – on the concepts of negative liberty[16] and efficiency.

A labour market in which workers are hired at extremely low wages and/or face poor and hazardous working conditions, a market for body organs or for blood, are all examples of how transactions can *rest*[17] on fundamental inequalities in social standing (power, income and assets). Matters are complicated by the fact that in some of these 'obnoxious markets' there is an additional consideration to reckon with: the transactions can often involve an element of harm.[18]

It is worth reiterating that weak agency may stem not just from cultural constraints, initial low levels of assets and resources but, also, from insufficient (or asymmetric) information, and limited cognitive capacity. Kanbur (2001) supports this view, stating that transactions that are conducted over long periods of time and that are bound up with uncertain outcomes are more likely than not to be thought of as 'obnoxious trades' because of weak agency.[19]

More generally, it is the poor, the vulnerable (children) and the most socially marginalized (women, low castes) who are the likeliest to be on the receiving end in the commoditization process (Radin and Sunder, 2004). It is their labour and their body parts that are more likely to be commoditized. And with commodification (privatization) it is they who are more likely to have worse access to health care, education and clean air than if our policies provided these 'goods' on the basis of rights. Treating other people, nature, or parts of our own bodies as things or objects is, it is argued, invariably associated with some kind of violence (or at least domination) and a restriction of the autonomy of the poorest and most marginalized.

So far I have argued that market expansion could be restricted on the grounds that they further, or are based on, significant inequalities (in income, power). A third possible reason relates to the fact that markets structure our self-perceptions, motivations and notions of personhood.

The parsimonious picture of individual agents in economic theory suggests that market participants are (or perhaps ought to be) autonomous, rational decision makers for whom culture, social relationships and identity are irrelevant to their decisions and self-understanding. It is not wholly surprising, therefore, that some people, linking theory to actual markets, believe that "the continuous production of loneliness as a fundamental underpinning of capitalism" (Crary, 2013, p. 116). Also, *homo economicus* is typically described by economists as being guided by a highly restricted motivational set (or self-interest, in plain terms).

Given that emphasis on self-interested market behaviour it is quite natural to believe that greater market expansion will have a profound and deleterious effect on our conceptions of the self, how we relate to other people, and how we conceptualize the good life. These implications form the basis of the view that market expansion should, to some extent, be limited.

Commodification can entail thinking of ourselves as 'objects', our relations with other people in purely transactional or instrumental terms, and goodness as something that is dependent on the consumption of commodities. But how, exactly, does commodification change our self-perceptions and the timbre of our social relationships? It is often argued that a central role is played by the commodification of labour power (and labour-time). Lukács (2013) writes, "Qualities and abilities are no longer an organic part of his [the labourer's] personality, they are things which he can 'own' or 'dispose of' like the various objects of the external world" (p. 100).

The commodification of labour is emblematic of a process which inclines us to think more in terms of abstract categories and less in terms of concrete persons living in (and shaped by) a particular, unique habitat. Under a market system, it could be argued, since my work has limited bearing or relation to my core, disembodied 'true self' it can be easily alienated. One consequence of this is that work becomes homogenized – standardized, measurable and therefore comparable across people. A second and much noted aspect of commodification is that because work is hardly ever thought of as an 'internal good' or a practice that is related to the good life (MacIntyre, 2003), it is easier for us to think of it as being alienable. And it is precisely this ability to alienate our labour in which our autonomy supposedly lies!

At a fundamental level a desiring self, negative liberty, and a particular liberal conception of property lends intellectual support to the process of commodification (Radin, 1987). But so too, I argue, does a narrow conception of the self since, according to Hegel, "my abilities acquire an external relation to the totality and universality of my being" (as cited in Radin, 1987, p. 1894).

Of course, the roots of the notion of 'externalization', the emergence of a 'detached self' – the false separateness between subject and object – does not have to be traced back exclusively to the expansion of markets – though commodification has undoubtedly helped further this tendency.[20]

Given that, it is now possible to think of some of the most obnoxious markets not simply in terms of harm or weak agency. In addition, we can think of the sale of body organs, sexual services and the commodification of education, health and care as being problematic because they rest on (and encourage) a narrow and false understanding of both the self and human flourishing. Commodification – market mentalities and market practices – can foster the idea that our body, labour and personal characteristics are somehow external to our 'inner' or 'thin' self – usually thought to be constituted by abstract reason or the will. The authentic self, then, is one that is abstracted from social reality and is neither formed by, nor dependent on, any genuine social relationships.[21]

Closely related to the last argument for limits to market expansion is the criticism that once an activity or an object becomes the subject of a monetary transaction, once we begin think of either as a mere commodity, their nature and our understanding and evaluation them is radically altered, tarnished or undermined. Sandel (2013) calls this process of degradation 'corruption'. Here the emphasis is not so much on what happens to individuals during the market transactions as it is on what happens to an object or activity as it becomes a commodity.[22]

Let's take three examples: surrogate motherhood, mercenary armies and the buying and selling of votes.[23] In all three instances it is quite plausible to view the critique of commodification in terms of the ways in which it alters human subjectivities[24] But it is just as correct to say that what gets corrupted is the concept and the social meaning[25] of 'motherhood', 'military duty' and 'political participation'.

To extend the argument: education is not the same thing when it takes on commodity form and is viewed as something to be consumed or invested in (human capital); military service, social care, and sex are not the same thing if they come attached with a price tag. Under commodification things never remain the same.

Hirsch (2015) is correct, therefore, to suggest that the social context of human relationships involved in the 'production' or 'supply' of some 'good' imparts to it a quality that is missing when it is provided by an impersonal, profit-driven system. So, even if we are not directly involved in the production (or consumption) of the commodity we can, and often do, feel that the social meaning and qualitative distinctiveness of something is diminished when it takes commodity form.

The argument for ethical limits to markets, therefore, rests on the conviction that there are certain moral, religious, aesthetic, cultural, civil and political 'goods' that should not be thought of in market terms. That argument does not depend on an essentialist notion of value but it does presuppose that the social meaning and intrinsic value we attach to particular ways of being in the world are degraded when the 'goods' in question become mere commodities, subject to monetary evaluation. It is important to distinguish this reason for the limitation of market expansion from more instrumental reasons.

The instrumental reason holds that market transactions should be limited because the quantity (and quality) of the 'good' may be reduced as they become commoditized. That kind of argument was central to Titmuss'(1997) critique of a market for blood but we can extend it to health care, education, or military service and easily imagine a decline in their effectiveness as the 'goods' become commodities under market provision.

But what if that is not the case? For example, with private provision health care may actually, in some sense, become more effective.[26] It is easy enough to imagine that under a market system more people's preferences are satisfied and commercial incentives may help foster competition and innovation in the sector, thereby improving quality. The question, then, is whether under those circumstances there is still good cause to pause and ask ourselves if something of distinct value, a particular approach to relating to other people and being in the world, is lost or 'crowded out' in the commodification process.

This loss of intrinsic value lies at the heart of the argument being made here for the limiting of market expansion, for what we need to register in this process is a shift to a different scale of meaning and value. We cannot, that is, think of aesthetic, cultural, civil and political 'goods' simply in terms of how they instrumentally contribute to efficiency or 'value'. G.A. Cohen (2013) rightly claims that we can value something – an aesthetic object, an institution, a way of life, perhaps – as the particular thing that it is, and not simply as a means to the accomplishment of some other end ('universal value'). And we can also recognize that thing as being important in a way that is independent of its personal value to us.

Acknowledging that a particular thing, with its distinct value,[27] may be tarnished in the process of commodification is not to argue that its preservation is the best thing to do, *all things considered*. It is merely to suggest that there is a reason for there being ethical limits to markets because commodification dissolves "the specificity of things (any specific things) in favour of their aggregation into classes of things" (Prudham, 2009, p. 129). Market exchanges require commensurability and, ultimately, quantification. And yet Wendell Berry (2015) is surely correct when he writes, "An economy operating on the basis of mere quantities runs oddly toward both infinity and nothing; limitless desires and final exhaustion" (p. 125).

3.4   The commodification of culture

Up until the end of the age of mass production in the early 1970s it could, with some justification, be said that the main forms of commodification revolved around the commodification of the factors of production: labour, land and capital. What I want to suggest in this section is that the scope of commodification has now widened and deepened to incorporate ever greater areas of our lives into the market order. These include not just health, education, care, military service, security and prisons; and not just the natural habitat, but human nature, too (biogenetic material, body parts, and intellectual capacities). It is, therefore, not just physical labour that is now commoditized but cognitive labour, human relationships and the very fabric of our personal and social lives.

For the sake of convenience I am bracketing some of these distinct dimensions of life (education, communication, art, literature and music etc.) under the broad, catch-all term 'culture'. The question is then: does this latest wave of commodification represent a further (and distinct) stage in the re-shaping of experience and perception, a disruption of our narrative selves, a more intense 'internal colonization' by the commodity form?

In terms of our relations with other people it has been argued that market exchange implies a false universality and a false notion of sociality since "it brings objectified human labour together socially, but at the cost of abstracting and emptying it of all substantial content" (Slater and Tonkiss, 2004, p. 161). In addition, in this stage of late capitalistic development commodities are produced, consumed and disposed of at ever-increasing speeds, thus undermining our own sense of durability and continuity. Seen in this light the commodification of culture – the aspect of our lives that we often think is both central to our humanity and to the orientation of our lives in the world – is leading to a hollowing out of the self[28] and to 'worldlessness' (Arendt, 1998).

It is worth stressing that the argument against commodification here is not just that culture shouldn't be treated as one commodity amongst other commodities because it represents something of higher and unique value. Instead, there are distinct arguments for ethical limits to the commodification of culture. First, it has been argued (Keat, 1999) that culture – along with other political, civil and moral 'goods' (trust, a fair judiciary, a political system that supports contracts and property rights) – is essential for the functioning of the market system itself. The argument, as we saw in the last section, is that markets themselves require some degree of limitation – non-commoditized spheres of social reality – to be successful. If the objective of markets is to enhance individuals' well-being and autonomy then it could be argued that cultural 'goods', by providing us an understanding of what constitutes a good life, can help us determine which commodities and which activities further our well-being.

A second argument holds that culture is not just important because it instrumentally enhances well-being by improving the quality of our preferences *within* a market system. In addition, culture is important because it can reveal the limitations of markets and a life geared exclusively to material pursuits. In this more direct sense an autonomous culture is important to individual and social well-being because it can critique and challenge the one-sidedness of capitalist development.

The problem with these two arguments in favour of culture is that they overlook the changes that have occurred in market societies in the post-Fordist era. It is now clear that culture itself is increasingly being assimilated into the structure of capitalist relations and even encourages individuals to 'buy into' the latter's values and rhetoric as well. It is worth recalling that the 'boundless' and 'impulsive' self (Bell, 1978) of the counterculture of the sixties has fed into, and even been encouraged by, changes in the structure of capitalism (Streeck, 2012). Thomas Frank (1994) may well be right to suggest that the 'permissive society' and a dissident, non-conformist culture with its "frenzied sensibility of pure experience, life on the edge, immediate gratification and total freedom from moral constraint" is actually just the "official style of consumer society". Nancy Fraser (2013) agrees, suggesting that in a post-Fordist regime of capital accumulation dominated by finance and signal-value, the emancipatory movements of the 1960s may have helped "dissolve the solidary ethical basis of social protection, thereby clearing a path for marketization".

What we are witnessing, then, is perhaps another, deepening stage of commodification, a process of progressive dematerialization[29] which is driven by the production of images, representations, brands, spectacles and events in an 'attention economy'. Although it is true that representations and wish-images have always been part of the commodification process it now appears as if the representations are almost autonomous, distinct from the material reality and contexts that produced them. Jean-Luc Marion (2004) is correct, therefore, to say that the image, by keeping up appearances in a 24/7 televisual order, dispenses with the real world.

3.5   Commodification as a process

In the analysis above I have said that commodification is a complex cultural, political and economic process. We have seen that at the conceptual level it is related to liberalism in the sense that both are inextricably bound to notions of rationality (self-interested maximization), freedom (negative liberty) and a decontextualized understanding of the individual. Furthermore, the notion of the boundless self, free from the restraints of tradition, social norms and ethical judgement is one that sits easily with both the spirit of contemporary society as well as with mainstream economic theory.

I have also argued that what were once considered non-commoditized realms are to significant extent being commoditized (culture, for example). Far from offering resistance to the inexorable growth of commodification culture, cognitive capacities and 'the social' are all being mobilized to support it.

In this section I briefly summarize a very fruitful way of describing a number of conceptual features of the commodification process and relate them to the analysis above.

Castree (2003) notes that there are several inter-linked dimensions of capitalist commodification. Firstly, commodification requires individuation. By this is meant the representation and material practices that separate something from its supporting context. This is somewhat similar to the subject/object dichotomy alluded to above. For instance, to denote something as 'land' is already to separate it from the history of its use and the specific mythological importance or religious significance it may have for certain communities. To speak of it as a thing, a discrete entity (and later as a factor of production) is to ignore the myriad ways in which our relationship to land has supported various ways of being in the world at any particular point in time and over time.

Other thinkers have called this aspect of commodification 'reification'. It entails that certain features of a thing are given prominence while others are considered irrelevant, vague, or contingent. This process necessarily involves, then, accentuating the 'separateness' of some features from other ones and from the whole.

This process is similar to what Radin (1987) calls thinking that is dominated by a 'market mentality', i.e. thinking of things and social relationships as if they were commodities. For us to conceive of something as a commodity requires the ability and the desire to abstract from certain features that are configured in a particular place at a specific time in history. Cultural and social norms may explain the meaning we attach to something or the appropriate way to value and interact with it. Included in that notion of value, therefore, is the idea of our relation to the thing in question.

As something becomes commoditized it loses its "organic, irrational and qualitatively determined unity" (Lukács, 2013, p. 88). And that fragmentation of the object goes hand in hand with other 'separations' and displacements. Commodification, then, also leads to the fragmentation of the subject as the worker's labour power is separated from his whole personality and to the separation of workers from one another ('atomization').

A second feature of the commodification process is privatization. This is a precondition of capitalist commodification since things are not produced and exchanged as commodities unless there is ownership. Again, it is worth stating that, like the subject-object dichotomy, private property is inextricably bound to liberalism.[30]

A third and closely related dimension of commodification is what Castree calls alienation. This is the ability and the right to exchange something.[31] A richer understanding of this process would have to incorporate an understanding of the actual historical economic and social processes that generate the possibility of alienation. Part of that richer approach would, I think, involve a discussion of the central role contracts have played in modern thought and practices and how contract is closely aligned to notions of an abstract individual who is pictured as being both appropriative and rational in an instrumental sense (Gauthier, 1977). If we reject the view of ourselves as being fundamentally asocial and infinitely desiring creatures then there would be less need for contracts in our interactions (Rosenfeld, 2010).

Another important dimension of commodification is abstraction. Whereas individuation brings about a separation of a distinct thing from its surrounding context abstraction reintegrates the qualitative specificity of a thing back into a broader abstract category. For example, 'land' is now a homogenous category which allows us to think of land in vastly different countries and over different periods of time as all being instantiations of this one, abstract notion of land.

Closely related to abstraction is the reliance on quantification, measurement, monetization and rationalization – which for simplicity we can subsume under the concept of 'standardization'. As with abstraction we should see this shift in emphasis in the context of wider social and cultural changes. It is, for example, possible to detect the same fundamental motives at play in the standardization of weights and measures as in the growth of the importance of population and land surveys, the design of cities and, more generally, of statistics (Hacking, 2010).

Such developments must have received great impetus from the actual development of market exchanges and from the state's desire to impose administrative uniformity (Scott, 2008). The measuring and codifying of landholdings, property rights, yields, wealth, assets and population are all fundamental pre-requisites of the state having any claim to furthering the 'wealth of nations'. Equally, market exchanges are severely hampered if property rights are not clearly defined and if measurements are either determined by local, contextual, time and place-bound procedures or impossible because of the qualitative and incommensurable nature of the goods being measured.

Abstraction, quantification and standardization,[32] then, are crucial for the development of markets and state and serve an important political goal of furthering the Enlightenment dream of producing a rationally ordered society of free and equal citizens under one law and one clearly recognized system.

3.6   Conclusion

We are witness to the unfolding of an historical process that we can characterize as a move from use-value to exchange-value and from that to sign-value. This has been matched by a shift in emphasis from the association of commodities with needs, then with wants (preference satisfaction and utility) and now with wishes, dreams and fantasies. It is hard to imagine how, in the midst of this proliferation of images, either genuine creativity, encounters and communication or a "collective overturning of omnipresent conditions of social isolation and economic injustice" (Crary, 2013, p. 108) can occur.

It follows that any discussion of the ethical limits to the *historical* process of market expansion has to take into account *modern* forms of commodification. That includes looking at the role of what Žižek (2009) calls pure enjoyment (*'jouissance'*), with its emphasis on an excessive hedonism that is not overly concerned with the possession of commodities, the achievement of utility or the relevance of commodities as markers of social status. It would also mean focusing ethical critiques on what seem to be increasingly larger problems in consumer society in advanced capitalist economies: hoarding, waste and addictions. For instance, are we now, as slaves of our desires, under a compulsion to enjoy? And it would also require us to look carefully at what Brockes (2015) calls 'hysterical consumerism' and brand extension, a process which leads to the "transference of one good thing to other, unrelated good things", this being part of "a peculiarly American urge to satisfy all appetites at once and its eroding the idea of pleasure as context-specific".

The commodification of culture is not a process that we can ignore since it effects the very fabric of our individual and social lives. The sheer scale and intensity of this process means that increasingly we think of religion, leisure, knowledge[33] and the arts in terms of the production and consumption of commodities and their representations.

Captivated by our own private dreams and engrossed by our screen technologies, it is difficult to imagine how, given the declining ability to see our situatedness in the world, we can collectively organize ourselves to delimit or challenge the process of market expansion. In addition to refusing to accept a form of relationality structured by the commodification process, we face the task of positively re-imagining a life lived in a more unstructured way, free from the dominance of capitalist relations.

In this chapter I have implicitly been asking the question of what space is left for the individual when he surrounds himself with things. Or, better: if commodities and the real world have become more ephemeral, has the individual disappeared[34] too? I now turn to that question.

Notes

1 Radin and Sunder (2004) argue that commodification entails a change in the way we understand human relationships.
2 The central questions are: who determines whether market transactions should be limited, and to what extent; and is there any consensus on the normative grounds for doing so?
3 The reasons for this shift are complex. It can only be explained the background of wider political, institutional and cultural changes over the last 30 years. As Le Grand (2013) makes clear, freedom of choice and competition have come to trump the older virtues and values associated with the public sector. Market practices, therefore, are inextricably bound to changes in attitudes, motivations, expectations, values and rhetoric (Radin, 1987). Also, see chapter 8.
4 Radin (1987) explores the idea that the concept of freedom cannot be reduced to the notion of freedom extolled by markets (i.e. negative liberty).
5 This view is similar to Adam Smith's insistence on the importance of free and formally equal relations in market societies compared to the hierarchical social relations and exclusionary practices found in feudal societies (Fraser, 2013).
6 For the historical dimension, see Pocock (2009) and Ignatieff (1994).
7 On how land was dissociated from a particular way of living and made into a mere 'factor of production' see (Hobsbawm, 2000). For a discussion on the earlier enclosure movement see Thompson (1993). Not unrelatedly, discussions over the extent to which food should be thought of as a 'natural commodity' whose distribution should be left to the vagaries of the market mechanism rather than as a political commodity, have always elicited fierce debates (Hont and Ignatieff, 1983; Davis, 2014) – and in some cases riots (see Thompson, 1993).
8 Although I'm only focusing on market expansion in this chapter a recurrent theme throughout this book is that it is the abstractions of the market *and* the state that undermine 'the social'. Gorz (1980) is correct, therefore, to maintain that the erosion of everyday culture, *metis* and vernacular know-how is only possible with the growth of economic *and* administrative power.
9 More recently, Sen (1997, 2015) has critiqued the idea that our exclusive focus should be on goods and services or the welfare/utility they promote. Instead,

we should look to what people can be and do – their 'functionings'. And some of those, such as friendship, meaningful work, and political participation are – or should be – relatively independent of the possession of commodities.

10 I say perhaps because in many respects the components of liberalism are actually conducive to commodification (Radin, 1987).

11 Mainstream economic theory also lends support to greater commodification. Since more is always better than less and since desires are potentially infinite, it is easy to see theory endorsing a never-ending expansion of markets. In addition, since individual, self-interested preferences/desires are the first and universal principle of action it is not easy to picture them being constrained by historically given social, cultural or institutional norms.

12 Social reproduction can be thought of as one dimension of culture (see section 4 below). It involves "the human capacities to create and maintain social bonds . . . reproducing the shared meanings, affective dispositions and horizons of value that underpin social co-operation" (Fraser, 2014, p. 542).

13 It could be claimed that the solution to this problem is simply better markets. The point I'm emphasizing is that in real-world economies markets are typically imperfect. Extending them *at the expense of* an effective public sector and social security mechanism can have serious distributive (ethical) implications.

14 These can be the result of for manifold causes: prior relations of debt, asymmetries in information, and differences in asset holdings or social power.

15 It is perhaps better to think of these decisions as 'tragic choices' (Nussbaum, 2000).

16 Radin (1987) argues that the underlying idea of negative freedom in liberalism makes it harder to justify inalienability.

17 The earlier argument against market expansion was that it can *perpetuate* inequalities.

18 In a similar vein, Larry Summers's efficiency argument for the transfer of 'dirty industries' to developing countries ignored that the transaction wouldn't be truly voluntary (being based on significant income differentials). It also glossed over the idea of 'harm'. See Hausman and McPherson (2010).

19 In developing countries long-term and 'tied' contractual landlord-worker relations can limit autonomy and restrict mobility even in the face of better outside opportunities (Banerjee and Newman, 1998).

20 The abstract, disengaged individual is central to some strains of modernity (Taylor, 1989) and can be thought to have political, scientific, religious and philosophical roots (see chapter 4). Arendt (1998), in this regard, calls modernity "the second turning inwards". Radin (1987) notes how the 'thin' notion of the Kantian self has animated (political) liberalism.

21 Such a view is, as we have already seen in the last chapter, not too dissimilar to the narrow understanding of rationality in economic theory. In the post-Fordist era, it is argued, attachments and relationships have weakened appreciably and been replaced by personal choice, the 'impulsive self' (Bell, 1978) and counter-cultural sentiments. This cultural shift in sensibilities has been exploited by producers (Streeck, 2012; Frank, 1994). The relation of the self to commodification in a late capitalist age dominated by images, representations and brands is taken up below (section 4).

22 In practice the distinction is a blurred one since what is ultimately changing under commodification is our relation to things of value – whether those be body parts, knowledge, work or civic duties.

23 Concerns about the pernicious effects of the influence of money in politics have been recently raised by Stiglitz (2013). Contrary to the market view, voting is an inalienable right that can both expresses strong political commitments and

reinforce deeply held notions of identity (citizenship). Voting, in that sense, is bound to a particular (democratic) understanding and evaluation of the political relation.

24 In each case the individual is, inappropriately, putting his or her private interests over publicly or socially approved ways of behaving. What emerges is the 'thin' conception of the individual who rationally maximizes his pay-offs. This is what Satz (2013) calls 'individual corruption'.

25 This is close to what Satz (2013) calls 'intrinsic corruption'

26 See Le Grand (2002).

27 To take another example, think of the process that transforms the various use values associated with a home to the singular and abstract market value of a house. On this transformation process, see de Soto (2000). As a home becomes a house, a commodity that we can 'consume', invest in or speculate against, it is less likely that the local and culturally specific ways of 'dwelling' will survive (Illich, 1992). A home can provide us with a sense of security, belonging and continuity over time; it is the locus of our first initiation into the importance of sociality, familiarity and togetherness; and it can profoundly give shape to our affective and moral life. See Bachelard (2013).

28 See chapter 4. As a result of commodification the relation between the 'I' and the world is loosened with the self retreating into its own private and narcissistic dream-world of fantasy and hedonism and the world itself losing its substantive reality as it becomes at once depthless and ephemeral, a surface on which spectacles are projected. On the emergence of 'virtual reality' see Crawford (2015).

29 It is not surprising, perhaps, that the Information Revolution and the digital economy have produced the myth of a seamless, shiny, frictionless and infinitely connected immaterial world. This goes hand-in-hand with the notion that the real source of value in the economy comes from intangible capital (human and social capital, creativity, organizational and R & D).

30 Any theoretical understanding of the commodification process has to take into account the successive attempts to privatize and enclose the commons under various private property regimes. Market economies are simply not possible without private property and the background legal and administrative apparatus that define and secure ownership.

31 It may be that alienation is already embodied in some notion of property but this is not necessarily so. For example, the ownership of land may give you use-rights over it but not the right of sale or transfer.

32 See de Soto (2000).

33 As we shall see in a later chapter, knowledge in the universities is well on the way to becoming a commodity as well.

34 Perhaps we are involved in a series of disappearing acts. The thinning out of non-human nature (chapter 9), the replacement of tangible books and knowledge by digital information, the substitution of artificial intelligence for human cognition, and the reduction of the body to its genetic code. If so, it could be that politics is today primarily about the administration of bare life, or of subjects without substance.

Bibliography

Ambedkar, B. R. (2001). *The Annihilation of Caste*. New Delhi: Blumoon Books.

Arendt, H. (1998). *The Human Condition*. Chicago, IL: University of Chicago Press.

Bachelard, G. (2013). *The Poetics of Space* (M. Jolas, Trans.). Boston, MA: Beacon Press.

Banerjee, A. V., and Newman, A. (1998). Information, the Dual Economy, and Development. *The Review of Economic Studies, 65*(4), 631–653. Retrieved from www.jstor.org/stable/2566906

Bell, D. (1978). *The Cultural Contradictions of Capitalism.* New York, NY: Basic Books.

Berry, W. (2015). *Our Only World: Ten Essays.* Berkeley, CA: Counterpoint.

Brockes, E. (2015, September 29). Hysterical Consumerism Ruins Food. And Holidays. And Books. *The Guardian.* Retrieved from www.theguardian.com/commentisfree/emma-brockes-column/2015/sep/29/hysterical-consumerism-ruins-food-and-holidays-and-books

Calhoun, C. J. (2012). *The Roots of Radicalism: Tradition, the Public Sphere, and Early Nineteenth-Century Social Movements.* Chicago, IL: University of Chicago Press.

Castree, N. (2003). Commodifying What Nature? *Progress in Human Geography, 27*(3), 273–297. doi:10.1191/0309132503ph428oa

Cohen, G. A. (2013). Rescuing Conservatism: A Defense of Existing Value. In M. Otsuka (Ed.), *Finding Oneself in the Other.* Princeton, NJ: Princeton University Press.

Crary, J. (2013). *24/7: Late Capitalism and the Ends of Sleep.* Verso.

Crawford, M. B. (2015). *The World Beyond Your Head: On Becoming an Individual in an Age of Distraction.* London: Penguin Books.

Davis, M. (2014). *Late Victorian Holocausts: El Niäno Famines and the Making of the Third World.* London: Verso.

De Soto, H. (2000). *The Mystery of Capital: Why Capitalism Triumphs in the West and Fails Everywhere Else.* New York, NY: Basic Books.

Frank, T. (1994). Dark Age. *The Baffler, 6.*

Fraser, N. (2013). A Triple Movement? *New Left Review, 81.* Retrieved from https://newleftreview.org/II/81/nancy-fraser-a-triple-movement

Fraser, N. (2014). Can Society Be Commodities All the Way Down? Post-Polanyian Reflections on Capitalist Crisis. *Economy and Society, 43*(4), 541–558. doi:10.1080/03085147.2014.898822

Fuller, P. (1985). *Images of God: The Consolations of Lost Illusions.* London: Chatto & Windus.

Gauthier, D. (1977). The Social Contract as Ideology. *Philosophy & Public Affairs, 6*(2), 130–164. Retrieved from www.jstor.org/stable/2264939

Gopnik, A. (2012, January 30). The Caging of America: Why Do We Lock Up So Many People? *The New Yorker.* Retrieved from www.newyorker.com/magazine/2012/01/30/the-caging-of-america

Gorz, A. (1980). *Ecology as Politics.* London: Pluto Press.

Graeber, D. (2015). *The Utopia of Rules: On Technology, Stupidity, and the Secret Joys of Bureaucracy.* Brooklyn, NY: Melville House.

Hacking, I. (2010). *The Taming of Chance.* Cambridge: Cambridge University Press.

Hausman, D. M., and McPherson, M. S. (2010). *Economic Analysis, Moral Philosophy and Public Policy.* Cambridge: Cambridge University Press.

Hirsch, F. (2015). *Social Limits to Growth.* Abingdon: Routledge.

Hirschman, A. O. (1982). Rival Interpretations of Market Society: Civilizing, Destructive, or Feeble? *Journal of Economic Literature, 20*(4), 1463–1484. Retrieved from www.jstor.org/stable/2724829

Hirschman, A. O. (1997). *The Passions and the Interests: Political Arguments for Capitalism Before Its Triumph.* Princeton, NJ: Princeton University Press.

Hobsbawm, E. J. (2000). *The Age of Revolution, 1789–1848*. London: Phoenix.

Hont, I., and Ignatieff, M. (1983). Needs and Justice in the Wealth of Nations: An Introductory Essay. In I. Hont and M. Ignatieff (Eds.), *Wealth and Virtue: The Shaping of Political Economy in the Scottish Enlightenment*. Cambridge: Cambridge University Press.

Hughes, M. V. (2005). *A London Child of the 1870s*. London: Persephone Books.

Hughes, R. (2012). *The Shock of the New: Art and the Century of Change*. London: Thames & Hudson.

Ignatieff, M. (1994). *The Needs of Strangers*. London: Vintage.

Illich, I. (1992). *In the Mirror of the Past: Lectures and Addresses, 1978–1990*. London: M. Boyars.

Kanbur, R. (2001). *On Obnoxious Markets*. Working Paper, Cornell University.

Keat, R. (1999). Market Boundaries and the Commodification of Culture. In L. Ray and A. Sayer (Eds.), *Culture and Economy After the Cultural Turn*. London: Sage.

Le Grand, J. (2002). The Provision of Health Care: Is the Public Sector Ethically Superior to the Private Sector? In B. New and J. Neuberger (Eds.), *Hidden Assets: Values and Decision-Making in the Nhs*. London: King's Fund. ISBN 978-1857174588

Le Grand, J. (2013). *Motivation, Agency, and Public Policy: Of Knights and Knaves, Pawns and Queens*. Oxford: Oxford University Press.

Lukács, G. (2013). *History and Class Consciousness: Studies in Marxist Dialectics*. Cambridge, MA: MIT Press.

MacIntyre, A. C. (2003). *After Virtue: A Study in Moral Theory*. Notre Dame, IN: University of Notre Dame Press.

Marion, J. (2004). *The Crossing of the Visible*. Stanford, CA: Stanford University Press.

McCloskey, D. N. (2007). *The Bourgeois Virtues: Ethics for an Age of Commerce*. Chicago, IL: University of Chicago Press.

Mitropoulos, A. (2012). *Contract & Contagion: From Biopolitics to Oikonomia*. Wivenhoe: Minor Compositions.

Nussbaum, M. (2000). The Costs of Tragedy: Some Moral Limits of Cost-Benefit Analysis. *The Journal of Legal Studies, 29*(S2), 1005–1036. doi:10.1086/468103

Pocock, J. G. A. (2009). *The Machiavellian Moment Florentine Political Thought and the Atlantic Republican Tradition*. Princeton, NJ: Princeton University Press.

Polanyi, K. (2014). *The Great Transformation: The Political and Economic Origins of Our Time*. Boston, MA: Beacon Press.

Prudham, S. (2009). Commodification. In N. Castree, D. Demeritt, D. M. Liverman, and B. L. Rhoads (Eds.), *A Companion to Environmental Geography*. Malden, MA: Blackwell.

Radin, M. J. (1987). Market-Inalienability. *Harvard Law Review, 100*(8), 1849–1937. doi:10.2307/1341192

Radin, M. J., and Sunder, M. (2004). *The Subject and Object of Commodification*. Working Paper No. 97, UC Davis Law.

Ray, D. (1998). *Development Economics*. Princeton, NJ: Princeton University Press.

Rieff, P. (2006). *My Life Among the Deathworks: Illustrations of the Aesthetics of Authority*. Charlottesville, VA: University of Virginia Press.

Rosenfeld, M. (2010). Hegel and the Dialectics of Contract. In D. Cornell, M. Rosenfeld, and D. G. Carlson (Eds.), *Hegel and Legal Theory*. New York, NY: Routledge.

Roux, C. (2005, March 12). The Freedom Years. *The Guardian*. Retrieved from www.theguardian.com/artanddesign/2005/mar/12/photography.art

Ruskin, J. (1967). *"Unto This Last": Four Essays on the First Principles of Political Economy*. Lincoln, NE: University of Nebraska Press.

Sandel, M. J. (2013). *What Money Can't Buy: The Moral Limits of Markets*. New York, NY: Farrar, Straus and Giroux.

Sassen, S. (2014). *Expulsions: Brutality and Complexity in the Global Economy*. Cambridge, MA: Belknap Press of Harvard University Press.

Satz, D. (2007). Liberalism, Economic Freedom, and The Limits of Markets. *Social Philosophy and Policy, 24*(1), 120–140. doi:10.1017/s0265052507070057

Satz, D. (2010). Ethics, Economics, and Markets: An Interview With Debra Satz. *Erasmus Journal for Philosophy and Economics, 3*(1), 68–88. doi:10.23941/ejpe. v3i1.40

Satz, D. (2012). *Why Some Things Should Not Be for Sale: The Moral Limits of Markets*. New York, NY: Oxford University Press.

Satz, D. (2013). Markets, Privatization, and Corruption. *Social Research: An International Quarterly, 80*(4), 993–1008. Retrieved from https://muse.jhu.edu/article/541984/pdf

Scott, J. C. (2008). *Seeing Like a State: How Certain Schemes to Improve the Human Condition Have Failed*. New Haven, CT: Yale University Press.

Sen, A. K. (1993). Markets and Freedoms: Achievements and Limitations of the Market Mechanism in Promoting Individual Freedoms. *Oxford Economic Papers, 45*(4), New Series, 519–541. Retrieved from www.jstor.org/stable/2663703

Sen, A. K. (1997). Goods and People. In *Resources, Values, and Development*. Cambridge, MA: Harvard University Press.

Sen, A. K. (2015). *Commodities and Capabilities*. Delhi: Oxford University Press.

Slater, D., and Tonkiss, F. (2004). *Market Society: Markets and Modern Social Theory*. Cambridge: Polity Press.

Stiglitz, J. E. (2013). *The Price of Inequality*. New York, NY: W.W. Norton & Company.

Streeck, W. (2012). Citizens as Customers: Considerations on the New Politics of Consumption. *New Left Review, 76*. Retrieved from https://newleftreview.org/II/76/wolfgang-streeck-citizens-as-customers

Taylor, C. (1989). *Sources of the Self: The Making of the Modern Identity*. Cambridge, MA: Harvard University Press.

Taylor, C. (2007). *Modern Social Imaginaries*. Durham, NC: Duke University Press.

Thompson, E. P. (1993). *Customs in Common*. London: Penguin Books.

Titmuss, R. M. (1997). *The Gift Relationship: From Human Blood to Social Policy* (A. Oakley, Ed.). New York, NY: The New Press.

Žižek, S. (2009). *The Parallax View*. Cambridge, MA: MIT Press.

4   Individualism and the self

A picture held us captive.

(Wittgenstein, 1967, p. 48e)

[In modern consciousness] there is not a common being but a self, and the concern of this self is with its individual authenticity, its unique irreducible character free from contrivances and conventions, the masks and the hypocrisies, the distortions of the self by society.

(Bell, 1978, p. 19)

The human figure is progressively disappearing from pictorial art, as no object is present except in fragmentary form.

(Ball cited in Appignanesi, 2004, p. 113)

4.0   Introduction

In this and the next chapter I turn to two of the three structuring assumptions underlying the economic point of view: the assumptions that economic agents are self-interested individuals. A comprehensive understanding of *homo economicus* would entail an analysis of the meaning of the two concepts (self-interest and individualism) in economic thought. It would also require a grasp of whether those meanings have in fact been stable over time or whether, and how, they are influenced by varying historical conditions. A more comprehensive view, then, would throw light on how our understanding of self-interest and the individual (in economic theory) is related to both notions of the individual in the broader history of intellectual ideas and to changes in social reality.

A further complication arises because self-interest and individualism are related to a whole host of distinct concepts: freedom, rationality,[1] equality, power, etc. A richer analysis, then, would not simply focus on the *empirical* validity of Edgeworth's proposition that economic agents are primarily self-interested. In addition, it would have to examine the reasons why that particular understanding of economic agents came to be legitimated.[2] Given these vastly complex difficulties I will simplify by concentrating on the term 'individualism' in this chapter, drawing out its characteristics and the role it plays in economic thinking.

Individual identity in economic theory is, problematically, portrayed as being devoid of social relations. Individuals make decisions with little reference to circumstances or the limitations on cognitive capacities that circumscribe choice; their goals are either defined too narrowly in terms of pleasure or too generally in terms of exogenously given all-things-considered preferences. And the possibility that personal identity might be forged out of social/practical identities that are reflexively endorsed is generally discarded (Davis, 2009). Furthermore, a relentlessly maximizing individual has only a questionable degree of freedom to stand back and evaluate preferences (Hodgson, 2013).

These characteristics of the individual, I suggest, are better understood if we look at the historical evolution of individualism, and so I start with a discussion on the dissolution of the relational subject ('the person') in the early modern period (section 1).

In section 2 I look at the key ways in which individualism has been understood in political and economic thought. I then look in more detail at how market economies and economic theory tend to rule out sociality by focusing on a narrow idea of individuality (section 3). In sections 4 and 5 I look at the rise and fall of the idea of self-interested individuals. What we're left with, I argue in section 6, is not so much as a desiring self as a desiring body. In the last section of the chapter I offer some final thoughts as way of a conclusion.

But before that I want to pause and ask how the notions of self-interest and individualism are connected to the main themes of this book.

Scarcity was initially thought of as a specific event that sporadically occurred throughout human history, a culmination of the role played by fortune or the greed of particular individuals such as merchants (Foucault, 2014). In chapter 2, however, I noted that scarcity gradually became accepted as an irreducible fact of human reality rather than a specific, historical event. This new, fundamental understanding of scarcity is not unrelated to the idea of the individual in economic thought and market economies. In chapter 1 I argued that an agent's lack of genuine social relations, the very fact that he was an asocial individual, is what (in part) generates the problem of scarcity.

We have seen in the second chapter that a central way of characterizing rationality in economic thought is to conflate it with self-interest maximization. And, as was also stated in that chapter, the dominant idea of reason in economics is firmly rooted in the notion of *individual* rationality: we reason alone.

Individuality is also central to the political[3] and moral weight we assign to freedom. A free individual, at least since the Enlightenment (Foucault, 1984a), has been characterized as an autonomous agent, someone who is not subject to social, institutional, religious or political determination.

The notion of the continuity of the self across time is a well-known philosophical problem. But what notion of the individual survives the break-up of narrative unity and our increasingly myopic frames of reference? In chapter 9 I will argue that both market economies and economic theory also present such a view of the disjointed individual, someone who is utterly distinct from nature and non-human beings alike. This lack of sociality is also responsible for us relating to other individuals – those currently existing as well as future generations – in an abstract way.

The dominant notion of the self or the individual in economic thought is also tied to the problem of commodification. We have seen that the 'thin' view of the self, found in both liberalism and in our conception of market agents, can favour a slide to ever-greater levels of commodification. This applies with particular force to our current predicament as the central dimensions of individual subjectivity are now becoming 'commoditized'. As culture, knowledge and sociality are commoditized the way in which we relate as individuals to ourselves, other people and things of beauty is grossly distorted.

In chapter 7 I look at the relation between market expansion and the decline of the public sector ethos. I ask: what kind of individual emerges with the decline of public man?

And finally, we can evaluate the economy by referring to equality or to the common good. In both cases our particular conception of the individual is crucial. For both equality and the common good, it will be argued, derive their moral importance from a relational understanding of human beings.

4.1 From the person to the individual

The idea of individualism in economic theory implies a particular way of relating both to other people and to the world. Economists are often guilty of believing that 'individuality' and 'self-interest' are ahistorical and universal concepts so that if we think hard enough we can see self-interested behaviour everywhere and if we look beyond the various social formations that have existed over the years we will detect the individual struggling to emerge from the morass of institutional distortions. We cannot, however, understand individuality without thinking about both history and society. The type of individualism that economists take to be 'timeless' is actually a cultural and social construct embedded in early capitalism's configurations of ideas and practices.

From a historical perspective both our sense of identity and our economic activities have typically existed within a given habitus: a dense network of formal and informal rules, norms, shared meanings, social relations and collective representations. In both contemporary peasant economies (see Platteau, 1991) and in the 'ancient economy' (Boldizzoni, 2011) we would be hard pressed to find the hard-headed, calculating, autonomous and self-interested individuals that are so familiar to us from economic theory. In fact, to echo James C. Scott (2014), for large swathes of time individuals have existed outside of the sphere of the state (and the market).

The challenge before us is to articulate a third way of thinking about human beings, to picture individuals between the state and the market, since these have, at their most extreme moments, led either to an almost pathological subservience to institutional life or to a free-floating and fragmentary autonomy.[4]

Individualism is a major element of our modern social imaginary and can be thought of as consisting of a number of distinct but related components: autonomy,[5] privacy, dignity and self-development or improvement (Marglin, 2010). In this chapter I'll take a stab at describing how this particular notion of individualism emerged. In summary, the stylized picture is this: there has been a transition from 'the person' to the asocial individual. But for large periods of time the bourgeois, self-interested individual has been an important self-conception. In late capitalism that conception is being replaced by a shadowy, insubstantial and contingent desiring 'self' which, by being equated with the body and its desires, is on the verge of disappearing.

Rowan Williams (2012), commenting from a religious perspective, notes that 'the person', as distinct from the individual, is not an abstract concept but, instead, the locus of a constellation of relationships (the most important of which is our relation to the divine since it structures all other relations). In this reading, the person is not a sealed-off and fully-formed personality who moves through a hostile environment that he must either control or retreat from by entering a private fantasy or an artificial 'world'.

Human beings are not defined by a particular capacity ('the thinking animal' for example) or a specific subjective experience but, instead, by the sum total of all they do, think and feel. There is no question, therefore, of a person existing (or flourishing)[6] outside of, or prior to, his social relations. We are not in any fundamental sense entities that interact, only grudgingly, with other abstract, decontextualized subjects. And neither can we be said to have 'perfect knowledge' at any juncture in time since our relationships are an ongoing project: we live and think *in* time.[7]

We cannot understand the person in this tradition, therefore, without reference to either her ultimate good or her social nature. As Maritain (1996) puts it, the person is metaphysically distinct from the individual. For the individual there is barely room for other people or a genuine attentiveness to their being. The person, on the other hand, is a contradiction in terms if she lives without communion, dialogue and mutual relations. If the person is by nature a relational being, someone whose personality is given weight and shape by his unique relation to God,[8] then to be an autonomous individual, free of deeply held attachments – to other people and to specific places – is in a sense to become rootless and not fully human. Without those textured relationships, without what Simone Weil called *metaxu*,[9] we only possess the weightless, phantom-like freedom of strangers and become "the docile slaves of artificial cadences" (Sutermeister, 2014). Human spontaneity, on the other hand, is the ability to respond to the given conditions of life.[10]

So, there is a religious tradition which posits that "a person is a being-in-relation that exists only in relation with others" (Bruni, 2012, p. 27). In the language of Etzioni (1990) there is no 'I' without a 'We', an 'other' that in an eminent sense is a 'Thou' but in a more mundane sense is what we might call the community. The social constitutes our sense of mutuality and our understanding of 'the good'. The question is then: how and why did the notion of an asocial individual emerge in place of 'the person'?

There are many possible answers to that questions, and they can include economic and political explanations (section 2). But, equally, we can think that this shift to the non-relational individual was presaged by changes in religious sensibilities and doctrines (Taylor, 2007a). In other words, the (modern) notion of individualism in general, and that of economic individualism in particular, "makes philosophical and theological claims about the nature of the shared world we inhabit" (Pabst, 2012, p. 4). We have moved, arguably, to a culture that is "permeated by nominalism, which grants real existence only to individuals and not relations" (Dumont, 1992, p. 11). This is in part because the beginning of modernity is marked by a shift in religious emphasis from the 'out worldly individual' to the 'in worldly individual' who is still moral, still in a relation with God but asocial and profoundly skeptical of any institutional supports (Dumont, 1992).[11]

Some thinkers have claimed that this tension between a realm of authentic and inner selfhood on the one hand, and a suspect and shadowy social world on the other is inherent to Christianity (Steiner, 1971). Or at least they maintain that this tension is not wholly unrelated to certain tendencies within the belief system (Brown, 1989). The point to stress here is that this 'inner-worldliness' stands at the beginning of modernity and that the tension (gnostic tendencies) can, at their worst, generate a kind of nihilism (Jonas, 1982). The independence and self-sufficiency of the individual, then, comes at the expense of a denigration of social and natural worlds. This notion of the disembedded or disengaged individual entails a scepticism towards the world and to other people. At best 'the social' is a necessary evil, an artificial construct which emerges to compensate for man's inherent weakness. Society, then, is either a fictitious body, a site of mutual indifference or, worse, another name for totalitarian order.

In this account of events that sees the emergence of a new kind of individual, spiritual life was thought to be deepened by making it narrower. Instead of religion standing at the apex of a hierarchy of values, interests and activities, instead of grace completing nature, the sober, prudent but isolated individual comes to live in divided and distinguished worlds. Hierarchy is replaced by "the conception of separate and parallel compartments which have no vital connexion with each other" (Tawney, 1926, p. 15). This sounds all too familiar to our modern ears (MacIntyre, 2000; Nagel, 2015).

So, we see the nascent idea of the individual emerge from an older notion of the person. It is tempting to see this decisive development in terms of a radical break from the past but some scholars have stressed deep continuities at work here. If the modern idea of the individual marks a departure from medieval conceptions of the person its emergence, as a distinct concept, also stands as the culmination of long-drawn out historical processes of religious and social change that were already at work during the medieval period itself.

The religious roots of the modern individual may pre-date the Reformation and stretch all the way back to the 12th century. The assumption of moral equality[12] under canon law gave weight to the belief "in a human agency prior to established social roles" (Siedentop, 2014, p. 218) – such as those corporate notions of society epitomized by the family, caste or tribe. Individualism and secular liberalism, then, may have been a reflection of the growing importance assigned to the freedom of the will in this period. This tendency can be seen in the shift from natural law as a set of commandments and prohibitions to an emphasis on an understanding of natural law as natural rights that privilege human freedom. Increasingly natural law is understood as a *power* to do good (Tierney, 2004). Or, to put it another way, human autonomy and choice are necessary but not sufficient conditions for an act to be praiseworthy. But once the idea of an objective good[13] becomes disreputable, once the will no longer needs to be guided by 'right reason' or be in conformity with the divine will, it is easy to see how human agency[14] becomes a source of value in itself.

4.2   Individualism in political and economic thought

In the analysis so far I have said that the transition from the person to the individual can be seen, at least in part, as being the result of changes within religion over an extended period of time. Of course, the growth of independent reason in the universities (Minogue, 2005; Keen, 1991), the replacement of the teleological conception of the universe by modern science and abstraction, and urbanization were also important factors.

The theorization of the modern individual is also linked to the political and economic changes that took place the 16th century. Since the moral worth of the individual is determined independently of her social role, individuality in the early modern sense is clearly associated with autonomy, the disengaged self and independent reason (all of which are features, as we know, of economic man). This turning of the tide away from the morality of community ties to the morality of free individual choices is a distinct shift in the pattern of moral belief that can be explained, as we have seen, by changes in religious concepts. It also depended on changes in socio-economic conditions. But what bearing did the political context have on the formation of the early modern individual?

For thinkers like Oakeshott there is a mutually reinforcing relation between government power and the character or dispositions of political subjects (Oakeshott, 1993). Under the new conditions of the 16th century, it is argued, individuals are defined less by a sense of a common good or by their communal ties and occupations, and more by their ability to freely pursue their own interests.[15] For Oakeshott this notion of a self-determined, desiring self is what underlies a political theory of individualism that stretches all the way back from Hobbes to Adam Smith. An individual's good is not a substantive concept but, instead, the freedom to pursue his interests.[16]

From now on any political theory that aimed to explain or justify political power would have to do so against this background notion of the individual. Given that background notion, it is not wholly surprising that a new form of government power would emerge, one that would come to emphasize the lack of any compelling or utopian vision of 'the good' society. Individuals should be taken as they *are*, warts and all, and not as they ought to be. From that it follows that governments should act more like a neutral umpire instead of trying to be the 'best' regime (Manent, 2000).

The proper scope of government is reduced to the formal one of defending individuals' rights. In Burke's words, "The office of government is not to determine the desires and activities of its subjects" (as cited in Oakeshott, 1993, p. 71). These sentiments, suitably modified, would find their way into any modern introductory economics textbook since it is widely believed by economists that the only function of the state is that of a night watchman and not the promotion of human excellence.[17]

Another theme of political individualism that will later loom large in economic theory is the emphasis on contractual relations. In fact, the expansion of contractual relations in market societies – at the expense of undermining older forms of social relations such as friendship, duties, obligations, pacts, covenants, mutual gratitude, gifts – and the central role they play in economic theory is now widely recognized (Bruni, 2016). The shift from social relations ('status') to contract in the modern period has been well commented on. From the point of view of this chapter the key is that contract fosters and represents an aloofness as well as a calculating spirit that eventually finds its home in the discipline of economics. But all that comes much later. At the beginning, contract is theorized from a *political* perspective. It is a form of immunization from the contact/violence of others, an institutional drawing of lines around the body that prevents the contagion[18] of death and also simultaneously enhances our sense of a private, interior 'self'.

From within the contractual perspective, initiated or at least represented by Hobbes, individuals in the original state are subject to fear. A desire for self-preservation and an acute sense of one's mortality is what drives individuals in this condition to enter civil society. What unites individuals is not a positive conception of their inherent sociality but, instead, their common fear of one another. Civil society is, therefore, a 'unity without relation' (Esposito, 2010). So, at the beginning of the modern period an entirely negative picture of human beings emerges for "Men now are associated in the modality of reciprocal dissociation, unified in the elimination of every interest that is not purely individual, artificially united in their subtraction from community" (Esposito, 2010, p. 27).

The theory of the individual, then, is arguably fundamentally a *political* theory since it implicates the state in its conception (and inception). The state signifies a unity (not a concord) of men, a collection of asocial individuals who, for the sake of protecting themselves from the violence of other men in their natural condition, are obedient to it. No wonder Simone Weil (2003), writing many centuries later, could write "in our age, money and the State have come to replace all other bonds of attachment" (p. 99) – an acute point if one thinks of the last two centuries being dominated by state capitalism. And to think along those lines is merely to recall Siedentop's (2014) observations about an earlier, pre-modern period, namely: the forging of inter-connections between sovereign power and individual subjects that would be carried over into modernity.[19] In fact, for thinkers like Schmitt (2008) the order of the early modern (Hobbesian) state was "an essential intellectual or sociological precondition for the technical-industrial age that followed" (p. 34). In that sense Leo Strauss (1965) is correct to see Hobbes as the founder of liberalism, initiating a political hedonism that entails "the lifting of all restrictions on the striving for unnecessary sensual pleasure" (p. 189).

Throughout this chapter I have argued that the type of paradigmatic individual who stands at the head of the project of modernity is someone who is not defined by any *substantive* notion of goals, preferences, or interests. Instead, what really counts is his freedom to choose his own values and ideals independently of any social determination.[20] Later on I will argue that over the last 70 years or so economic theory returns us to this view of the asocial individual. But that only comes about only after the notion of the self-interested individual with his substantial interests (welfare, happiness, etc.) is eclipsed (section 5).

4.3   Individualism and sociality

As we have seen above, the idea of the individual, disconnected[21] from the world, nature and other people, may originally have derived from religious or political theorizing. But, equally, we cannot discount the role of abstraction in 17th century scientific thought (Willey, 1972) and contemporary philosophical thought[22] in generating notions of the 'punctual self' (Taylor, 1989). In this section I want to underline the paramount importance of individualism to modernity and how it sits at odds with a relational or inter-subjective notion of individuality.

Gellner (1998) is right to suggest that there are two ways of looking at life – individualism and holism/sociality – and that these two ways have implications for, and are expressed in, the differing ways in which we think about knowledge, reason, society, politics and economic life. Two ways, we might say, of being in the world.

For Gellner the individualistic-atomistic-universalist conception presents a 'thin' view of the self, one that stands apart from, or even opposed to, culture, institutions, customs, tradition and the social perspectives that underwrite the social. According to this conception the world is a colder, more abstract place, with a limited role for the passions and emotions in any comprehensive notion of the good life. Nevertheless, it appeals to us since it extolls the virtues of equality, individual rights, and freedoms. It can (and has) served as a vehicle for constraining authoritarian tendencies.

One strand of our earlier discussion about the historical roots of individualism maintains that even as far back as the medieval period learning was becoming more speculative as reason gradually unloosened itself from the hold of theology and revelation (Keen, 1991). For Gellner (1998) this culminates in the modern view, shared by the Romantic hero: "We discover truth alone" (p. 3). This is in conflict with what we can broadly call the holistic or social point of view of knowledge which, fed by poetic, communitarian and mystical impulses prioritizes being over thought (or, alternatively, emphasizes 'lived thought' over abstract thought). According to the holistic view the idea of a purely individual, pre-social or non-social[23] form of understanding is mistaken.[24]

Since economic theory is founded on methodological individualism it is no surprise that economic agents can be characterized as having 'algorithmic knowledge' (Marglin, 2010). This implies two things. Firstly, individual behaviour can be mathematically represented in large part because we typically simplify things by not taking into account experiential or vernacular knowledge. An economic actor's history, character and experience of living in real time (with all the implications that that holds for uncertainty, learning through an ongoing and creative engagement with other people and the world) is ignored.[25] Instead, we have an atomistic, optimizing individual who supposedly has perfect knowledge, foresight and cognitive capacities. Economic theory's understanding of individual behaviour, therefore, has the alleged advantages of being mathematical, cerebral, theoretical, rigorous, impartial, abstract and universal. Far from analytical intelligence or algorithmic knowledge being a narrow approach to understanding human behaviour it improves – or so it is claimed – the possibility of prediction, the taming of chance and standardization.

Secondly, a focus on algorithmic knowledge tends to diminish the importance of the social.[26] *Individuals* decide and they do not, in the standard framework, make choices guided by norms, tradition, socially-informed habits, rules of thumb, emotions, cultural identity, duty to others, conventions, or shared, tacit understanding. The fact that within the algorithmic system of knowledge we 'discover truth alone' reminds us of the asocial nature of the enterprise.

The narrow characterization of the individual in economic theory is not, however, an isolated phenomenon since it draws upon a wider tradition that disparages the social aspects of our lives (*philia, agape* and benevolence). These anti-social fictions and theories (the 'veil of ignorance', for example) give the impression that the aggressive and competitive behaviour that pits individual against individual is natural and/or desirable.

Having dismissed the idea of 'the person' (and the transcendent,[27] to which it was related), the individualistic tradition also denies the primacy of the social bond. Todorov (2001) is right to claim, therefore, that the modern individual has, in some profound sense, replaced an emphasis on the cosmic and social realms –'being' and 'existing'– with an emphasis on the animal realm.[28] He suggests that our inter-subjective relationships are at the root of our humanity since a fundamental lack in my being requires the complementarity of an 'other' (or others). But this dependency[29] on others, and this radical insufficiency, far from signifying a purely negative condition (a 'wound' in Bruni's, 2012 terminology) also constitutes a blessing since "the relationship to another enlarges the self" (Todorov, 2001, p. 14). Attachments to, and affection for, specific people, places and objects – and not the pursuit of maximizing abstract value – are crucial, therefore, to the formation of a richer kind of individuality.

We need – and perhaps 'need' is a better word than 'desire' – a witness to our being, just as we need to bear witness ourselves if we are to achieve a fuller understanding of individuality. It could be argued that the need to both give and receive recognition and respect – without subsuming other people's interests and goals to our own – is one of humanity's deepest instincts. To exist in a field of mutual gazes[30] is radically at odds, then, with being part of an economic system whose guiding principles are competition, rivalry and vanity. Instead, if "Man is not born of a struggle but out of love" (Todorov, 2001, p. 23), as symbolized but not reduced to the mother-child relationship, then an ethical approach could be said to involve both looking at the world and other people in the right way.[31]

In practical terms, is there much chance of recovering a richer, socially embedded and ethical notion of the individual? I think the ability to think about the social or communal faces formidable obstacles in our times. As we have already seen, the asocial notion of the individual draws on deep-rooted political and economic theorizing. Furthermore, that theoretical picture is well-entrenched in liberal societies, given the widespread prevalence and success of both democratic forms of organization and market societies.

In fact, we might even be witnessing the disappearance of the individual. That the causes of this disappearance are the brutality of the 20th century and the influence of Darwin and Freud is not in question. But from the perspective of this book our focus is on how the economic system itself along with changes in economic theory have contributed to the de-centering of the self.

If Iris Murdoch is correct in her assessment then I think the recovery of a relational way of being will be an uphill task.[32] The reasons for this, according to Sennett (2013), are a result of a compounding of three inter-related changes within the dynamics of capitalism:[33] rising inequality, changes in the labour market and a culture of withdrawal from others that is expressed in boredom, narcissism and mutual indifference.

The very material conditions of everyday life generated by capitalist production is a main contributory factor to the lack of social relationships.[34] The commodification and division of labour along with the rise of bureaucratic control limits the scope for contextual knowledge, genuine autonomy, and non-instrumental reasoning, thus hollowing out individuality.

For Sennett these tendencies have been exacerbated in the era of late capitalism. Long-term unemployment, precarious work (short-term contracts), and globalization have all contributed to a weakening sense of attachment to a particular place of work. This is conflated with rapidly changing technologies/knowledge that make the notion of a permanent job, a well-defined career, and an enduring professional identity[35] less likely (unlike in the solid stage of capitalism where occupations and social roles were more stable). As capital has become impatient the very structure of work and our attitudes to it are changing.

But if we increasingly find our jobs pointless can we turn to culture in order to give meaning, continuity and structure to the world we live in? Perhaps not, since culture and leisure have come to be associated with the private self, passivity and consumerism as well. As Marcuse (2009) acutely remarks, "culture means not so much a better world but a nobler one: a world to be brought about not through the overthrow of the material order of life but through events in the individual's soul. Humanity becomes an inner state" (p. 76).

4.4   The emergence of self-interest

In this section I want to backtrack somewhat and suggest that the asocial individual we've just looked at, though a theoretical possibility, doesn't actually fully emerge until the dissolution of the self-interested individual. So, the individual in the early modern period is largely only *theorized* as someone whose moral or religious worth lies in being free to make decisions independently of social and institutional constraints. Despite that moral ontology individual identity for all practical purposes continued to be embedded in social frameworks up until the 20th century. For all our talk of the isolated will it is worth recalling that the self was for large periods of time inextricably bound to language, national and local identity, occupational status, class, tradition, custom, religion and family.

It is perhaps fair to say, then, that in reality the individual up until the 20th century was not "frightened and alone" (Murdoch, 1999) but held secure by God, Reason and Society. If art provides insights into social history then we might think that the portraits of the practical, solid-looking bourgeoisie in the 17th century indicate the emergence of sober, quietly confident individuals (Clark, 2005). And it could be argued that such similar individuals – even though forming a narrow class – would continue well into the period that Bauman (2000) calls the 'solid stage of capitalism'.

If we turn to how we conceptualize individuals in the market from the 17th century onwards we would be led to conclude that far from leading to disruption, self-interested behaviour was a force for stability. This is corroborated by Hirschman (1982) and McCloskey (2007) who inform us that self-interested market activity in the early modern period was intertwined with commendable characteristics or virtues such as reliability, punctuality, sobriety and reasonableness. In fact, the market according to Charles Taylor (2007b) came to play such a central role in our imagination and practices precisely because it offered a model of how we might live ordinary,[36] predictable and productive lives. Here there was no Hobbesian "war of all against all" to be resolved by obedience to the Leviathan; instead, the market was a place in which the possible ruinous effects of conflict might be diminished (Hobbes, 2003). Even better – and more radically – the pursuit of self-interest would, it was believed, lead to harmony and the public good.

In the section below I want to suggest that this particular incarnation of the desiring self – the self-interested agents that populate our economics textbooks – offer us a picture of a relatively stable individual existing in a relatively stable world. That stability was no doubt partly a product of the fact that individual desires and interests were still hemmed in by the norms set by the family, communal expectations, property, institutional constraints, reason and religion. The limited scope of self-interest is, interestingly, reflected in the fact that up until the final third of the 20th century economic theory did not maintain that rational, self-interested choice could explain *all* social and political behaviour. Furthermore, even within the economic realm proper, it was not always clear whether the idea of self-interested behaviour was limited to exchange and trade relations or whether it could fruitfully be extended to production as well (Sen, 2009).

The stability I've just mentioned was also partly a product of the shift in our language from erratic and even irrational desires/passions to the cooler language of interests, interests that were not ephemeral and that were also to a large degree knowable and predictable. The question arises, however, whether in an era of 'liquid modernity'[37] (Bauman, 2000) another notion of the desiring self hasn't emerged. If it has then the standard picture we have of *homo economicus* (self-interested individuals) is an anachronistic one and in need of drastic revision.

I'll return to those questions in section 7. But before doing so let's spend a little more time examining the notion of self-interest since it has played such an important role in structuring how economists think about human behaviour.

4.5   The eclipse of self-interested individuals and the emergence of the desiring self

To summarize, I have argued that early modernity starts with an emphasis on the idea of an abstract, asocial individual who is theorized as being in conflict with other people. This way of thinking about individuality runs throughout modernity. Autonomy, the essential quality of this individual, is pictured as entailing a freedom from all social scripts, allegiances, obligations and ties of identity. However, the concept of the individual that *actually* prevailed for much of the time sat somewhere between this purely free-standing, isolated hedonistic individual and the individual formed in a web of tradition, custom, inherited social and moral norms. I called that person the self-interested individual.

In fact, as Appiah (2005) informs us, there's always been the possibility of a Millian individual occupying this middle ground, a person whose 'experiments in living' entail giving a shape to one's life from within the 'language' or set of available *social* forms, practices and models. In this reading, desire or preferences are neither merely 'wanton' nor 'given', but part of a life plan that takes form as a result of our reflective choices and commitments. Those choices involve our feelings, judgements and other capacities that have to be cultivated *over* time. That pleasure itself varies in quality gives greater scope for the development of *individual* reason and competencies to determine what really matters in one's life.[38] The self, then, is both historically and dialogically constituted by the horizons of the world it finds itself in.

Somewhat similar to the Millian individual – at least in certain respects – the theoretical picture of self-interested economic actors, up until the 20th century, was also 'worldly': possessive perhaps, but moderate and realistic (since he was cooperative and social – at least in some minimal sense of those terms). One could still say – at a stretch – that the individual possessed some psychological depth and didn't pursue mere whims or fancies. As long as his utility retained the semblance of a substantive perspective the pursuit of self-interest could be seen to be, in a non-trivial way, good for both himself and for society. And in practical terms, as I've already commented, economic life found its orientation from within the limits and narratives provided by culture, customary expectations, settled purposes and the relative stable identities imposed by the regularities of family life, work and social norms.

But I want to now tentatively suggest that in our contemporary situation the very notion of a stable self, as described above, is being called into question. Since the last third of the 20th century we've seen both a fragmentation around racial and gender identities as well as a weakening of class identities. Other developments around this time have been significant: rising inequalities that have contributed to the thinning out of social/public identities;[39] the ever-greater penetration of markets into private, social and political spheres of life; and the increasingly imperialistic reach of economic theory.[40] But if social and political identities are ultimately a matter of our optimizing choices, and if we can think of them simply as if they are commodities that can be traded-off against actual commodities in a preference function, then we are less likely to have a sense of an enduring, stable self. In some sense, in our late capitalism era *homo economicus* is devouring himself.

Some commentators have argued that from the early 20th century onwards there has been a disjunction between the unrestricted, boundless and creative self in culture and the more prudential, bourgeois individual found in the economy. Associated with the former conception of the self is an emphasis on speed, immediacy and a simultaneity of perspectives; the obliteration of distance between subject and object (mirrored by the erasure of distinctions between the private and the public realms); and the disruption of narrative time in favour of the fragmentary and the discontinuous. On the other hand, the solid economic agent, the bourgeois individual, was defined more by restraint and seriousness than 'release' and enjoyment.

As the economy changed gears over the second half of the last century – via globalization and financialization – this space-time compression was accentuated in the economic sphere as well (Harvey, 1989; Streeck, 2012) and to such an extent that economy and culture seemed less distinguishable (Slater and Tonkiss, 2004). In fact contemporary economic and cultural systems may be leading us to a situation in which evaluative distinctions cease to be of importance.[41]

This transition from self-interested individuals to the desiring self is expertly explored by Bauman (2008). He first notes a change in self-conceptions from 'Being'– which is associated with notions of virtue, the good life – to 'Having', which is akin to the possessive individualism of *homo faber* that closely resembles the self-interested behaviour we see in the solid stage of capitalistic development. In both stages individuals still exist in an entanglement of dependencies and relationships (on other people in the one, and on commodities in the other). In the 'having' stage human conduct and desire are still framed by discipline, institutional norms, cultural expectations, calculation, routines and instrumental rationality.

But what happens in the advanced stage of capitalistic development is that both the individual and desire get uncoupled from this relatively solid framework so that the desiring self that emerges increasingly comes to resemble the cultural self described by Daniel Bell above.[42]

The idea of a relatively stable self-interested individual, whose desires were still bound by moral and cultural norms, comes into question since desires are no longer underwritten by the notions of usefulness, satisfaction, reason or possessiveness (property) that still might have connected the individual to the world.

What emerges in the advanced stage of capitalism is, interestingly, the idea that we are driven not so much by self-interested desires but by wishes, fantasies and dreams. Consumption, or so it is believed, is no longer related to the *attainment* of pleasure, satisfaction, happiness, utility or the accumulation of possessions so much as it is about the freedom to *pursue* whatever one wants. Given that, the idea that self-interested individuals rationally chose means to maximize their welfare seems woefully anachronistic.

For some of the harshest critics of our current situation the displacement of the creedal self ('the person') by the inner-worldly ascetic of the early modern period is eventually followed by the emergence of a transgressive, hedonistic self, for whom there are no ethical limits to desire. The result of all those changes is, according to Rieff (2007), that by being "endlessly innovative and experimentally unstable" (p. 133) individuals lack all self-identity and inwardness. Since what matters now is the production of desire – whence the emphasis on "eroticism and its publicity" (Rieff, 2007, p. 12) – the desiring self is, it is argued, held captive by spectacles and the 'erotic dazzle of power' and 'stars'.[43]

To 'be held captive' suggests that we are increasingly becoming slaves of our desires (and so it is worth keeping one eye on addictions and our apparently ever-greater craving for excitement and stimulation). Such a dark possibility was hinted at many years ago by the conservative critics of liberalism who saw it as a creed that dissipates and relaxes.[44] Whether we've reached that stage or not is a moot point. However, it is fair to say that technology, mainstream culture and the economy are pushing us in a direction that leads to the dissipation, blurring, or disappearance of the self.

But can a 'self' shorn of its religious, social and ethical dimensions really be said to exist in any coherent, non-contingent fashion? Should we say with Bauman (2002), in a world of ephemeral relationships, skills, possessions and neighbour-hoods, the only stable frame of reference is the living body? Or, alternatively, without a coherent self and a shared, common world are we just thinking robots?[45] I will take up these questions in section 6.

In the light of these changes the assumption of self-interested behaviour fails in a number of ways. Firstly, economic theory assumes we aim to satisfy our 'given' self-interested preferences when it could be argued that the real dynamism of capitalism – at least in its present form – derives from our desire to escape the realm of instrumentality and rational calculation (Knight, 1997). Desire – impulsive, instinctual and perhaps even compulsive – is what drives us forward, and not our cool, predictable interests. What matters now, from the perspective of the perpetuation of the economic system, is pure desire itself in all its momentariness and inexhaustibility. Or, as Bauman (2001) writes, "Consumption ought to be an absolute end in itself" (p. 39) if capitalism is to reproduce itself. The market system in this reading is actually more innovative and dynamic than the standard, self-interest model suggests. Markets foster novelty, rapid obsolescence, and the creation of new desires. They are not, as economic theory claims, mechanical, coordinating system that equilibrate individuals' *given* desire.

A second shortcoming is that the standard approach, by assuming consumer sovereignty and perfect knowledge, ignores a more realistic depiction of our actual current situation. Consumers in advanced capitalism cannot always be said to know what their desires are, or if they are really even their own rather than the product of manipulation, deception and the social construction of distractions (Akerlof and Shiller, 2016).

A third source of limitation is that the approach implicitly assumes a stable notion of the self over time. So, for example, individuals invest in projects that yielded a future (known) return. But it could be said that with space-time compression and the collapse of narratives in liquid modernity the very notion of identity and the persistence of a self over time is brought into question.[46]

Do the limitations of the self-interest assumption reduce the ability of economic theory to both explain how we ought to act as well as describe how we actually act in reality? Yes, to the extent that economic theory relies on an idea of exogenously 'given', self-interested preferences it doesn't adequately explain choice in our contemporary situation. However, since the beginning of the 20th century economic theory has included an alternative way of thinking about preferences, a way that has jostled with the self-interest conception for centre-stage.

At the level of theory this new way of thinking has replaced the idea that individuals are governed by psychological egoism. Previously, it was believed that economic agents were propelled to maximize utility – where utility did not signify 'usefulness'[47] but, instead, a substantive (though abstract) value such as 'pleasure', 'happiness' or 'satisfaction'.[48]

From the beginning of the 20th century, an alternative[49] way of thinking about preferences and choice emerges. According to this alternative view, axiomatic utility theory, any remnants of psychology from economics are eliminated (Bruni and Sugden, 2007). Utility is no longer a substantive concept but a mere mathematical representation of our preferences. Accordingly, whereas in the older formulation of utility we could still reasonably talk about human subjectivity and subjective inwardness, in the newer one agents' preferences, devoid of any subjective content, suggest the existence of individuals with very little inner life.

Economic agents, then, come to resemble (and draw upon) the theoretical picture of the abstract, atomistic, asocial individual that emerged at the beginning of modernity and that was described in section 2 above. But what arguably separates them from this earlier characterization of the individual is that the nature or content of his desires, passions or preferences become less important in explaining his behaviour. In place of such explanations economic theory increasingly relies on the *formal*[50] properties of preferences (Davis, 2003). In fact, there has been a tendency to think of choice independently of the context of those choices (internal consistency) and, in some cases, an attempt to do away with the reliance on preferences altogether (as in the idea of revealed preferences).

We are in the midst of profound changes in our self-conceptions. Individuals in late capitalism are really constantly moving desiring machines for whom the only relevant consideration is the perpetuation of desire itself (irrespective of its ends). Such an individual, devoid of any 'inwardness' or social relations marks what I have called 'the disappearance of the self'. This trend is matched in the development of axiomatic economic theory in the second half of the 20th century since all that matters for the asocial individuals in our models is the rational structure of their preferences (and not their content).

From the perspective of economic theory a realistic explanation of mental processes isn't even important as long economic models accurately *predict* (not explain) human behaviour. In addition, this viewpoint is very much in line with the popular notion that the mind is simply a computer and that thought can be described by algorithmic procedures. What economists are really modelling, it transpires, is not *human* behaviour but a set of interactions between robots.[51]

The metaphor of economic agents as robots, however, mistakenly assume that the self has a stable frame of reference from which it can mechanically and rationally calculate its best options. In reality the formal view of utility and the actual dynamism of real-world market economies push us to a different conclusion: what ultimately matters is only the freedom of the isolated and abstract will to choose.

Do we need another metaphor that captures something of our contemporary situation? Could it be, as Bauman (2002) suggests, that the only constant frame is my living body and that the only source of continuity is the body, not the self?

4.6   The life of the body

Some academics have argued that economic theory needs to move away from its reliance on mechanical metaphors and incorporate biological ones instead (Bronk, 2009). Doing so would have the advantage of moving us in the direction acknowledging individuals are complex, dynamically and dialogically constituted beings; it would also entail giving up the notion that we have exogenously 'given' preferences that we unreflectively aim to maximally satisfy. Both of those amendments would make economic theory more realistic. But such an approach still neglects ethical considerations as long as it avoids considering the varying historical relation between the body (and 'life') to capitalistic development.[52]

One way of reading this history is to suggest that the record of capitalistic development can be seen as involving a number of transitions: from the notion of a 'higher' life (contemplation, a relation to the divine), to a socially defined way of life; and from that to the natural life of the body. And, it should be emphasized, this bare body has no relation to any higher truth (or morality), no longer bears the character of gift, and is not socially related to other bodies. The only commonality we share is that of our animal nature.

We can think of the long history of capitalistic development, then, as being synonymous with the emergence of the biopolitical. The latter phenomenon describes the techniques and apparatus that incorporate 'life' – individual bodies (via discipline) and the collective body (via the regulation of population) – into systems of knowledge, power and economic functionality.

The incorporation of the body into the polis is, however, not without its tensions and contradictions. Firstly, the biopolitical can refer to the animal body (*zoe*) and its desires – as they supposedly just factually *are*, independent of any rational, social, ethical, religious or cultural norms and values that might give weight and direction to them. And yet far from fostering emancipatory possibilities, biopower has attempted to produce bodies by harnessing the body's energies to the capitalist goal of greater productivity, profits and consumption. It may be that what is ultimately esteemed is a life of endless bodily pleasures, a "body stripped of its guilt, an end in itself" (Hughes, 2012, p. 152). But if that attitude is an outcome of the logic of capitalistic expansion it can hardly be said to be a reflection of autonomous and emancipatory possibilities.

Secondly, in the early stages of capitalism the inscribing of the body into the political was predominantly achieved by the micro-mechanisms of disciplinary power (Foucault, 1984b). But in late capitalism the emphasis is less on repressions and more on the invention of an empty, indeterminate and perpetually desiring body.[53] This sets up a difficulty for the organization of desire and the conversion of the body's energies into economic value since animal spirits, passions and desires are precisely what escape the control of reason. In other words, the idea of the unrestrained body with its infinite and unpredictable desires might serve as the ideal model of a consumer; but it doesn't carry over well into the realm of production and the creation of economic value.

The production of value, it is now increasingly understood, depends less on the management of pure life (*zoe*) and more on the subsumption of distinct human ways of life (*bios*) to the interests of capital – whence the great importance given to human, social and cultural capital[54] in our times. But this leads us to a third source of tensions.

In the solid stage of capitalism, where 'having' is still of paramount importance, it is restraint, sobriety, the utilizing and disciplining of the body's forces that matters since there's still an ostensible end-goal in sight: a secular form of redemption (wealth, happiness, welfare, or the quality of life). As we move into the last third of the 20th century, into liquid modernity, it is pure desire itself – groundless, excessive and transgressive – that is at the heart of a consumer society. In fact, 'excessive' and 'transgressive' are probably not the best way to describe the phenomena since they are only meaningful concepts against prior notions of norms and limits, and it is precisely such notions that are negated.[55]

But this emphasis on the release of the animal body's fleeting and limitless desires in effect leads to the repudiation of social relations as well as the disruption of the narratives[56] that go to make-up the *bios*. Instead of a solid, durable and common world, instead of the dense accumulation of meanings associated with a particular place over time, we have a network or space of flows. And yet the appropriation in late capitalism of 'living labour' (the *bios*) depends precisely on the continued existence of social relations (Harvey, 2008), unique habitats and the commons – the collectively formed potential for thinking, speaking, remembering and acting (Fleming, 2015).

All of these three factors are inter-related with one another. For example, the loss of our bearings in space – what some have called 'free-fall' (Steyerl, 2012) – is not solely down to changing work conditions but also includes factors such as technology, a culture of withdrawal/narcissism *and* changing conceptions of the body. For sure, technological developments mean that we live amidst a proliferation of words (even as the contract between word and world has been broken

Steiner, 1986), a relentless spectacle of 'breaking news', entertainment, frivolity, banality and the hyper-inflation of images that, relieved from the burden of representation, now form a virtual world, our empire of signs. But the loss of a sense of place (stable property, attachments to the land) is both cause and effect of "a new alliance between the body and the virtual" (Juvin, 2010, p. 54).

The cult of the life of the body (*zoe*) and the libidinal economy that promotes it whittles away at our sociality and solidarity (attachments, bonds, obligations to other people); and as it posits a body free from the sense of identity (or belonging) and independent of the rhythms of the earth,[57] it drastically alters our understanding of longing, weight and duration that formerly gave us our image of the body.

It is hard not to see this as the culmination of a line of thought that stretches back to the origins of modernity and the birth of the individual, for it appears that what was central to the Hobbesian worldview "was a universe that is nothing but bodies and their aimless motions" (Strauss, 1965, p. 172).

What is left of the individual but the exposed body, raw flesh?[58] Perhaps not even that. A depthless subject, almost out of time, whose bodily desires signify nothing beyond themselves is really at the point of disappearing.

Which painters best typify this situation? Not Hopper, the great painter of estrangement and distances between sad and forlorn people. Perhaps Schiele for in his angular, narcissistic, slightly neurotic and vulnerable individuals we see the body as the self – a body that is broken and torn. His bodies, displayed in all their isolation from any relation to the world, in all their heightened fragmentariness, point to nothing more than the existence of crucified bodies without the cross. Or maybe Abstract Expressionism in the second half of the 20th century was symptomatic of that feeling. Perhaps Robert Hughes (2012) was right when he wrote of a David Hockney painting: we see "the body, as it is swallowed by the blue, a vanishing-act watched by absences" (p. 422).

4.7 Conclusion

The old metaphysical notion of an individual with a given nature – what I earlier called 'the person' – is now largely held to be a historical fiction. The idea of an order of being (intellect-soul-body) and even the solid, prudent bourgeois individual of the industrial or solid stage of capitalism has given way to a much more ephemeral 'self'. This unstable, fleeting and fragmentary entity, far from being a mere conjecture of post-modern thought, is both a reflection and a product of late capitalism. In other words, this continually shifting self, lacking continuity or identity as it comes under the influence of the tyranny of the 'now', mirrors the shape-shifting, directionless world it finds itself in. Human subjectivity, then, loses its depth and is flattened out to a surface, which explains the current emphasis on the body and on the screen. What is the 'self' but a moving tissue of images and a series of unrelated and rapidly changing bodily pleasures?

From within this current (broken) picture of the 'self' it could be argued that the mind is itself merely an epiphenomenon of the body. Is that the logical conclusion of historical developments that have entailed the progressive hollowing out of the individual by denying his aspirations any substantive content? Perhaps it is true that from early modernity to our own day the individual has only been defined negatively, as someone who is free as long as he is free *from* community, nature and world. The result of thinking of freedom in terms of separation (rather than in terms of connectivity) is that the individual is deprived of any enduring psychological or ethical substance. We are left with an individual for whom inwardness is simply a *direction* and not a description of particular states of being (Davis, 2003), and for whom weightlessness and lightness[59] were perhaps always the ideals.

The great danger posed by the elimination of substantial notions of the individual is that he is replaced either by a mere natural body or a machine-like cyborg, both of which lack inwardness. Anxieties about the disappearance of the individual extend beyond concerns over the implications of the rise of artificial intelligence on health and education (Ford, 2016), or on jobs (Haldane, 2015). Our anxieties are actually a reflection of our inability to answer the profound question: what is left of the image of Man?[60]

Notes

1 On the important ways in which standard, axiomatic approaches to reasoning misrepresent or ignore aspects of our actual individuality see Davis (2015). Reconceptualizations of individuality that rely on game theory, experimental and behavioural science, complexity modelling or neuroscience may still fail to capture the specifically social/ethical dimension that we are concerned about (Davis, 2011).

2 How and why any particular understanding of a concept comes to be accepted as the orthodox interpretation cannot, I believe, be explained in a systematic or *a priori* fashion. For example, the narrowing down of all human motivations to self-interest offers the obvious advantages of simplicity and tractability to a discipline that has scientific pretensions. On the other hand, Keynes (2008) reminds us of an alternative explanation: "That it [economic orthodoxy] afforded a measure of justification to the free activities of the individual capitalist, attracted to it the support of the dominant social force behind authority" (p. 30).

3 The recognition of a pre-political moral individual may pre-date the Enlightenment (Murdoch, 1993). Market economies are also seen as promoting process and opportunity freedoms (Sen, 1993). That they do is of some moral import.

4 The reality, of course, is more complex with the distinct possibility that the supposedly autonomous individual of the market is caught in an increasingly complex web of bureaucratic control (Graeber, 2015).

5 Taylor (2007a) relates this to a revolution in devotion in the early modern period, to an idea of nature that doesn't necessarily reflect the divine or 'the good'. The greater emphasis on the ordinary lives of particular individuals is foreshadowed in art by a more realistic portrayal of the suffering, human Christ as opposed to the transcendent, timeless, *Christ Pantocrator* (Graham-Dixon, 2000).

6 The concept of flourishing draws us to the insight that we cannot talk about the person without a particular notion of 'the good' (see chapter 10). As Bruni (2012) notes, for the individual (as opposed to the person) only *his* good counts. The individual is either indifferent or opposed to 'the good' of others and to the common good.

7 See chapter 2 for the implications of this view on how we think about economics and more generally (Löwith, 1942).

8　"The pattern of our beliefs composes our sense of self" (Hoggart, 1999, p. 18).

9　"No human being should be deprived of his *metaxu*, that is to say of those relative and mixed blessings (home, country, tradition, culture, etc.) which warm and nourish the soul and without which, short of sainthood, a *human* life would not be possible" (Weil, 1952, p. 202).

10　For a remarkable example of freedom being eked out from the narrowest conditions of life see Rosenzweig (1998).

11　Also see Dumont (1977) where he writes: the individual is "given in relation to God and his fellow men, and, thanks to the relation to God, the abstract relation between members of the human species can be substituted for the links within a community" (p. 59).

12　For Adam Smith the idea of moral equality plays an important role in the justification of the markets against the hierarchies and dependencies of feudal power.

13　Strauss (1965), writing of changes at the dawn of the modern period, says "No objective criterion henceforth allowed the distinction between good and bad choices" (p. 18). This is a view that would come to dominate the economics discipline in the form of a commitment to the idea that preferences or tastes are simply 'wanton' or 'given', and not subject to ethical judgement.

14　It could be argued that market economies and liberal societies are the ultimate expression of the idea that choice is *in itself* good.

15　We look at interests and their relation to political order in more detail in section 5.

16　As Broome (1999) argues, 'the good' is a purely formal concept in economics.

17　It is not surprising, given that context, that one will struggle to find barely a mention of the role of state in the development process in Ray's (1998) otherwise excellent *Development Economics*.

18　In chapter 1, I argued that the invention of scarcity was partly a response to the fear of contagion.

19　It should be noted that the notion of self-interest also has a political dimension. In the final section it will be argued that the 'neoliberal self' cannot be understood without analysing political developments (neoliberalism).

20　Hobbes (2016) writes: "Whatsoever is the object of any man's Appetite or Desire; that is it, which he for his part calleth *Good*. . . . There being nothing simply and absolutely so; nor any common Rule of Good and Evill, to be taken from the nature of the objects themselves; but from the Person of the man" (Chapter VI. Of the Interior Beginnings of Voluntary Motions, Commonly Called the Passions; and the Speeches by which They are Expressed).

21　It is this disembedded and asocial individual that we typically encounter in economic theory. It is not surprising that there is such little emphasis on culture, identity, social class, ethnicity and power relations in the economist's explanation of exchange and production.

22　Arendt (1998), in The Human Condition writes of how modern philosophy initiates a "second turning inwards".

23　Rose (1999) relates this emphasis on *individual* knowledge to liberation/understanding as "Gnosticism".

24　See Kerr (1997), Crawford (2015) and Reed (1996). Chamberlain (2007) informs us of an older, pre-modern tradition that was in stark opposition to the individualistic approach to thinking found in Descartes. Instead of the *cogito* the Russians might have said: 'I am, therefore I think'. Or, even better, as if to emphasize the social dimension to our understanding: 'we are, therefore I think'. In chapter 2 we looked at the critiques of the notion of individual rationality. It is an intriguing question whether the logical conclusion of progressively greater levels of abstraction and disengagement from the social world is tantamount to the production of a virtual reality. And if so, within that reality does reasoning become robotic, does desire become mechanical?

25 On "vernacular knowledge" see Illich (1981). For a critique of the idea that algorithmic knowledge is a uniquely valid approach to understanding human behaviour see Cartwright (1999).

26 The Robinson Crusoe-like sovereign, rootless individual ushered in by politics (contracts) and markets is a potentially universal figure (according to economic theory) since contracts and trades are not restricted by time or place. It is hard to see how economics can be a *social* science when, as Douglas (1998) writes, "no-one else is there".

27 Nowhere is this disappearance of the transcendent dimension more visible than in Holbein's great painting, 'The Death of Christ'. Kristeva (1992) argues that the painting represents a grim acceptance of finitude. That modernity starts with the erasure of the sense of immortality is powerfully argued by Jonas (2001).

28 I return to this point in section 6. Arendt (1998) also writes about a 'modern reversal': a decline in the importance of contemplation in favour, at first, of the durable social world of work and then, later, of the laboring animal in a consumer society. The ramifications of this emphasis on the animal body are profound. If biological life and the body are the true locus of meaning, what is the structure of our narrative lives, our relations to other people and the world around us? Is it possible to conceive an ethical economy when bodily desires are all that matter?

29 See MacIntyre (2011) for a discussion of why to be part of a web of relations, dependent on others, and also depended upon, is central to a notion of human flourishing.

30 This mutuality is not dualistic but chiastic: a simultaneity of overlapping *and* distinctive perspectives or, in the language of Etzioni (1990) : I *and* We. As Todorov (2001) says: "In the communion one is not ignorant of the fact that the other is other" (p. 69). A brilliant illustration of this attitude can be seen in Rembrandt's painting, 'The Jewish Bride'.

31 Murdoch (2001) gives a remarkable account of what this entails since all depends on M looking at D "not just to see D accurately but to see her justly or lovingly" (p. 22).

32 "Perhaps the individual liberated or created by capitalism had a golden age of integral being and virtuous idealism, . . . but now, it is said, has disintegrated and become unconfident, and even corrupt" (Murdoch, 1993, p. 352).

33 The emphasis in late capitalism on a narrow form of intelligence and short-term perspectives also makes solidarity, connectedness and cooperation less likely.

34 We are in danger of becoming the isolated, acquisitive and asocial individuals that theory suggested we were all along. That may explain why loneliness and mental illness are increasingly a major problem (Monbiot, 2016) and why conflict seems so natural: me against the world; me against nature; and me against my father. The only form of relationality we accept can be subsumed under the conceptual categories of rivalry, strategic interaction and submission.

35 The existence of the freelancer, the temp, the migrant worker and the consultant testifies to the continued decline in our ability to identify with any organization on a long-term basis. Coupled with the decline in trade unions it is not surprising that workplace solidarity seems like a thing of the past.

36 This was reflected in the emphasis on unheroic subjects and ordinary objects in Dutch art in the early modern period (Herbert, 2012).

37 Will we look back, Adam Gopnik muses (Hughes, 2005) to our shared and inherited bourgeois pleasures and possessions, to our world of solid and durable commodities, with a sense of nostalgia as our lives become more precarious in liquid modernity?

38 Appealing as this picture of the Millian individual is, Sugden (2003) offers another interpretation, suggesting that for Mill autonomy is not merely important because its employment helps us to attain what reason or ethical reflection may determine

as the 'best' choice within the set of choices. The very act of choosing is, according to Sugden, what Mill esteemed.

39 See Sennett (2017). In chapter 7 I discuss this in more detail.

40 The market, now no longer restricted to a specific place, has become a metaphor for all social, political and ethical relations.

41 In economic theory, too, an all-things-considered understanding of utility precludes us from assigning any fundamental importance to distinctions in the sources of value.

42 This shift is mirrored in academic economics itself as the notion of pluralistic and socially/institutionally embedded markets is replaced by the universal and timeless market formed by the interaction of atomistic individuals (Rodgers, 2011).

43 For the latter phenomenon see Steyerl (2012).

44 "Liberalism can prepare the way for . . . the artificial, mechanized, or brutalized control which is a desperate remedy for its chaos" (Eliot, 1949, p. 12).

45 Davis (2003) writes that the contemporary, post-modern self sows the seeds of its own destruction and replacement by a machine-like cyborg devoid of inwardness.

46 This has wide implications not only for how we think about the fate of future generations, but also for how we think about our own lives in the future (think of saving, borrowing and educational investment decisions, for example).

47 See the discussion between Broome (1991) for the different historical understanding of the term 'utility'.

48 This view was contested, of course. Butler claimed that what we first desire are specific objects and that the pleasure we derive from them is derivative on the first desire (Blackburn, 2009).

49 Both views are deeply problematic since preferences are not open to rational scrutiny. The individualistic basis of preferences means there is little scope for thinking about relationality.

50 Similarly, before the increasing formalism and abstraction took root in economic theory during this period markets were for a large time conceived of as pluralistic, imperfect and socially embedded (Solow, 1997).

51 Robert Lucas famously took this position (see Davis, 2003).

52 I gloss over many important facets of that history – such as its connection to racism and gender discrimination.

53 Both the entertainment industry and business organizations must, therefore, "incite, excite and provoke the body" (Juvin, 2010, p. 155) in order to 'liberate' the body's impulses.

54 See chapter 7 for a further discussion of this point.

55 What Rieff (2006) calls the negation of the negations.

56 The counter-society of the permanently available naked body, with its useless, arbitrary, unproductive, transgressive, excessive and wasteful pleasures is brilliantly dissected by Hénaff (1999). The Sadean emphasis on the absolute freedom of the body stands diametrically opposed to the lyrical body of expressive signs. The lyrical body is not something that can be accounted for in economic theory's model of contractual exchange.

57 The human body has, over time, adapted itself to the ebb and flow of terrestrial life (Russell, 2006).

58 Franzen (2006): "To be all meat ad raw nerve is to exist outside of time and – at least momentarily – outside of narrative" (p. vii). This ties in with Fuller's (1985) description of the work of the painter Francis Bacon. For Bacon, whose life seems to have been dedicated to futility and chance, depicts the naked reality of the human body without any moral or spiritual values.

59 See Calvino's (1996) thought-provoking *Six Memos for The Next Millennium*, where both of these ideas are discussed.

60 This image is, according to Marion (2004), being destroyed by the 'televisual order': "Every perception of the world is reduced to an expression of the monad

itself . . . the *libido vivendi*, which satisfies itself with the solitary pleasure of the screen, does away with love by forbidding sight of the other face – invisible and real" (p. 54). Contrast this with an aspect of what in chapter 3 we called 'austerity', namely, what Illich (1995) calls restraint in *Guarding the Eye in the Age of Show*.

Bibliography

Akerlof, G. A., and Shiller, R. J. (2016). *Phishing for Phools: The Economics of Manipulation and Deception*. Princeton, NJ: Princeton University Press.

Appiah, K. A. (2005). The Ethics of Individuality. In *The Ethics of Identity*. Princeton, NJ: Princeton University Press.

Appignanesi, L. (2004). *The Cabaret*. New Haven, CT: Yale University Press.

Arendt, H. (1998). *The Human Condition*. Chicago, IL: University of Chicago Press.

Bauman, Z. (2000). *Liquid Modernity*. Malden, MA: Polity Press.

Bauman, Z. (2001). *(Un)Happiness of Uncertain Pleasures*. Copenhagen: Sociologisk Laboratorium, Aalborg Universitet.

Bauman, Z. (2002). *Society Under Siege*. Cambridge: Polity Press.

Bauman, Z. (2008). *Consuming Life*. Cambridge: Polity Press.

Bell, D. (1978). *The Cultural Contradictions of Capitalism*. New York, NY: Basic Books.

Blackburn, S. (2009). *Ruling Passions: A Theory of Practical Reasoning*. Oxford: Clarendon Press.

Blake, W. (2016). *There Is No Natural Religion*. Retrieved December 26, 2017, from http://ramhornd.blogspot.com/2016/09/no-natural-religion.html

Boldizzoni, F. (2011). *The Poverty of Clio: Resurrecting Economic History*. Princeton, NJ: Princeton University Press.

Bronk, R. (2009). *The Romantic Economist: Imagination in Economics*. Cambridge: Cambridge University Press.

Bronk, R. (2013). Reflexivity Unpacked: Performativity, Uncertainty and Analytical Monocultures. *Journal of Economic Methodology, 20*(4), 343–349. doi:10.1080/1350178x.2013.859404

Broome, J. (1991). Utility. *Economics and Philosophy, 7*(1), 1–12. doi:10.1017/s0266267100000882

Broome, J. (1999). *Ethics Out of Economics*. Cambridge: Cambridge University Press.

Brown, P. (1989). *The World of Late Antiquity 150–750*. New York, NY: W.W. Norton & Company.

Bruni, L. (2012). *The Wound and the Blessing: Economics, Relationships, and Happiness*. Hyde Park, NY: New City Press.

Bruni, L. (2016, October 11). *A Nobel for the Economics that Gathers Ashes*. Publication. Retrieved from www.edc-online.org/en/publications/articles-by/luigino-bruni-s-articles/avvenire-editorial/12490-a-nobel-for-the-economics-that-gathers-ashes.html

Bruni, L., and Sugden, R. (2007). The Road Not Taken: How Psychology Was Removed From Economics, and How It Might Be Brought Back. *The Economic Journal, 117*(516), 146–173. doi:10.1111/j.1468-0297.2007.02005.x

Calvino, I. (1996). *Six Memos for the Next Millennium*. London: Vintage.

Cartwright, N. (1999). *The Dappled World: A Study of the Boundaries of Science*. New York, NY: Cambridge University Press.

Chamberlain, L. (2007). *Motherland: A Philosophical History of Russia*. New York, NY: Rookery Press.

Clark, K. (2005). The Light of Experience. In *Civilisation: A Personal View*. London: John Murray.

Crawford, M. B. (2015). *The World Beyond Your Head: On Becoming an Individual in an Age of Distraction*. London: Penguin Books.

Davis, J. B. (2003). *The Theory of the Individual in Economics: Identity and Value*. New York, NY: Routledge.

Davis, J. B. (2009). Identity and Individual Economic Agents: A Narrative Approach. *Review of Social Economy, 67*(1), 71–94. Retrieved from www.jstor.org/stable/41288440

Davis, J. B. (2011). *Individuals and Identity in Economics*. Cambridge: Cambridge University Press.

Davis, J. B. (2015). Bounded Rationality and Bounded Individuality. In L. Fiorito, S. Scheall, and C. E. Suprinyak (Eds.), *A Research Annual* (Vol. 33, Research in the History of Economic Thought and Methodology, pp. 75–93). Bingley: Emerald Group Publishing Limited.

Douglas, M. (1998). *Missing Persons: A Critique of the Social Sciences*. Berkeley, CA: University of California Press.

Dumont, L. (1977). *From Mandeville to Marx: The Genesis and Triumph of Economic Ideology*. Chicago, IL: University of Chicago Press.

Dumont, L. (1992). Introduction. In *Essays on Individualism: Modern Ideology in Anthropological Perspective*. Chicago, IL: University of Chicago Press.

Eliot, T. S. (1949). *Christianity and Culture: The Idea of a Christian Society and Notes Towards the Definition of Culture*. New York, NY: Harcourt, Brace & Company.

Esposito, R. (2010). *Communitas: The Origin and Destiny of Community*. Stanford, CA: Stanford University Press.

Etzioni, A. (1990). *Moral Dimension: Toward a New Economics*. New York, NY: Free Press.

Fleming, P. (2015). *Resisting Work: The Corporatization of Life and Its Discontents*. Philadelphia, PA: Temple University Press.

Ford, M. (2016). *Rise of the Robots: Technology and the Threat of a Jobless Future*. New York, NY: Basic Books.

Foucault, M. (1984a). What Is Enlightenment? In P. Rabinow (Ed.), *The Foucault Reader*. New York, NY: Pantheon Books.

Foucault, M. (1984b). *The Foucault Reader* (P. Rabinow, Ed.). New York, NY: Pantheon Books.

Foucault, M. (2014). *Security, Territory, Population: Lectures at the Collège de France, 1977–1978* (F. Ewald, A. Fontana, and M. Senellart, Eds.). Basingstoke: Palgrave Macmillan.

Franzen, J. (2006). Introduction. In F. Dostoyevsky (Author) and H. A. Aplin (Trans.), *The Gambler: A Novel (From a Young Man's Notes)*. London: Hesperus Press.

Fuller, P. (1985). *Images of God: The Consolations of Lost Illusions*. London: Chatto & Windus.

Gellner, E. (1998). *Language and Solitude: Wittgenstein, Malinowski and the Habsburg Dilemma*. Cambridge: Cambridge University Press.

Graeber, D. (2015). *The Utopia of Rules: On Technology, Stupidity, and the Secret Joys of Bureaucracy*. New York, NY: Melville House.

Graham-Dixon, A. (2000). *Renaissance*. Berkeley, CA: University of California Press.

Haldane, A. G. (2015, November 12). *Labour's Share*. Speech presented in Trades Union Congress, London. Retrieved from www.bankofengland.co.uk/-/media/boe/files/speech/2015/labours-share.pdf?la=en&hash=D6F1A4C489DA855C8512FC41C02E014F8D683953

Harvey, D. (1989). *The Condition of Postmodernity: An Enquiry Into the Origins of Cultural Change*. Cambridge, MA: Blackwell.

Harvey, D. (2008). *Spaces of Hope*. Berkeley, CA: University of California Press.

Herbert, Z. (2012). *Still Life with a Bridle*. London: Notting Hill Editions.

Hénaff, M. (1999). *Sade: The Invention of the Libertine Body*. Minneapolis, MN: University of Minnesota Press.

Hirschman, A. O. (1982). Rival Interpretations of Market Society: Civilizing, Destructive, or Feeble? *Journal of Economic Literature*, *20*(4), 1463–1484. Retrieved from www.jstor.org/stable/2724829

Hobbes, T. (2003). *Leviathan*. London: Penguin Books.

Hobbes, T. (2016). Chapter VI. Of the Interior Beginnings of Voluntary Motions, Commonly Called the Passions; And the Speeches By Which They Are Expressed. *Leviathan*. Retrieved from https://ebooks.adelaide.edu.au/h/hobbes/thomas/h68l/index.html

Hodgson, G. M. (2013). *From Pleasure Machines to Moral Communities: An Evolutionary Economics Without Homo Economicus*. Chicago, IL: University of Chicago Press.

Hoggart, R. (1999). *First and Last Things: The Uses of Old Age*. London: Aurum Press.

Hughes, M. V. (2005). *A London Child of the 1870s*. London: Persephone Books.

Hughes, R. (2012). *The Shock of the New: Art and the Century of Change*. London: Thames & Hudson.

Illich, I. (1981). The War Against Subsistence. In *Shadow Work*. Boston, MA: Marion Boyers.

Illich, I. (1995). Guarding the Eye in the Age of Show. *RES: Anthropology and Aesthetics*, *28*, 47–61. Retrieved from www.jstor.org/stable/20166929

Illich, I. (1999). The Shadow Our Future Throws. *New Perspectives Quarterly*, *16*(2), 14–18. doi:10.1111/0893-7850.00216

Jonas, H. (1982). Gnosticism, Existentialism, and Nihilism. In *The Phenomenon of Life: Toward a Philosophical Biology*. Chicago, IL: University of Chicago Press.

Jonas, H. (2001). *The Phenomenon of Life: Toward a Philosophical Biology*. Evanston, IL: Northwestern University Press.

Juvin, H. (2010). *The Coming of the Body*. London: Verso.

Keen, M. H. (1991). *The Penguin History of Medieval Europe*. London: Penguin Books.

Kerr, F. (1997). Chapter 1. In *Theology After Wittgenstein*. London: SPCK.

Keynes, J. M. (2008). *General Theory of Employment, Interest and Money*. New Delhi: Atlantic & Distributors (P) LTD.

Knight, F. H. (1997). *The Ethics of Competition*. Piscataway, NJ: Transaction.

Kristeva, J. (1992). *Black Sun: Depression and Melancholia* (L. S. Roudiez, Trans.). New York, NY: Columbia University Press.

Löwith, K. (1942). M. Heidegger and F. Rosenzweig or Temporality and Eternity. *Philosophy and Phenomenological Research*, *3*(1), 53–77. doi:10.2307/2103129

MacIntyre, A. C. (2000, October 13). *A Culture of Choices and Compartmentalization*. Lecture, Notre Dame. Retrieved from http://brandon.multics.org/library/macintyre/macintyre2000choices.html

MacIntyre, A. C. (2011). *Dependent Rational Animals: Why Human Beings Need the Virtues*. Chicago, IL: Open Court.

Manent, P. (2000). The Authority of History. In *The City of Man*. Princeton, NJ: Princeton University Press.

Marcuse, H. (2009). The Affirmative Character of Culture. In J. J. Shapiro (Trans.), *Negations Essays in Critical Theory*. Colchester: MayFly.

Marglin, S. A. (2010). *The Dismal Science: How Thinking Like an Economist Undermines Community*. Cambridge, MA: Harvard University Press.

Marion, J. (2004). *The Crossing of the Visible*. Stanford, CA: Stanford University Press.

Maritain, J. (1996). *The Person and the Common Good*. Notre Dame, IN: University of Notre Dame Press.

McCloskey, D. N. (2007). *The Bourgeois Virtues: Ethics for an Age of Commerce*. Chicago, IL: University of Chicago Press.

Minogue, K. (2005). *The Concept of a University*. New Brunswick, NJ: Transaction.

Monbiot, G. (2016, October 12). Neoliberalism Is Creating Loneliness. That's What's Wrenching Society Apart. *The Guardian*. Retrieved from www.theguardian.com/commentisfree/2016/oct/12/neoliberalism-creating-loneliness-wrenching-society-apart

Murdoch, I. (1993). *Metaphysics as a Guide to Morals*. London: Penguin Books.

Murdoch, I. (1999). *Existentialists and Mystics: Writings on Philosophy and Literature*. New York, NY: Penguin Books.

Murdoch, I. (2001). *The Sovereignty of Good*. London: Routledge.

Nagel, T. (2015). The Fragmentation of Values. In *Mortal Questions*. Cambridge: Cambridge University Press.

Oakeshott, M. (1993). *Morality and Politics in Modern Europe: The Harvard Lectures*. New Haven, CT: Yale University Press.

Pabst, A. (2012). *The Crisis of Global Capitalism: Pope Benedict XVI's Social Encyclical and the Future of Political Economy*. Cambridge: James Clarke & Co.

Platteau, J. (1991). Traditional Systems of Social Security and Hunger Insurance: Past Achievements and Modern Challenges. In E. Ahmad, J. Drèze, J. Hills, and A. K. Sen (Eds.), *Social Security in Developing Countries*. Oxford: Clarendon.

Ray, D. (1998). *Development Economics*. Princeton, NJ: Princeton University Press.

Reed, E. S. (1996). *The Necessity of Experience*. New Haven, CT: Yale University Press.

Rieff, P. (2006). *My Life Among the Deathworks: Illustrations of the Aesthetics of Authority* (K. S. Piver, Ed.). Charlottesville, VA: University of Virginia Press.

Rieff, P. (2007). *The Crisis of the Officer Class: The Decline of the Tragic Sensibility* (A. Woolfolk, Ed.). Charlottesville, VA: University of Virginia Press.

Rodgers, D. T. (2011). The Rediscovery of the Market. In *Age of Fracture*. Cambridge, MA: Harvard University Press.

Rose, G. (1999). *Paradiso*. London: Menard Press.

Rosenzweig, F. (1998). *Franz Rosenzweig: His Life and Thought* (N. N. Glatzer, Ed.). Indianapolis, IN: Hackett.

Russell, B. (2006). *The Conquest of Happiness*. London: Routledge.

Schmitt, C. (2008). *The Leviathan in the State Theory of Thomas Hobbes: Meaning and Failure of a Political Symbol* (G. Schwab and E. Hilfstein, Trans.). Chicago, IL: University of Chicago Press.

Scott, J. C. (2014). *Two Cheers for Anarchism: Six Easy Pieces on Autonomy, Dignity, and Meaningful Work and Play*. Princeton, NJ: Princeton University Press.

Sen, A. K. (1993). Markets and Freedoms: Achievements and Limitations of the Market Mechanism in Promoting Individual Freedoms. *Oxford Economic Papers*, 45(4), New Series, 519–541. Retrieved from www.jstor.org/stable/2663703

Sen, A. K. (2009). Introduction. In A. Smith (Author), *The Theory of Moral Sentiments*. New York, NY: Penguin Classics.

Sennett, R. (2013). *Together: The Rituals, Pleasures and Politics of Cooperation*. New Haven, CT: Yale University Press.

Sennett, R. (2017). *The Fall of Public Man*. New York, NY: W.W. Norton & Company.

Siedentop, L. (2014). *Inventing the Individual: The Origins of Western Liberalism*. Cambridge, MA: Harvard University Press.

Slater, D., and Tonkiss, F. (2004). *Market Society: Markets and Modern Social Theory*. Cambridge: Polity Press.

Solow, R. (1997). How Did Economics Get That Way and What Way Did It Get? *Daedalus*, *126*(1), 39–58. Retrieved from www.jstor.org/stable/20027408

Steiner, G. (1971). *In Bluebeard's Castle: Some Notes Towards the Redefinition of Culture*. New Haven, CT: Yale University Press.

Steiner, G. (1986). *Real Presences*. Cambridge: Cambridge University Press.

Steyerl, H. (2012). *The Wretched of the Screen*. Berlin: Sternberg Press.

Strauss, L. (1965). *Natural Right and History*. Chicago, IL: University of Chicago Press.

Streeck, W. (2012). Citizens as Customers: Considerations on the New Politics of Consumption. *New Left Review*, *76*. Retrieved from https://newleftreview.org/II/76/wolfgang-streeck-citizens-as-customers

Sugden, R. (2003). Opportunity as a Space for Individuality: Its Value and the Impossibility of Measuring It. *Ethics*, *113*(4), 783–809. doi:10.1086/373953

Sutermeister, W. (2014). Gustave Thibon and Human Freedom. *Obsculta*, *7*(1), 49–60. Retrieved from http://digitalcommons.csbsju.edu/obsculta/vol7/iss1/6

Tawney, R. H. (1926). *Religion and the Rise of Capitalism*. New York, NY: Harcourt, Brace & Company.

Taylor, C. (1989). *Sources of the Self: The Making of the Modern Identity*. Cambridge, MA: Harvard University Press.

Taylor, C. (2007a). *A Secular Age*. Cambridge, MA: Harvard University Press.

Taylor, C. (2007b). *Modern Social Imaginaries*. Durham, NC: Duke University Press.

Tierney, B. (2004). The Idea of Natural Rights-Origins and Persistence. *Northwestern Journal of International Human Rights*, *2*(1), 1–13. Retrieved from https://scholarlycommons.law.northwestern.edu/cgi/viewcontent.cgi?article=1005&context=njihr

Todorov, T. (2001). *Life in Common: An Essay in General Anthropology*. Lincoln, NE: University of Nebraska Press.

Weil, S. (1952). *Gravity and Grace*. London: Routledge & Kegan Paul.

Weil, S. (2003). *The Need for Roots: Prelude to a Declaration of Duties Towards Mankind*. New York, NY: Routledge.

Wiggins, D. (2009). *Ethics: Twelve Lectures on the Philosophy of Morality*. Cambridge, MA: Harvard University Press.

Willey, B. (1972). *The Seventeenth-Century Background: Studies in the Thought of the Age in Relation to Poetry and Religion*. Harmondsworth: Penguin Books.

Williams, R. (2012, October 1). *The Person and the Individual: Human Dignity, Human Relationships and Human Limits*. Lecture presented at The Fifth Theos Lecture in Methodist Central Hall, Westminster.

Wittgenstein, L. (1967). *Philosophical Investigations* (G. E. Anscombe, Trans.). Oxford: Blackwell.

5 Motivations

Self-interest, sympathy and commitment

The first principle of economics is that every agent is actuated only by self-interest.

(Edgeworth cited in Sen, 1977, p. 317)

Identity is located not in the impulses of selfhood but in deliberately maintained connections.

(Berry, 2010, p. 45)

We are not 'utility monsters', or relentless consumers or atomistic individuals . . . we are, pretty much, the complex, primarily social, moral and intellectual beings we always thought we were.

(Fleischacker, 2005, p. 69)

5.0 Introduction

In the previous chapter we looked at the rise of self-interest as a concept and also how it was coming under strain given the changes in late capitalism. In this chapter I want to re-trace our steps and first examine how self-interest came to be such a powerfully structuring concept in economic thought (section 1).

In section 2 I look at the relationship between markets and ethics. At issue here is the question of whether markets are exclusively based on self-interested behaviour and if so what the implications of that are. One way of framing the relationship between ethics and markets is to ask the question of whether the deepening of market economies, supposedly based exclusively on self-interested motivations, can lead to a 'crowding-out' of ethical behaviour and perspectives. The arguments here run parallel to recent concerns over the impact of unbridled individualism on the social fabric of society (Putnam, 2007).

Alternatively, we can think of the ethics-market relation in another way: perhaps moral behaviour, codes and norms actually lead to markets working in a more effective way? I tackle this question by turning to the social capital literature (sections 3 and 4).

In the last chapter I stated that the standard economics paradigm, centred on a notion of a stable self with known and predictable interests, now appears dated given the state of the world we currently live in. The arguments against the idea that we're always self-interested were largely empirical in nature. In the fifth and sixth sections I examine alternative critiques that draw upon both the recent experimental literature and the idea of endogenous preferences.

In section 7, I look at some of the ethical critiques of the idea of self-interest. Since our desires and preferences are dependent on, and ultimately a reflection of, who we are economic theory has to take account of our social nature and our social preferences. Before concluding I look at two ethical perspectives (sympathy and commitment) in section 8.

5.1 A brief history of self-interest

In the early modern period the notion of self-interest came to play an increasingly important role in how we think about our motivations and how we ought to relate both to other people and to things in the world. In this section I'll try and flesh out that statement.

For the most part economists have been inclined to think that self-interested motivations underlie *all* of economic behaviour. The aspiration to universality is even extended to ascribing self-interest and market behaviour to the distant past.[1] The ahistorical view of a natural propensity to truck and barter conveniently ignores the role of commercial society, institutions and market-oriented policies in actually shaping our self-interested outlook. It also masks the fact that, historically speaking, human behaviour has been influenced by a variety of factors: sympathy, altruism, compassion, commitment and kindness, etc. Well could Grotius write, "The saying that every creature is led by nature to seek its own private advantage, expressed thus universally, must not be granted" (as cited in McCloskey, 2015, p. 23). So, if not a natural propensity, how did self-interest emerge as the paradigmatic way of thinking about human action?

Interest and calculation started to be thought of as the prime mover in all human affairs – and not just in the economic realm of property and finance – in the early decades of the 17th century (Gunn, 1968). Here we are looking at one of those momentous shifts in human psychology that is both a product of, and determining factor in, changes to the polity and the economy.

As we saw in the previous chapter, modernity ushered in both new ways of talking about the self as well as new socio-economic relations. The emergence of atomistic, self-centred individuals helped undermine the weight previously assigned to duty, hierarchy and social relations in the old order. For the self was no longer born into a given sea of obligations and in order to flourish the person was no longer dependent on other persons (Baier, 1991). The need for others, formerly a principle of solidarity, could now be dispensed with under the reign of self-interest (Hont and Ignatieff, 1983). And the dignity and identity of the self no longer resided in its relation to an antecedent order of value or 'the good'.

What, precisely, were these alterations in human psychology, though? For Rousseau the notion that self-interested motives stood behind all behaviour was coterminous with the rise of commercial or civilized society itself. In the early stages of human history[2] *amour de soi* (the instinctive self-preservation of the 'primitive') comes to be dominated by the *amour-propre* (self-love) and pity of the 'savage' (Force, 2007). At this earlier stage, however, self-love is still disinterested and only morphs into the more familiar economist's version of self-interest as human reason, calculation and civilization develops.

For Adam Smith self-interest or *amour-propre* (vanity) is also associated with commercial society and is not a universal principle of action. The solitary individual may live well within himself, content with the satisfaction of his or her needs. There is, on the other hand, always a hint of superficiality or artificiality associated with men living in (commercial) society, driven as they are by comparisons with other people. Lurking behind the glamour of commercial society is the shadow of false consciousness, alienation and corruption; a life that depends on self-display, a life of surface appearances such that the exhibition of wealth and pleasures externalized in commodity form reigns, is a life that is lived in the constant gaze of the other, beset by the anxious need for the esteem and recognition[3] of other people.

Both Rousseau (pity) and Smith (sympathy) recognized the existence of other-regarding motivations and that they could not be reduced to, or explained by, self-interest (Smith, 2009).[4] But equally, pity and sympathy eschew the idea that identification with the other is simply a matter of an emotional contagion of feelings. Both pity and sympathy require reflection and mental representation, a certain 'distancing'[5] from both the other person's emotions and from our own direct feelings (Paganelli, 2010). The key point remains that in a commercial society, predominantly driven by self-interest and rational calculation, the natural sentiments of pity and sympathy would inevitably become weaker and play a diminished role in influencing human behaviour.

I'll return to the idea that self-interest can crowd out other motivating factors below. For economists, though, moral sentiments (such as pity and sympathy) might simply be dismissed as not playing an important role in explaining economic choices. All that matters are commodities, states of the world and a self-regarding perspective. Or, alternatively, every economic choice can be explained by employing an extended notion of interest. Under this wider conception of interests – one that is reflected by a broader definition of utility – *whatever* I decide to do is, tautologically, a reflection of me pursuing my interests. I'll return to the broader view below (section 7).

The appeal of the narrow understanding of self-interest rests largely on the prospect it offers for more accurate predictions,[6] the attraction of parsimonious explanations, rather than on its empirical plausibility. Helvetius, writing in 1758, could opine: "If the physical universe be subject to the laws of motion, the moral universe is equally so to those of interest" (as cited in Force, 2007, p. 8). But even if self-interest is the strongest motivation underlying economic behaviour it doesn't follow that it is the 'highest': *is* does not imply *ought*.

The narrow notion of self-interest has led to a serious aberration of our understanding of deeply held notions (such as sympathy and pity). For if self-interest holds sway then what are we to make of the distinction between concepts such as 'selfish' and 'unselfish', and of the attitudes or judgements of blame and praise we typically associate with them? (Ben-Ner and Putterman,

1998a). It is fairer to say, therefore, that social and moral norms are distinct from self-interest in the sense that they are not always a rationalization of self-interest, they are not always followed out of it, and they do not necessarily promote it (Elster, 1989). The narrow view is also of questionable scientific merit. To say that all behaviour is, logically, derived from self-interest doesn't seem like an *explanation* of behaviour.

So far the discussion has been confined to the human mind and its need to identify a simple, predictable and stable principle of behaviour. Because interests supposedly do not err, and because interests are *knowable* to the subject, the concept of self-interest satisfies that need. Allayed with reason,[7] self-interest helps dispel the confusion arising from the pull of contradictory inclinations and helps the mind order its thoughts by narrowing the opportunity for being swayed by unruly passions and emotions. Instead of living in a dappled world of diverse experiences, some degree of uniformity of behaviour might be expected under its tutelage.

Whilst all of that might be eminently plausible at its own level it fails to explain how the self-interest doctrine is shaped by political institutions, education and language (Mathiowetz, 2011)

It appears that for some thinkers (Hobbes) the lack of an original or natural concord precluded the possibility of a sociable commonwealth – based on genuine mutuality and the common good – from being established. Instead, fear and pride/vanity (*amour-propre*) could only be overcome by a union brought about by the state[8] (Sahlins, 2005; Hont, 2015). For Rousseau, on the other hand, a society given over to the emulation and envy of *amour-propre* could only be stabilized by an egalitarian republic of virtuous citizens. Self-imposed austerity by virtuous citizens, a republic of fixed and limited needs and state redistribution might limit inequality and competition, thus taming our potentially insatiable and relative desires. So, the problem of political stability in a world dominated by self-interest has been with us for a long time.

For Adam Smith, however, the pursuit of self-interest would not necessarily lead to the dissolution of society or the weakening of the political realm – and since then we've almost taken it for granted that free markets and democracy flourish hand-in-hand. In fact, for Smith the endless pursuit of our interests would not lead to chaos, conflict or a zero-sum game but, quite remarkably, to an unsocial sociability and political stability. It has to be noted, therefore, that one of the main reasons for the spectacular rise of self-interest as a principle of behaviour stems from the belief in its political usefulness (Fleischacker, 2005)

According to Hirschman's (1997) classic account of self-interest, the desire to possess more wealth, commodities, or pleasure is politically associated with the need to improve statecraft[9] and the governments' desire for peace, order and stability. Since stability could not be guaranteed by the old mechanisms of duty and organic hierarchy our selfish, competitive and acquisitive drives, once repressed by normative constraints, might be employed along with a "political arithmetic built on the power of interest" (Gunn, 1968, p. 563) to stabilize the polity.

The thesis, however, that "harnessing shabby motives to elevated ends" (Bowles, 2010, p. 5) and a 'constitution for knaves' could lead to the collective good of society would have hardly have gained traction unless it was justified in some way (philosophically or religiously).

One plausible method of justification was to think of some appetites (greed, avarice and the love of money) as interests, *natural* interests that stood in stark contrast to our unruly "passions [that] were 'divers' (Hobbes), capricious, easily exhausted and suddenly renewed again" (Hirschman, 1997, p. 52). Interests, thus reformulated, could be thought to be independent of both moral considerations and the untamed passions that often result in momentary and arbitrary decisions. From now on prices and appeals to self-interest could do the work previously done by morality, or so it was believed.

Interests, then, could be seen as nicely fitting the requirements for order and stability since they were held to be universally valid, permanent, continuous, predictable, calculable and transparent.[10] Without the guarantee of a divine or natural order humans faced the risk of being swept away by *Fortuna*. The idea of self-interest, it was thought, helped introduce single-mindedness, realism, prudence, efficiency and regularity into human affairs. And, as Hirschman (1982) argues elsewhere, market societies based on self-interest would favour the flourishing of gentleness and peacefulness.[11]

To the old political question of what binds a people together the advocates of the self-interest doctrine would offer the astonishing answer: the individual pursuit of pleasure and money instead of being a "semi-criminal, semi-pathological propensity" (Keynes, 1932) would establish more lasting ties than friendship and affection. This ever-present desire for abstract wealth (money) initiates an age of scarcity and is as foundational to economic theory (see Chapter 1) as it is to the political order. But for Keynes and moral theorists after him, there was nothing natural or inevitable about our love affair with filthy *lucre*.

5.2 Markets and ethics: crowding-out

One way of thinking about how the relation between self-interested market behaviour and ethics/sociality is constituted is to consider the possibility of ethical limits to market transactions (see chapter 3). In fact, it could be argued that up until recent times religious and political thought have often drawn tight boundaries around the scope of market activity.[12]

Alternatively, we can think of how ethical behaviour, moral values (such as fairness, honesty) and social capital (trust) can play a role in generating better *economic* results (efficiency, growth). This holds with special relevance to real-world economies which are characterized by market imperfections (asymmetric or poor information, incomplete contracts, and Knightian uncertainty).

In this section I conceptualize the relation between ethics and economics along other lines still. The extension of markets and self-interested behaviour into areas of social/political life can lead to the 'corruption' of moral and political virtues.[13] Concerns about crowding-out draw on a long history of religious and philosophical suspicion towards the negative effects that naked self-interest, money and calculation have on our moral, social, economic and political lives.

The expansion of markets might have a deleterious effect on morality, partly because the greater competition associated with markets can be a destabilizing factor.[14] Unfettered markets (based on self-interested behaviour) can also have serious long-term *economic* consequences. It is now widely recognized that in settings of poor or asymmetric information the existence of either public goods or non-tradeable 'positional goods' (Sen, 1983). The pure and relentless[15] pursuit of self-interest may not always result in economically optimal outcomes.

Titmuss (1997) also famously argued that the voluntary system of blood donations produced good outcomes because it was infused with moral values: the desire to help other people, the emphasis on truthfully revealing information. The introduction of a market for blood (payment for blood) would, he argued, crowd out moral behaviour (gift-giving) as well as lead to less efficient outcomes.

In a similar vein, the dangers of self-interest were crucial to Polanyi's (2014) critique of untrammeled markets. The fictitious commodification of land, labour and money would have disastrous effects on the very fabric of social life and meaning since all three were deeply embedded in society and not merely abstract economic factors of production.

Without resistance, a counter-reaction – one strand of Polanyi's 'double movement' (Polanyi, 2014) – a purely self-regulating market would end up destroying the economy *and* society.[16] The point is this: land, labour, money, as they have been historically constituted, are each associated with a specific set of values, evaluative standards, and notions of relationality. These may stand in stark contrast to the self-interested motivations and competitiveness of the market. The introduction or expansion of markets can, therefore, change how we relate to and our affection for, other people, the world and things of value. 'Crowding-out' is just another name for this process.

The term 'crowding-out' suggests a relatively benign process. Polanyi warns us, however, that the actual process may actually be *disastrous*.[17] If we include social reproduction/affective labour and nature as part of the structural conditions necessary for the success of market societies then we can usefully incorporate contemporary expulsions, precarious work, the simultaneous crises in housing, education, care and ecology, within an integrated Polanyian framework (Fraser, 2016).

We can also start to think about how commodification and the dominance of self-interest in one area of social reality has an impact on other dimensions of our lives. For example, financialization and austerity can put pressure on care; the undermining of a stable natural habitat can increase labour precarity (migration being a case in point); and the depletion of care (dependent on shared meanings, common horizons, affection,[18] and a sense of continuity) can exacerbate the climate change crisis by reducing our concern for future generations.

Most economists, however, argue that self-interested market interactions are a good thing overall because they help promote economic growth, welfare and process freedoms (Keat, 2012). Both supporters and detractors of the market, it should be noted, assume they're driven by self-interested behaviour. But is it empirically true that ethical considerations have an insignificant role in the actual decisions of economic agents in real-world markets? And if so, has that *always* been the case? It is to these questions that I now turn.

5.3   Can ethical behaviour lead to a flourishing economy?

Markets have historically been underpinned by moral and social norms, legal institutions and power relations.[19] They have been circumscribed by cultural norms that shape preferences, influence redistribution, and determine who engages in what kind of work.[20] Transactions between economic agent have often been at least partly determined by the moral and social norms that find expression in notions of reciprocity, gift, ideas of fairness, redistribution etc. Over both time and wide geographical areas exchange has been linked with kinship, status, identity, ritual, collective bonds, the desire to minimize conflict and the need to maintain a level of equality and solidarity in the community.

Since economic transactions have for large parts of our history been embedded in a wider social, moral and political framework the idea that self-interest is a ubiquitous and 'natural' (Graeber, 2014) feature of our motivational make-up seems highly implausible.[21]

Given that, it is fair to say that the idea and reality of the market as a moral-free zone of interactions between asocial, self-interested individuals is a relatively recent phenomenon.[22] The attempt to substitute historically constituted markets with 'the market', such that each particular market was guided by the same behavioural assumptions and the same disregard for institutional and cultural specificities, would lead, Polanyi argued, to disastrous social ramifications.

How are markets actually constituted in the real world today? Markets are still, despite what mainstream economic orthodoxy maintains, to some extent socially embedded[23] institutions.

In the last chapter I argued that the self-interested individuals that populated economics textbooks hardly resemble the economic agents we find in our contemporary situation: the neoliberal self whose life is bound to the interests of production or the figure of the empty, endlessly desiring body at the heart of consumer culture. I want to now temper the argument somewhat and suggest that although that's undoubtedly the dominant *trajectory* of modernity, older forms of the self continue to exist. In practice, in market societies and economies we still find individuals guided by a mix of self-interest and moral/social norms.[24] The dissipation of the self is a powerful trend in modern society but not an accomplished fact; nor is it either inevitable or irreversible.

To summarize the argument: historically speaking, neither production for markets nor the pure pursuit of self-interest have been central features of economic transactions. More interestingly, in both rural economies and advanced capitalist economies today self-interest is not the only factor that guides economic behaviour. The rules governing our transactions in a modern economy may indeed be of a legal and contractual nature, but they can just as well contain informal, conventional or customary elements.[25]

Any attempt to move to a more realistic economic theory would entail, therefore, acknowledging that non-self-interested motives (ethical, impersonal, professional, etc.) can and do exist in market societies. Actual market economies are an amalgamation of different distribution mechanisms over a diverse array of 'goods'. Typically, pure market exchange co-exists – at least at some level – with command-and-control as well as reciprocity (Akerlof, 1982). Our social and economic lives are much more intertwined than we are led to believe.

And to repeat Polanyi's point: the existence of non-self-interested motives and their institutional expression (e.g. the police, judiciary and polity) are necessary for the flourishing of both the economy and society. Successful economic transactions depend on trust and moral/social norms of fairness, decency, reciprocity and honesty.[26] This holds with particular force, as we will see below in the discussion on social capital, when there are serious imperfections in various markets.[27]

Markets, if they are to avoid predatory and rent-seeking elites from using fraudulent means or violence to pursue their own interests[28] need principled actors, since contracts are only made possible by a regulation which is *social* in origin (Besley, 2009). To work effectively they also need state involvement in redistribution, the provision of public goods, and possibly in the promotion of innovation as well (Mazzucato, 2013).

Economic success depends, then, on a whole host of factors that convert potential assets into functioning assets (or capital), namely: formal contracts, abstraction and property rights that are both clearly defined and well-enforced (De Soto, 2000). Apart from an effective state and institutions (Acemoglu, Johnson and Robinson, 2005) social capital, networks and moral virtues *can*, under some circumstances, lead to good economic outcomes. Such a view does not, of course, imply that the *reason* for those ethical motives is success – either at the individual or the group level. But the main point remains: self-interested behaviour cannot, on its own, explain the remarkable economic growth of the west or of East Asia (Stiglitz, 1998) and Japan.[29]

5.4   Social capital

The standard neoclassical model is built on a number of assumptions. First, individuals have self-interested preferences. Second, agents choose amongst those preferences as independent, autonomous and asocial *individuals*. Economic interactions typically take the exclusive form of impersonal contractual exchanges amongst strangers. The classical figure of Robinson Crusoe looms large in economic theory: an abstract, solitary and isolated individual oblivious of his social context[30] and concern for other people

Third, agents have perfect knowledge over those preferences and have the rational capacities to make decisions upon the perfect information available to them. Fourthly, preferences are taken as exogenously given. And finally, it is assumed that the contracts governing economic relations are complete and can be enforced in a costless fashion. Everything related to our economic relations can, that is, be perfectly specified *ex ante* and an agent's actions can be monitored, outcomes verified, so that something as simple as a handshake seals the agreement between contracting parties.

These assumptions, despite their lack of realism,[31] underlie the way in which we model market interactions. This approach may have a certain appeal because of its abstractness,[32] tractability and generality. It has also helped simplify analysis by putting to one side the various non-economic motives such as moral norms.[33]

The assumption of the model that I want to turn to in this section relates to the idea of non-contractual social relations. In actual (second-best) economies incomplete contracts – imperfections in information and knowledge, costly enforceability, the inability to specify or measure what is contracted for – may be the prevalent, with non-contractual relations commonly observed in firms, families and credit markets.[34]

In the presence of incomplete contracts social capital and community organization may provide tangible economic benefits even though they also have their costs. In a relatively small, closed developing economy with low-level technologies and limited outside trading opportunities nothing much is lost (and much is gained) by organizing economic activities within a community framework. But as those opportunities and technologies improve, the economies of scale make impersonal market organization, despite the greater likelihood of opportunistic behaviour, much more attractive. Social capital and community networks that embody it may in those circumstances lock people into a low-level equilibrium and inefficient activities (Munshi and Rosenzweig, 2006; Banerjee and Newman, 1998) as potentially productive investments and innovation are blocked (Acemoglu & Robinson, 2000).

As economies become more advanced it becomes increasingly difficult, *ex ante*, to specify what in a job constitutes a 'good performance' – especially if the work involves creativity, care or innovation. Some of those features are non-tangible and cannot be contracted for. Contracts that eschew vagueness in favour of quantification and ever-great specification may not only be difficult and costly to draw up and verify; in addition, they may reduce agents' autonomy and have a demotivating effect. In advanced economies, then, "most economic interactions are governed by a heterogeneous set of formal and informal rules reflecting aspects of markets, states and communities" (Bowles, 2009, p. 493).

It may not be very realistic, for example, to think that labour activities related to production can be explained *exclusively* in terms of self-seeking behaviour. A fair share of the co-ordination of economic activity in the firm depends on non-economic factors: teamwork and control, which should be incorporated into mainstream theory (Sen, 1983; Marglin, 1974). Furthermore, in social reproduction ('care') and the health and education sectors there is no fully specified contract – and nor could there be. There is, however, the (taken-for-granted) assumption of professionalism, sympathy and commitment.

Another glaring example of contractual incompleteness is climate change. Here the problem is not just that uncertainties make it difficult to specify beforehand the appropriate actions in a contract; nor is it that the global enforcing agencies are weak; it is, rather, that a crucial dimension of the climate change problem involves future generations and it is hard to conceive how they can possibly be part of a contractual arrangement with the present generation.

Summarizing the argument in this section, let us admit that the unrestrained pursuit of self-interest in real-world economies may necessitate monitoring, the writing of detailed contracts, mechanisms to detect and prevent fraud, opportunism and deceit; it may also require the establishment of systems of contract enforcement. All of which are time-consuming and costly. Social and moral norms may, given market imperfections, provide a less costly way of facilitating exchanges and promoting economic prosperity. Whether the social is ultimately destroyed in being made over into capital (social capital) in this way is something I return to in a later chapter.

5.5 Critique of self-interest (I): evidence from experimental literature

A richer and more realistic approach to economic theory and the understanding of human behaviour involves a modification of how we conceptualize preferences. In this section I suggest we question the dominance[35] of self-interest by examining the empirical evidence for 'social preferences'. In the next section I look at another modification: the idea of endogenous preferences.

The point to note is that when we think about reasons for choice we are confronted with a wide range of disparate motivations that cannot be equated with narrowly defined self-interested preferences. Behind our choices and behaviour lie tastes (wanton preferences), compulsions, habits, social norms, emotions (fear, anger, etc.), moral inclinations (concern for others, commitment), reflective (informed) preferences, rule-following behaviour,[36] identification with social groups (class, clan, community) and the demands of acting professionally or in accord with our character.

Social preferences can encompass a wide variety of reasons for behaviour. They can include process-regarding reasons such as fairness. We can also think of numerous types of other-regarding reasons for behaviour (pecuniary emulation, envy, altruism, inequality aversion, a regard for others that is not reducible to our own interests or vanity). Individuals can also exhibit strong reciprocity, where a strong reciprocator is someone who is willing to sacrifice resources (money, welfare) to be kind to someone who has been kind to them and to punish those who are unkind to her. She is, contrary to the assumption of self-interest, willing to forego resources to reward (punish) behaviour even though this is costly to her, and even though it provides neither present nor future benefits.

Recent experimental literature in experimental labour markets, ultimatum games and public goods games suggests the evidence for other-regarding preferences is quite strong (Gintis, Bowles, Boyd and Fehr, 2005). In the labour market game employers' offers of a high wage-effort contract only make sense if they think employees were not driven by self-interest but by strong reciprocity. In the ultimatum game, despite interesting cross-cultural variations, the self-regarding outcome is hardly ever obtained, which suggests that considerations of fairness are important.

In the Public Goods Game there is more cooperation than would be expected if the actions of individuals were determined by self-interested preferences alone.

In summarizing the experimental evidence we could say that belief in the assumption that agents are exclusively self-interested in certainly strained. Individuals' choices in these experiments may be determined by the kind of preferences they hold, their habits or, indeed, the level of agents' cognitive abilities (Ben-Ner and Putterman, 1998b).

5.6   Endogenous preferences

In this section I want to return to the assumption that individuals have exogenously 'given' preferences. The standard view of human beings in economic models envisages the individual economic agent being autonomous, his preferences determined independently of communitarian, political or social identities. In fact, society and community are little more than fictions or constructs according to this view.

It could be argued that such a pared down description of atomistic and mechanistic individuals is a necessary simplifying assumption of economic theory. But if we actually *are* relational and socially constituted beings a more realistic account of behaviour requires us to modify our understanding of preferences by accepting that we are, at least in part, influenced by our social circumstances. Our social identities and ethical outlook shape who we are and the kind of preferences we endorse. The economic system of production and distribution, and the institutional arrangements, social norms and customary expectations in society, can influence the evolution of values, tastes, identity, preferences and personality. This can occur in many different ways.

First, social institutions can (and do) influence who we meet, what kind of exchanges/work is deemed acceptable as well as the appropriate rewards to various activities. For example, historically speaking, certain trades have been blocked or looked down upon; certain segments of society may have relatively rigidly defined roles along gender[37] or ethnic lines. Rewards to investments can partly be determined by the social definition of property rights and/or the emphasis that a society places on redistribution.

Second, if our experiences over time affect learning and self-understanding, preferences may also change[38] and not be 'given'. Thirdly, individuals do not determine their own preferences in a sovereign fashion if they are manipulated or if they are subject to addictions.[39] And fourthly, Bowles (1998) suggests that through cultural transmission, either via exposure or indoctrination, individuals internalize a particular perspective. So, for Bowles it is not simply the case that behaviour becomes more self-interested because the net economic pay-offs of doing so *becomes* attractive; instead, the cultural transmission mechanism has changed so that 'higher economic pay-offs' becomes the relevant criteria when it comes to determining appropriate behaviour.

Summarizing the above points, a richer and more complex picture of individuals entails thinking about the connection between individual preferences on the one hand, and institutions, modes of exchange, economic policies, identity and education on the other. Different rules or 'constitutions' may determine what counts as a good distributive principle of 'goods' and what stands as appropriate behaviour in different spheres of economic and social life. Against that background picture the economist's idea that asocial individuals simply maximize their *given* preferences seems like a drastically limited way of understanding human behaviour.

Since there is no such thing as an individual with values, inclinations and preferences wholly separate from historical social formations economic theory needs a relational 'I-we' perspective. The 'I' and 'we' terms must mutually refer to one another: "If friends make gifts, gifts make friends" (Sahlins, 1974, p. 186).

Communities, the state, educational and cultural systems, and the market itself all play a role in the formation and justification of our preferences and identities. A study of the complex interaction between these factors and the co-evolution of preferences, institutions and ideas over time would require of us to acknowledge the fact that preferences are not simply exogenously 'given'.[40]

5.7 Critique of self-interest (II): the role of ethics

I have argued that a more nuanced and realistic picture of human psychology and preference formation involves taking account of the fact that economic choices are sometimes guided by ethical considerations and not just self-interested ones. But can an ethical outlook be incorporated into the concept of preferences?

Economists can cynically maintain that moral motivations are really a veiled form of self-interest. Altruism or reciprocity exist, they might say, because the giver expects the receiver to help them out in their time of need (or, alternatively, they receive a 'warm glow' from helping them). Morality, in that understanding of things, is only necessary if it leads to good consequences. Wiggins (2006) is surely correct to see in all this the desire to find

> a single rule for the determination of overall rightness that will replace the multiplicity of ways that are sanctioned by practices . . . by notions of morality and reasonableness that take it for granted that morality itself fills out our idea of reasonableness.
>
> (p. 218)

Thinking about ethics as an individual choice rather than as an imperative can be understood in two ways. Firstly, the inescapable fact that I chose to act ethically must ultimately imply that I *wanted* to. Secondly, the empirical fact that I made the decision surely entails that the act, at some level, is undeniably interwoven with *my* interests and my welfare. Let's take up these two arguments in turn.

The second argument is a weak one. That what I desire must of necessity refer back to the empirical subject and her agency does not in any way imply any determination of the actual nature or substance of those desires or preferences. If I desire *x* it is quite plausible that what I'm fundamentally concerned about is a state of the world in which *x* occurs. My pleasure or satisfaction is derivate on the primary desire of wanting that state of the world to come about. In fact, a state of the world in which *x* occurs may be a good thing even if I'm not around to witness it or even if I play a small role in bringing such a state of affairs about. The fact that we are troubled if someone is content with the mere pleasure of believing *x* has come about, when in reality it hasn't, suggests that it isn't always the *individual's* pleasure/welfare that is paramount.

What primarily moves us to act in this case is an interest in particular objects, specific people or states of the world and not the pleasure, happiness or state of my mind that *I* experience as a consequence of those interests being satisfied. In other words, the fact that the self has interests does not in any way imply that those interests are self-interested or self-regarding ones. If I seek a thing there must be an 'I' that is involved in the seeking and that is necessary to deliberative action. But it does not follow that it is *my* good/pleasure that I aim at. The narrow form of self-interest, psychological egoism, is implausible.

So, other-regarding preferences may refer in a weak sense to the 'I' but the motivational force of the desires/preferences depends precisely on me shifting my attention away from myself and from *my* satisfactions. Which is another way saying, in the language of Bernard Williams (1973), that the self can have 'non-I desires'.

I think the first argument is not so easy to dismiss, however, because of its association with ordinary ways of speaking. The fact that I *want x* to come about surely implies at some level that it is *my* desire, interest, advantage or preference that is involved in that proposition? If that is true then even moral motivations can possibly be incorporated in to a wider notion of utility (an all-things-considered-preference function). Put plainly, it is not, as in the previous argument, the inescapability of individual agency in any decision that concerns us. It is, rather, that my *desire* for the advantage or good of another person is evidently of some concern to *me*. In this reading I still aim to maximally satisfy *my* preferences/utility/interests but by doing so I do not necessarily maximize my welfare or level of satisfaction.

Under this broader conception, utility is simply a mathematical representation of my preferences (which I aim to maximally satisfy) and it is not related to any substantive notion, such as welfare, 'the good', or pleasure. This actually makes it *harder* to believe that moral motivations, ethical or aesthetic values, can be accounted for by economic theory since utility and 'the good' under the broad notion of preferences are now simply formal concepts. Morality, on the other hand, can hardly be construed as being an *individual* choice that is independent of our life as a whole, our social relations, our social nature, and the *substantive* notion we have of both ourselves and of 'the good'.[41]

In contrast to the idea of 'moral preferences' I would suggest that moral deliberation and action depend ultimately on the idea of 'being' (Spaemann, 2000). If action follows being we are drawn to an objective-list account of desires such that we desire something *because* it is good (and not the other way around).[42] The latter view which is close to the mainstream economic position is also very much in line with the widely held view of the self under emotivism, which makes it all the more difficult to question (MacIntyre, 2003).

In addition, the *structure* of moral behaviour precludes any easy incorporation of morality into preference theory. Firstly, when we think of preferences over commodities we make no *qualitative* distinction between increments in utility (arising from having more of the commodity) and reductions of utility (from having less of the commodity). Morality doesn't work in the same way. There is an imperative aspect of morality that is not captured by this idea of an easy reversibility. We would, for example, find it odd to say that stealing something and then returning it leads to no change in utility. Secondly, we typically think of marginal changes in the consumption of commodities and continuous utility functions. When it comes to morality, however, we are more inclined to think in discrete terms: it is hard to imagine ourselves having a continuous preference over different levels of honesty.

Thirdly, the existence of different arguments in a utility function suggests an inherent ability to make trade-offs between commodities. It is not at all clear, however, that we think we should so easily be able to make trade-offs between morality and commodities. Relatedly, by including morality in our preference function we are implicitly assuming that morality has a relative price, which is not something we are usually at ease with.

Fourthly, as already argued, in economic theory preferences as typically exogenously given and a preference relation over commodities expresses our relative valuations at a given point in time. Morality, on the other hand, cannot be regarded something as merely unreflectively 'given'.

In the following section I want to highlight an additional problem: the individualistic basis of preferences in economic theory.

5.8 Sympathy, identity and commitment

Part of the problem of incorporating ethical considerations into economic theory arises from the latter's assumption that we are autonomous, asocial and separative selves (England, 2005). And this distorted picture of the human subject is not simply a problem for economic theory. In late capitalism, it is argued, the economy and society are made up of 'atomistic' individuals (Klamer, 2001). Instead of a relational being we have, in economic theory, the empty subject; in the economy itself, a man of no qualities for whom history, tradition and moral sentiments no longer bind him to anyone else[43]; and in society little more than individual agents making choices in a fragmented future (Strathern, 1999).

It follows that any rethinking of the role of ethics – both in economic theory and in actual economies – has to address not just whether our preferences are exogenously given and self-interested; in addition, the dominance of an individualistic perspective has to be questioned. Can two great economists, Adam Smith and Amartya Sen, throw any light on this problem?

It is now recognized that Smith was a much deeper thinker than the caricature of him that has been handed down to us by economists (Sen, 2009) would lead us to believe. For example, Smith claimed that commercial societies, based on self-interest, might in fact encourage delusions, (Gerschlager, 2008) but these would also work towards the progress of mankind (Manent, 2000). More importantly, perhaps, commercial societies encouraged an egalitarian emancipation from hierarchical dependencies. Benevolence in small societies was not desirable; in complex, commercial ones, too weak to be effective (Fleischacker, 2005).

Since market societies lead to good outcomes could it be that the lack of sociability in them means there is a moral role for social distance? (Hill, 2011). Distance here doesn't imply invisibility, since the propriety and praiseworthiness of our actions requires other spectators (and, ultimately, an 'impartial spectator'). And praiseworthiness is not reducible to the approval of self-interested actions since the 'most perfect virtue' depends on the combination of self-interest with sympathy (Sen, 1986). But can a preference function represent a combination of a moral sentiment such as sympathy alongside self-interest?

Some have argued that altruism or sympathy can be expressed by interdependent utility functions (Collard, 1975). For Smith's notion of sympathy in particular, and for a broad class of ethical dispositions in general, such an attempt is likely to miss the mark. It is not simply that sympathy cannot be reduced to self-interest, as Griswold's (1999) trenchant analysis demonstrates, and as I have argued in the previous section. It is, rather, that the *individualistic* basis of economic theory precludes the incorporation of morality/sympathy into a preference relation.

For Smith the possibility of morality depends on reflexivity, inter-subjectivity and imagination (Brown, 2016). Sympathy, for example, depends on not just me imagining what you're feeling in your situation or what I might feel in your situation; it can also involve a change in person and character so that I imagine myself as you in your situation. In the latter case I must, to some extent, identify with the other person to enter his perspective; on the other hand, I can only reflectively and normatively sympathize with the other and endorse or disapprove of his feelings/actions if I can maintain the 'distance' implied by having my own perspective. Sympathy in this sense is a bridge which simultaneously allows for imaginative participation in the life of another while at the same time maintaining the distance required for judgement. It is hard to see how a preference function can capture all of these nuances.

In some sense the matter is more complicated since there is no 'I' who exists independently of both the other's perspective and the sympathetic act. The self does not exist isolated and fully formed at a particular point in time; instead, any understanding of who I am depends on an ongoing effort over time to 'see myself as you'.[44]

In relation to the main theme of this book the problem is that for Smith sympathy and gratuitous reciprocal giving remain separate from market transactions (Bruni and Sugden, 2008). Also, although in a 'fatherless world' we might find the inter-subjective features of sympathy and moral sentiments to be appealing, they are neither grounded on a religious notion of relationality ('I-Thou') nor are they inscribed in any actually existing social and political relations (Pabst, 2011).

The inability of the individualist perspective to accommodate the ethical is also apparent in Sen's work on commitment. As with Smith's idea of sympathy, commitment implies a particular understanding of the self, reason and imagination (Sen, 1977). For Sen, commitment can involve going against not only our self-welfare goals but also, more controversially, against our own broadly construed goals as well. Reasonable action, then, can involve making counter-preferential choices (where preference is understood in the narrow sense of my own welfare but *also* in the stronger sense of all-things-considered preferences (Hausman, 2005)).

The idea of commitment (which can be understood as being related to moral obligations/duty, but also to an adherence to social rules) has been criticized by some thinkers because it creates a wedge between individual choice and goals (Pettit, 2005; Schmid, 2005). To pursue another person's goals without integrating them into my own suggests, problematically, that I can intend something other than my own goals.

From Sen's perspective, though, the criticism is misplaced (Sen, 2007). Firstly, an act with another person's goals in mind is still my own intentional act. Secondly, if we consider a relational perspective then it is not the case that I, as a private individual, endorse another person's goals at the expense of my own; rather, because I identify with a social group I can think about promoting and endorsing *our* shared goals. But this formation of 'we-intentions' (Lewis, 2009) is not in opposition to individuality and reason. So, thirdly, it is precisely because I can subject my own goals to reasoned scrutiny that I can avoid relentlessly maximizing them and freely and reflectively bind myself to the content of collective intentions (Davis, 2007). *Individual* rationality and *social* identification can go hand in hand. Moreover, reasoning itself can be a social process, a conversation (as we saw in chapter 2).

Fourthly, an emphasis on reason can in some contexts lead to me restraining myself in the pursuit of my own goals without necessarily endorsing the goals of others. Commitment in this scenario would mean I simply think it is reasonable to follow a social rule without actively *pursuing* your goals or making them my own.

Both Smith's concept of sympathy and Sen's notion of commitment can move us to a relational notion of the self. And both suggest, therefore, that the purely individualistic basis of preferences limit the ability of economic theory, as it stands, to incorporate ethics.

5.9 Conclusion

In this chapter we have seen that far from being a universal and timeless disposition self-interest actually only comes to prominence with the advancement of market societies. But its growing importance in our lives can have the perverse effect of undermining the sociality (social capital, moral norms and relationality) that are necessary for the flourishing of both economy and society.

In our own day it is argued that there is a diminished role for self-interest[45] – both in advanced capitalist economies and in economic theory. Given that, there is a need to rethink preference theory. In particular, it was questioned whether the theory, as it stands, can accommodate ethical considerations (sympathy and commitment) given its individualistic foundations.

The relation between subjective interests and common projects, individual intentions and the common good, was at the heart of the discussion on sympathy and commitment. But it can be extended to another important area of what we commonly take to be an aspect of the good life, namely: meaning.

The ability to determine what we really care about (Wolf, 1986), to evaluate and re-evaluate our 'ends', is surely fundamental to any conception of person and to how we think we should shape our lives (Frankfurt, 1971). And a central component of such a life is an active engagement in worthwhile and meaning-ful projects, a life in which "subjective attraction meets objective attractiveness" (Wolf, 2015, p. 211). These activities or projects – whether intellectual, aesthetic or religious – are often social in nature and represent a good that, to some extent, lies outside of oneself (Wolf, Macedo and Koethe, 2010). This is another way of saying that we need to take relationality seriously: our 'I-we' relations, and how I (and we) relate to the common good.

Notes

1 See Finley (1999) and Boldizzoni (2011) for trenchant criticisms of this position.
2 It appears that Rousseau's reference to the 'primitive', 'savage' and 'sociable' stages of mankind are not meant to depict stages of an actual historical develop-ment; they are, instead, mental constructs (Todorov, 2004).
3 In *Frail Happiness,* Todorov (2004) claims that Rousseau did not advocate a return to the natural state but, instead, suggested that a 'third way' was possible: a reconciliation of his solitariness and his sociability. This tension between indi-viduals and citizens in a society increasingly dominated by money and commerce is outlined in Ignatieff's (1994) brilliant The Needs of Strangers.
4 For Smith (2009) see *The Theory of Moral Sentiments;* for Rousseau see Force (2007).
5 Also see Hill (2011).
6 That is, by ignoring factors apart from self-interest or treating them as constant. See Sutton (2002) on this point. And predicting behaviour is not always the same as explaining it. See Pfleiderer (2014).
7 That self-interest is often conflated with reason is made clear by Sen (2013).
8 Compare this to the anarchist idea of mutuality without hierarchy in Scott (2014).
9 See Foucault's (1991) notion of the 'reasons of state' in *The Foucault Effect, Stud-ies in Governmentality.*
10 A society governed by interests would be held together, in Burke's formulation from a later time period, solely by contractual obligations and the desire for mutual advantage; it would then be a society of 'sophisters, economists and calculators' (Berlin, 2013).
11 This line of reasoning is consistent with McCloskey's (2008) idea in *Not by P Alone* that self-interest (her 'P' variable) could go hand-in-hand, or even require, other values (her 'S' variable).
12 See Tawney's (1926) *Religion and the Rise of Capitalism* as well as chapter 10 for a discussion of boundaries.
13 See Ignatieff (1994), 'The Market and the Republic' in *The Needs of Strangers* and Pocock (2009).
14 See Shleifer (2004) for the example of child labour.
15 The relentless pursuit of the maximal satisfaction of our self-regarding preferences can lead to socially sub-optimal outcomes, which is another way of stating the

result of the Prisoners' Dilemma. We might also add that sometimes our goals are achieved obliquely, by our not *directly* pursuing them (see Kay, 2012).

16 It is worth noting that 'society' or social relations can also be hierarchical and exclusionary. Fraser (2013) is, therefore, correct to suggest that we need to think along the lines of a 'triple movement' so as to include emancipation (freedom from domination) along with solidarity when we think about social relations.

17 It is worth thinking of the historical continuities here. In the 19th and early 20th century, it has been argued (Sen, 1981; Davis, 2014), market expansion helped create severe famines and thereby laid the foundations for poverty in 20th-century India.

18 See Berry's (2012) lecture, "It all turns on Affection" in *It all Turns on Affection: the Jefferson Lectures* for the profound import of this sentiment.

19 On how power can have an effect on economic outcomes via differing rates of technology adoption see Acemoglu and Robinson (2000).

20 On how labour markets may be influenced by identity see Akerlof and Kranton (2000). More specifically, some of the development literature now looks at the role of ethnicity in labour and credit markets (see Munshi and Rosenzweig, 2006; Borjas, 1991).

21 On the dubious attempt to trace purely economic motivations back to antiquity see Finley (1999).

22 See Braudel (1992) for the limited scope of markets.

23 See Granovetter (1985) and Platteau (1994). See Hausman and McPherson (2010) for a discussion of how positive and normative economics are often intertwined.

24 This is another way of stating Appiah's (2005) thesis that in liberal societies the individual self exists within the bounds of "qualified horizons" (p. 46).

25 Real-world markets are riddled with imperfections in information, incomplete contracts, uncertainty, social norms, power relations and a wide array of motivations beyond self-interest. In fact, in our post-financial crisis world behaviour includes: robbery, thievery, swindling, corruption, usury, predation, violence, coercion, manipulation, market cornering and price-fixing (Harvey, 2014).

26 Doing the right can involve following a rule or principle that you think no one could reasonably reject or that you think accords with your reasoned goals/ purposes (Taylor, 1997). Following Elster (1989) I think one should be wary of the idea that all social norms can be reduced to one's interests and expediency.

27 In imperfect credit, insurance and labour markets why should economic agents do what is contractually expected of them? That is, in finitely repeated interactions with limited reputational effects, poor information and weak enforcement mechanisms the triumph of pure self-interest over moral and social obligations may lead to dysfunctionality.

28 At the time of writing this Moody's, a major credit rating agency, was fined over $850 million for its role in the recent financial crisis. In a similar vein, the world's largest rating agency, S&P, was fined $ 1.35 billion for deceiving investors ("Moody's $864 million fine for ratings in run-up to 2008 financial crisis", 2017).

29 Morishima (2003) and Sen (1995) argue that the Japanese economy flourished under a motivational structure that had little resemblance to pure self-interest.

30 Gauthier (1986): "Each person is thus a Robinson Crusoe, even in the market" (p. 91). For an enlightening discussion of the relation between Robinson Crusoe and capitalism see Moretti (2014).

31 Who, for example is the 'auctioneer' in exchange theory and what is the *market* process that gets us to a general equilibrium (assuming it exists)? In the wake of the financial crisis this has become an ever-more pressing concern, see Pfleiderer (2014). And for a stinging criticism of macroeconomic models see Romer (2016).

32 Writing in 1873, Walras (2013) claimed that we may go so far "as to abstract from entrepreneurs and simply consider the productive services as being, in a certain sense, exchanged directly for one another" (p. 225).

33 "Attempts have indeed been made to construct an abstract science with regards to the actions of an 'economic man' who is under no ethical influences and who pursues material gain mechanically and selfishly" (Marshall, 2009, p. v).

34 Inter-linked, repeated credit transactions and informal, community arrangements can alleviate some of the problems (poor information, monitoring costs, and the lack of collateral) in rural credit markets. See Ray (1998), Aleem (1990) and Udry (1990). In fact, loans may be given along the lines of caste or ethnicity (Munshi and Rosenzweig, 2009) or between friends and family (Banerjee and Duflo, 2007).

35 This dominance matches a profound scepticism towards the existence of kindness (Phillips and Taylor, 2009) and sociality.

36 Given uncertainties and complexities in the economy it may be easier to avoid the rigorous demands of a calculating rationality and rely, instead, upon rules of thumb, social norms, habits or tradition.

37 On how the poor and women may have adaptive preferences according to their situation see Sen (2011).

38 See Gerschlager (2008).

39 Are we increasingly addicted to work? For a fascinating discussion of this see Stiglitz (2010).

40 For the classic statement of this view see Stigler and Becker (1977).

41 Under the broad view of utility there could be no rational justification for ethical preferences (Keat, 1997).

42 This is too stark a contrast, as Griffin (1986) reminds us. In reality, desire and reason/understanding, the will and a vision of 'the good', are much more inter-mixed. But since economic theory brackets the possibility of an objective nature of man and an objective good all we are left with are purposeless pleasures, unorganized desires and an unconditioned freedom. On the latter see Eagleton's (2005) brilliant *Holy Terror*.

43 Hyde (2008) argues that gift economies, guided by *eros*, lead to more enduring social and spiritual bonds. Market economies are, in contrast, acquisitive, possessive and divisive.

44 Much of the preceding ideas were gleaned from Fleischacker's (2015) remarkable talk, "Empathy and Perspective, a Smithian Conception of Humanity". The fact that we *come to* an understanding of another person and her situation suggests that the sympathetic process depends on both the social context and the narrative structure of a person's life. This characterization of sympathy implies that it is not simply spectatorial or 'objective'; it also requires of us the ability to listen rather than the capacity to take a purely detached stance. In fact, as Iris Murdoch (1993) wrote, "the quality of our attachments is the quality of our understanding" (p. 295).

45 In fact, with the loss of the metaphysical subject, historical narratives and the idea that individuality truly flourishes within the horizon of social relations, what remains of the self? Are we left with only a narcissistic self and mindless pleasures (Blackburn, 2014)?

Bibliography

Acemoglu, D., Johnson, S., and Robinson, J. A. (2005). Institutions as the Fundamental Cause of Long-Run Growth. In P. Aghion and S. Durlauf (Eds.), *Handbook of Economic Growth*, 1A. Amsterdam: Elsevier: North-Holland. Available at: https://doi.org/10.1016/S1574-0684(05)01006-3

Acemoglu, D., and Robinson, J. A. (2000). Political Losers as a Barrier to Economic Development. *The American Economic Review*, 90(2), 126–130. Retrieved from www.jstor.org/stable/117205

Akerlof, G. A. (1982). Labor Contracts as Partial Gift Exchange. *The Quarterly Journal of Economics*, 97(4), 543–569. Retrieved from www.jstor.org/stable/1885099

Akerlof, G. A., and Kranton, R. E. (2000). Economics and Identity. *The Quarterly Journal of Economics*, 115(3), 715–753. Retrieved from https://public.econ.duke.edu/~rek8/economicsandidentity.pdf

Aleem, I. (1990). Imperfect Information, Screening, and the Costs of Informal Lending: A Study of a Rural Credit Market in Pakistan. *The World Bank Economic Review*, 4(3), 329–349. Retrieved from www.jstor.org/stable/3989880

Appiah, K. A. (2005). *The Ethics of Identity*. Princeton, NJ: Princeton University Press.

Baier, A. (1991). A Naturalist View of Persons. *Proceedings and Addresses of the American Philosophical Association*, 65(3), 5–17. doi:10.2307/3130139

Banerjee, A. V., and Duflo, E. (2007). The Economic Lives of the Poor. *Journal of Economic Perspectives*, 21(1), 141–167. doi:10.1257/jep.21.1.141

Banerjee, A. V., and Newman, A. (1998). Information, the Dual Economy, and Development. *The Review of Economic Studies*, 65(4), 631–653. Retrieved from www.jstor.org/stable/2566906

Ben-Ner, A., and Putterman, L. G. (Eds.). (1998a). *Economics, Values, and Organization*. Cambridge: Cambridge University Press.

Ben-Ner, A., and Putterman, L. G. (1998b). Values and Institutions in Economic Analysis. In A. Ben-Ner and L. G. Putterman (Eds.), *Economics, Values, and Organization*. Cambridge: Cambridge University Press.

Berlin, I. (2013). *Against the Current: Essays in the History of Ideas* (2nd ed.). Princeton, NJ: Princeton University Press.

Berry, W. (2010). *What Matters?: Economics for a Renewed Commonwealth*. Berkeley, CA: Counterpoint.

Berry, W. (2012). It All Turns on Affection. In *It All Turns on Affection: The Jefferson Lecture and Other Essays*. Berkeley, CA: Counterpoint.

Besley, T. (2009). *Principled Agents?: The Political Economy of Good Government*. Oxford: Oxford University Press.

Blackburn, S. R. (2014). *Mirror, Mirror: The Uses and Abuses of Self-Love*. Princeton, NJ: Princeton University Press.

Boldizzoni, F. (2011). *The Poverty of Clio: Resurrecting Economic History*. Princeton, NJ: Princeton University Press.

Borjas, G. (1991). Ethnic Capital and Intergenerational Mobility. *The Quarterly Journal of Economics*, 107(1), 123–150. doi:10.3386/w3788

Bowles, S. (1998). Endogenous Preferences: The Cultural Consequences of Markets and Other Economic Institutions. *Journal of Economic Literature*, 36(1), 75–111. Retrieved from http://citeseerx.ist.psu.edu/viewdoc/download?doi=10.1.1.335.7577&rep=rep1&type=pdf

Bowles, S. (2009). *Microeconomics: Behavior, Institutions, and Evolution*. Princeton, NJ: Princeton University Press.

Bowles, S. (2010, January). *Machiavelli's Mistake: Good Incentives Are No Substitute for Good Citizens*. Lecture presented at The Castle Lectures in Yale University, New Haven, CT.

Braudel, F. (1992). *Civilization and Capitalism, 15th–18th Century, Volume II: The Wheels of Commerce* (S. Reynolds, Trans.). Berkeley, CA: University of California Press.

Brown, V. (2016). The Impartial Spectator and Moral Judgement. *Economic Journal Watch, 13*(2), 232–248.

Bruni, L., and Sugden, R. (2008). Fraternity: Why the Market Need Not Be a Morally Free Zone. *Economics and Philosophy, 24*(1), 35–64. doi:10.1017/s0266267108001661

Collard, D. (1975). Edgeworth's Propositions on Altruism. *The Economic Journal, 85*(338), 355–360. doi:10.2307/2230997

Davis, J. B. (2007). Identity and Commitment: Sen's Fourth Aspect of the Self. In F. Peter and H. B. Schmid (Eds.), *Rationality and Commitment*. Oxford: Oxford University Press.

Davis, M. (2014). *Late Victorian Holocausts: El Niäno Famines and the Making of the Third World*. London: Verso.

De Soto, H. (2000). *The Mystery of Capital: Why Capitalism Triumphs in the West and Fails Everywhere Else*. New York, NY: Basic Books.

Eagleton, T. (2005). *Holy Terror*. Oxford: Oxford University Press.

Elster, J. (1989). Social Norms and Economic Theory. *Journal of Economic Perspectives, 3*(4), 99–117. Retrieved from http://dlc.dlib.indiana.edu/dlc/bitstream/handle/10535/3264/Elster.pdf

England, P. (2005). Separative and Soluble Selves. Dichotomous Thinking in Economics. In M. A. Fineman and T. Dougherty (Eds.), *Feminism Confronts Homo Economicus Gender, Law, and Society*. Ithaca, NY: Cornell University Press.

Finley, M. I. (1999). *The Ancient Economy*. Berkeley, CA: University of California Press.

Fleischacker, S. (2005). *On Adam Smith's Wealth of Nations: A Philosophical Companion*. Princeton, NJ: Princeton University Press.

Fleischacker, S. (2015, August 4). *Empathy and Perspective: A Smithian Conception of Humanity*. Lecture presented in The University of Melbourne, Melbourne.

Force, P. (2007). *Self-interest Before Adam Smith: A Genealogy of Economic Science*. Cambridge: Cambridge University Press.

Foucault, M. (1991). Governmentality. In G. Burchell, C. Gordon, and P. Miller (Eds.), *The (Michel) Foucault Effect: Studies in Governmentality. With 2 Lectures By and an Interview With Michel Foucault*. London: Harvester Wheatsheaf.

Frankfurt, H. (1971). Freedom of the Will and the Concept of a Person. *The Journal of Philosophy, 68*(1), 5–20. doi:10.2307/2024717

Fraser, N. (2013). A Triple Movement? *New Left Review, 81*. Retrieved from https://newleftreview.org/II/81/nancy-fraser-a-triple-movement

Fraser, N. (2016). Contradictions of Capital and Care. *New Left Review, 100*. Retrieved from https://newleftreview.org/II/100/nancy-fraser-contradictions-of-capital-and-care

Gauthier, D. P. (1986). *Morals By Agreement*. Oxford: Clarendon Press.

Gerschlager, C. (2008). *Foolishness and Identity: Amartya Sen and Adam Smith*. DULBEA Working Papers, 3rd ed., Vol. 8, ULB, DULBEA. Retrieved from https://dipot.ulb.ac.be/dspace/bitstream/2013/13590/1/dul-0073.pdf

Gintis, H., Bowles, S., Boyd, R., and Fehr, E. (2005). Moral Sentiments and Material Interests: Origins, Evidence, and Consequences. In H. Gintis, S. Bowles, R. Boyd, and E. Fehr (Eds.), *Moral Sentiments and Material Interests: The Foundations of Cooperation in Economic Life* (pp. 3–40). Cambridge, MA: MIT Press.

Graeber, D. (2014). *Debt: The First 5,000 Years*. Brooklyn, NY: Melville House.

Granovetter, M. (1985). Economic Action and Social Structure: The Problem of Embeddedness. *American Journal of Sociology, 91*(3), 481–510. Retrieved from www.jstor.org/stable/2780199

Griffin, J. (1986). *Well-being: Its Meaning, Measurement and Moral Importance*. Oxford: Clarendon Press.

Griswold, C. L. (1999). *Adam Smith and the Virtues of Enlightenment*. Cambridge: Cambridge University Press.

Gunn, J. (1968). 'Interest Will Not Lie': A Seventeenth-Century Political Maxim. *Journal of the History of Ideas*, 29(4), 551–564. doi:10.2307/2708293

Harvey, D. (2014). *Seventeen Contradictions and the End of Capitalism*. Oxford: Oxford University Press.

Hausman, D. M. (2005). Sympathy, Commitment, and Preference. *Economics and Philosophy*, 21(1), 33–50. doi:10.1017/S0266267104000379

Hausman, D. M., and McPherson, M. S. (2010). *Economic Analysis, Moral Philosophy and Public Policy*. Cambridge: Cambridge University Press.

Hill, L. (2011). Social Distance and the New Strangership in Adam Smith. In F. Forman-Barzilai (Ed.), Adam Smith Review (Vol. 6). London: Routledge.

Hirschman, A. O. (1982). Rival Interpretations of Market Society: Civilizing, Destructive, or Feeble? *Journal of Economic Literature*, 20(4), 1463–1484. Retrieved from www.jstor.org/stable/2724829

Hirschman, A. O. (1997). *The Passions and the Interests: Political Arguments for Capitalism Before Its Triumph*. Princeton, NJ: Princeton University Press.

Hont, I. (2015). *Politics in Commercial Society: Jean-Jacques Rousseau and Adam Smith*. Cambridge, MA: Harvard University Press.

Hont, I., and Ignatieff, M. (1983). Needs and Justice in the Wealth of Nations: An Introductory Essay. In I. Hont and M. Ignatieff (Eds.), *Wealth and Virtue: The Shaping of Political Economy in the Scottish Enlightenment*. Cambridge: Cambridge University Press.

Hyde, L. (2008). *The Gift Creativity and the Artist in the Modern World*. New York, NY: Vintage Books.

Ignatieff, M. (1994). *The Needs of Strangers*. London: Vintage.

Kay, J. A. (2012). *Obliquity: Why Our Goals Are Best Achieved Indirectly*. New York, NY: Penguin Books.

Keat, R. (1997). Values and Preferences in Neo-Classical Environmental Economics. In J. Foster (Ed.), *Valuing Nature?: Economics, Ethics and Environment*. London: Routledge.

Keat, R. (2012). *Market Economies as Moral Economies: The Ethical Character of Market Institutions* (Publication). University of Edinburgh.

Keynes, J. M. (1932). Economic Possibilities for Our Grandchildren. In *Essays in Persuasion* (pp. 358–373). New York, NY: Harcourt, Brace & Company.

Klamer, A. (2001). Late Modernism and the Loss of Character in Economics. In S. Cullenberg, J. Amariglio, and D. F. Ruccio (Eds.), *Postmodernism, Economics and Knowledge*. New York, NY: Routledge.

Lewis, P. (2009). Commitment, Identity, and Collective Intentionality: The Basis for Philanthropy. *Identity, Interests, and Philanthropic Commerce*, 6. Retrieved from www.conversationsonphilanthropy.org/journal-contribution/commitment-identity-and-collective-intentionality-the-basis-for-philanthropy/

MacIntyre, A. C. (2003). *After Virtue: A Study in Moral Theory*. Notre Dame, IN: University of Notre Dame Press.

Manent, P. (2000). *The City of Man*. Princeton, NJ: Princeton University Press.

Marglin, S. A. (1974). What Do Bosses Do? *Review of Radical Political Economics*, 6(2), 60–112. doi:10.1177/048661347400600206

Marshall, A. (2009). *Principles of Economics* (8th edition). New York, NY: Cosimo Classics.

Mathiowetz, D. (2011). Chapter 5: Historiographies of Liberal Interest and the Neoliberal Self. In *Appeals to Interest: Language, Contestation, and the Shaping of Political Agency*. University Park, PA: Pennsylvania State University Press.

Mazzucato, M. (2013). *The Entrepreneurial State: Debunking Public vs. Private Sector Myths*. New York, NY: Anthem Press.

McCloskey, D. N. (2008). Not By P Alone: A Virtuous Economy. *Review of Political Economy, 20*(2), 181–197. doi:10.1080/09538250701819636

McCloskey, D. N. (2015). Max U Versus Humanomics: A Critique of Neo-Institutionalism. *Journal of Institutional Economics, 12*(1), 1–27. doi:10.1017/s1744137415000053

Moody's $864m Penalty for Ratings in Run-Up to 2008 Financial Crisis. (2017, January 14). *The Guardian*. Retrieved from www.theguardian.com/business/2017/jan/14/moodys-864m-penalty-for-ratings-in-run-up-to-2008-financial-crisis

Moretti, F. (2014). *The Bourgeois: Between History and Literature*. London: Verso.

Morishima, M. (2003). *Why Has Japan "Succeeded"?: Western Technology and the Japanese Ethos*. Cambridge: Cambridge University Press.

Munshi, K., and Rosenzweig, M. (2006). Traditional Institutions Meet the Modern World: Caste, Gender, and Schooling Choice in a Globalizing Economy. *American Economic Review, 96*(4), 1225–1252. doi:10.1257/aer.96.4.1225

Munshi, K., and Rosenzweig, M. (2009). *Why Is Mobility in India So Low? Social Insurance, Inequality, and Growth*. Working Paper No. 14850, NBER. doi:10.3386/w14850

Murdoch, I. (1993). *Metaphysics as a Guide for Morals*. London: Penguin Books.

Pabst, A. (2011). From Civil to Political Economy: Adam Smith's Theological Debt. In P. Oslington (Ed.), *Adam Smith as Theologian*. New York, NY: Routledge.

Paganelli, M. P. (2010). The Moralizing Role of Distance in Adam Smith: The Theory of Moral Sentiments as Possible Praise of Commerce. *History of Political Economy, 42*(3), 425–441. doi:10.1215/00182702-2010-019

Pettit, P. (2005). Construing Sen on Commitment. *Economics and Philosophy, 21*(1), 15–32. doi:10.1017/S0266267104000367

Pfleiderer, P. (2014). *Chameleons: The Misuse of Theoretical Models in Finance and Economics* (Working paper No. 3020). Stanford University Graduate School of Business. Available at: https://www.gsb.stanford.edu/faculty-research/working-papers/chameleons-misuse-theoretical-models-finance-economics

Phillips, A., and Taylor, B. (2009). *On Kindness*. New York, NY: Farrar, Straus and Giroux.

Platteau, J. (1994). Behind the Market Stage Where Real Societies Exist – Part I: The Role of Public and Private Order Institutions. *Journal of Development Studies, 30*(3), 533–577. doi:10.1080/00220389408422328

Pocock, J. G. A. (2009). *The Machiavellian Moment Florentine Political Thought and the Atlantic Republican Tradition*. Princeton, NJ: Princeton University Press.

Polanyi, K. (2014). *The Great Transformation: The Political and Economic Origins of Our Time*. Boston, MA: Beacon Press.

Putnam, R. D. (2007). *Bowling Alone: The Collapse and Revival of American Community*. New York, NY: Simon & Schuster.

Ray, D. (1998). *Development Economics*. Princeton, NJ: Princeton University Press.

Romer, P. (2016, September 14). *The Trouble With Macroeconomics*. Lecture presented at The Commons Memorial Lecture in New York University, New York City, NY. Retrieved from https://paulromer.net/wp-content/uploads/2016/09/WP-Trouble.pdf

Sahlins, M. D. (1974). *Stone Age Economics.* New York, NY: Routledge.

Sahlins, M. D. (2005, November 4). *Hierarchy, Equality, and the Sublimation of Anarchy the Western Illusion of Human Nature.* Lecture presented in The University of Michigan, Ann Arbor, MI. Retrieved from https://tannerlectures.utah.edu/lecture-library.php

Schmid, H. (2005). Beyond Self-Goal Choice: Amartya Sen's Analysis of the Structure of Commitment and the Role of Shared Desires. *Economics and Philosophy, 21*(1), 51–63. doi:10.1017/S0266267104000380

Scott, J. C. (2014). *Two Cheers for Anarchism: Six Easy Pieces on Autonomy, Dignity, and Meaningful Work and Play.* Princeton, NJ: Princeton University Press.

Sen, A. K. (1977). Rational Fools: A Critique of the Behavioral Foundations of Economic Theory. *Philosophy & Public Affairs, 6*(4), 317–344. Retrieved from www.jstor.org/stable/2264946

Sen, A. K. (1981). Ingredients of Famine Analysis: Availability and Entitlements. *The Quarterly Journal of Economics, 96*(3), 433–464. doi:10.2307/1882681

Sen, A. K. (1983). *The Profit Motive.* Publication No. 147, Lloyds Bank Review.

Sen, A. K. (1986). Adam Smith's Prudence. In P. Streeten, S. Lall, and F. Stewart (Eds.), *Theory and Reality in Development: Essays in Honour of Paul Streeten.* Houndmills, Basingstoke, Hampshire: Palgrave Macmillan.

Sen, A. K. (1995). Moral Codes and Economic Success. In S. Brittan and A. P. Hamlin (Eds.), *Market Capitalism and Moral Values: Proceedings of Section F, Economics of the British Association for the Advancement of Science, Keele, 1993.* Brookfield, VT: E. Elgar.

Sen, A. K. (2007). Why Exactly Is Commitment Important for Rationality? In F. Peter and H. B. Schmid (Eds.), *Rationality and Commitment.* New York, NY: Oxford University Press.

Sen, A. K. (2009). Introduction. In A. Smith (Author), *The Theory of Moral Sentiments.* New York, NY: Penguin Classics.

Sen, A. K. (2011). *The Idea of Justice.* Cambridge, MA: Belknap Press of Harvard University Press.

Sen, A. K. (2013). *On Ethics and Economics.* Malden, MA: Blackwell.

Sen, A. K., and Development Economics Research Programme (1993). *Moral Codes and Economic Success.* Development Economics Research Programme, Suntory-Toyota International Centre for Economics and Related Disciplines, London.

Shleifer, A. (2004). Does Competition Destroy Ethical Behavior? *American Economic Review, 94*, 414–418. doi:10.3386/w10269

Smith, A. (2009). *The Theory of Moral Sentiments.* New York, NY: Penguin Classics.

Spaemann, R. (2000). *Happiness and Benevolence.* Edinburgh: Clark.

Stigler, G., and Becker, G. (1977). De Gustibus Non Est Disputandum. *The American Economic Review, 67*(2), 76–90. Retrieved from www.jstor.org/stable/1807222

Stiglitz, J. E. (1998, October 19). *Towards a New Paradigm for Development: Strategies, Policies, and Processes.* Lecture presented at Prebisch Lecture in UNCTAD, Geneva. Retrieved from http://citeseerx.ist.psu.edu/viewdoc/download?doi=10.1.1.199.9708&rep=rep1&type=pdf

Stiglitz, J. E. (2010). Toward a General Theory of Consumerism: Reflections on Keynes's Economic Possibilities for Our Grandchildren. In L. Pecchi and G. Piga (Eds.), *Revisiting Keynes: Economic Possibilities for Our Grandchildren.* Cambridge, MA: MIT Press.

Strathern, M. (1999). *After Nature: English Kinship in the Late Twentieth Century.* Cambridge: Cambridge University Press.

Sutton, J. (2002). Chapter 1. In *Marshalls Tendencies: What Can Economists Know?* Cambridge, MA: MIT Press.

Tawney, R. H. (1926). *Religion and the Rise of Capitalism.* New York, NY: Harcourt, Brace & Company.

Taylor, C. (1997). *Philosophical Arguments.* Cambridge, MA: Harvard University Press.

Titmuss, R. M. (1997). *The Gift Relationship: From Human Blood to Social Policy* (A. Oakley, Ed.). New York, NY: The New Press.

Todorov, T. (2004). *Frail Happiness: An Essay on Rousseau* (J. T. Scott and R. D. Zaretsky, Trans.). University Park, PA: Pennsylvania State University Press.

Udry, C. (1990). Credit Markets in Northern Nigeria: Credit as Insurance in a Rural Economy. *The World Bank Economic Review, 4*(3), 251–269. Retrieved from http://documents.worldbank.org/curated/en/165311468759320928/Credit-markets-in-Northern-Nigeria-credit-as-insurance-in-a-rural-economy

Walras, L. (2013). *Elements of Pure Economics.* New York, NY: Routledge.

Wiggins, D. (2006). *Ethics: Twelve Lectures on the Philosophy of Morality.* Cambridge, MA: Harvard University Press.

Williams, B. (1973). Egoism and Altruism. *Problems of the Self,* 250–265. doi:10.1017/cbo9780511621253.017

Wolf, S. R. (1986). Self-Interest and Interest in Selves. *Ethics, 96*(4), 704–720. Retrieved from www.jstor.org/stable/2381095

Wolf, S. R. (2015). Happiness and Meaning: Two Aspects of the Good Life. In *The Variety of Values: Essays on Morality, Meaning, and Love.* Oxford: Oxford University Press.

Wolf, S. R., Macedo, S., and Koethe, J. (2010). *Meaning in Life and Why It Matters.* Princeton, NJ: Princeton University Press.

6 An unequal world[1]

Each human life has its own propensity for illumination.

(Berger, 2008, p. 98)

An economic transaction is a solved political problem.

(Lerner, 1972, p. 259)

Of the tendencies that are harmful to sound economics, the most seductive, and in my opinion the most poisonous, is to focus on questions of distribution.

(Lucas, 2004, p. 8)

6.0 Introduction

In this chapter, I look at two basic and inter-related questions: what is equality (what are the evaluative dimensions of it?) and why is it important? They're inter-related questions because we – and how this 'we' is constituted is also of crucial importance – may think one particular dimension of equality is more important than another.

In section 1, I look at why equality (or, to put it the other way around, why inequality) is important. In the context of this book's main thesis inequality is important for a number of diverse reasons. Relative inequalities between people, for example, can be the source of our idea of scarcity (chapter 1). They can also be linked to the commodification process (chapter 3). Inequality is also a central issue in the analysis of climate change (chapter 8) since only relatively few countries produce the lion's share of pollution; and the impacts of climate change are likely to disproportionately affect the poor. In addition, the weight we give to the welfare of future generations in any inter-temporal policy analysis is partly a reflection of our concerns about the *distribution* of income across generations.

Equality, as a relational concept, is also key to understanding the importance of the public good (chapter 7), the common good (chapter 10) and our notions of the person/individual (chapter 4).

We live an unequal world. That is simply an inescapable fact of our current predicament, and perhaps an inevitable feature of the economic system, capitalism, as well. And so economic theory's traditional and continuing neglect of inequality in the face of very stark divergences of fortunes is deeply perplexing.

If the issue *is* addressed by economic theory at all it is usually in the context of economic outcomes – how the distribution of income is related to income growth – and so I summarize the literature on this in sections 2 and 3. But if we think the idea that the importance of inequality stems from of its impact on growth is a narrow one then we need to take a more pluralistic approach to understanding inequality. I briefly allude to that point in section 1, arguing that because inequality is a multi-dimensionality concept it is a complex one. And part of the complexity arises from the way in which inequality in one dimension is related to inequality in another so that the poorest can face a cluster of disadvantages.

In section 4 I argue that focusing too closely on the distributive aspects of inequality – in whatever dimension – misses out on a fundamental reason why, in fact, we're concerned about inequality. Ultimately, it is argued, inequality is important because we want to live in a society of equals. Equality, that is, is of value because it expresses a moral and social relation.

If market economies generate more inequalities (in the distributive sense) then they can reduce equality in the normative sense in that they diminish the possibility of a society of equals from taking root. And mainstream economic theory's neglect of inequality can only further that sense of diminished possibilities since it provides us with few intellectual resources to adequately address the problem. This is just another way of restating the main thesis: market economies and economic theory profoundly alter the way in which we relate to one another and the world around us.

Section 5 concludes with some thoughts about why social equality is so important.

6.1   Why is inequality important?

It is estimated that the eight wealthiest people in the world have the same amount of wealth as the poorest 3.6 billion people in the world (Hardoon, 2017). The total gross income of the richest 1 percent in the U.S. doubled over the period 1979–2012 (Atkinson, 2015).[2] We live in a vastly unequal world in which people face radically different opportunities to live flourishing lives. That in itself requires us to pay attention to the problem of inequality but how, exactly, do we make sense of such a complex issue?

First of all, one way to start is to note that inequality is a multi-dimensional concept. We can fruitfully think about inequalities in various dimensions of our economic, social and political lives; there are, for example, inequalities in incomes, assets, power, happiness, opportunities and nutrition. Secondly, we should also think about how those inequalities in the different dimensions (or evaluative spaces) are related to one another. Thirdly, we should be aware that there are different ways of *measuring* a distribution (are we concerned about the relative shares of income, say, between the top 1 percent and the bottom 40 percent of a population, or should we be looking at the distribution of income across the *whole* population?). Fourthly, what is the appropriate unit of our analysis? It is quite obvious that inequalities can exist between individuals, gender and ethnic groups as well as across households, regions and countries. And fifthly, there is a temporal dimension to inequality since it often persists over generations.

So, whenever we talk about inequality we should be cognizant of its complex nature. For some thinkers there isn't one overall and fixed context-independent criteria which determines how things should be distributed. Instead, the principles of distributive justice are pluralistic in form because we attach different meaning to different social goods (Walzer, 2010). For Sen (1979) that complexity is added to because individual heterogeneity means there are variations in the ways in which different individuals rank the importance of equality in different areas of social life.

That still leaves us with the question of why we should necessarily think inequality is an important issue. One possible reason why we do so is because inequality is of instrumental importance, in the sense that inequality can severely reduce social cohesion and solidarity, deplete democratic institutions and lead to a number of social problems (Wilkinson and Pickett, 2009). Later on, however, I will argue that it is better to think of equality as being part of an intrinsic feature of good social relations rather a *cause* of them (Norman, 1997).

More typically though, economists have historically only been concerned about inequality – if at all – to the extent that it promotes or hinders economic growth, efficiency, or the maximizing of aggregate utility in society. Let's just take stock of the way in which economists (and economic theory) has narrowed their (its) focus when it comes to inequality.

Firstly, since economics is an allegedly positive science it has not really been concerned with the distribution of economic outcomes (income, say) *per se* because that would involve it in normative questions. So – and this is the second point – it has focused more on trying to explain the *causes* of inequality than on any (moral) assessment of unequal outcomes. But these causes are, of course, usually economic in nature; so, trade, savings rates, globalization or technology (and differential returns to skill) rather than social, geographical and political features.[3] Institutions, governance, culture, power, class, other-regarding motives and public policy necessarily feature less in any explanation of inequality (though at the research level and in particular in development economics that is changing).

Some of these economic causes might be seen as exogenous (savings rates, technological changes) but more generally economists tend to think of inequality as being simply the result of people with differences in talent, effort or risk-taking inclinations making rational choices under perfect market conditions.

Thirdly, not much emphasis was given to history, inheritance and to the inter-generational transmission mechanisms that could lead to the persistence of inequality since it was usually assumed that under perfect market conditions there would eventually be convergence between countries or that there would be a 'trickle down' effect within them.

Fourthly, economists have usually restricted themselves to focusing on one variable: income. The only inequalities that count are income inequalities; and they count not because of their relation to distributive justice (point one above) but more prosaically because they might hinder the future growth in income.

In summary, the determination of *personal* income distribution has not been central to mainstream classical economic theory (Atkinson, 1997; Sandmo, 2014). In fact, taking property rights, class background and the distribution and ownership of assets as given necessarily limited the scope for bringing political and ethical considerations into economic analysis.

On the other hand, it has been argued that economics was not initially concerned about distributive justice for sound moral reasons. Up until the time when industrialization was in full swing it could, perhaps with some justification, be thought that markets, private property[4] and contract opened up liberating possibilities.[5] In a world of self-employed artisans, farmers and proprietors (Adam Smith's bakers, butchers and brewers) autonomous economic agents were not subject to the hierarchical dependencies that were associated with benevolence[6] and feudal class relations; but neither were they yet constrained by the 'private government' of work discipline in the factory[7] (Anderson and Macedo, 2017).

It is not hard to see, then, how in economies in which production was typically small-scale, market relations might come to represent the morally appealing values of independence, equal dignity and equal standing, or what Elizabeth Anderson (2015) calls 'commercial republicanism'.

For much of the 20th century, inequality has continued to be ignored by neoclassical theory (Atkinson, 2015). In general equilibrium theory, for instance, there is little mention of distribution. The issue of intra-household inequalities was only addressed at a relatively late date and, typically, macroeconomics rules out concerns about distribution by assuming a representative agent. Perhaps the most glaring example of the neglect of inequality at the theoretical level, however, is the omission of questions about power relations and authority from the analysis of the organization of production within the firm.

Part of the problem has been that economics has typically attempted to model the labour contract along the lines of commodity exchange under perfect market conditions. Under those conditions, it is usually argued, voluntary transactions between independent agents preclude the existence of power relations.

What that ignores, of course, is that in real-world economies the governance structure of most productive enterprises is best characterized by hierarchy and authority, an asymmetry of power relations such that wage labourers are subject to discipline, control, supervision, domination and, in the worst case scenarios, exploitation. This implies that any theory of the firm has to acknowledge that production is organized under a governance relation of subordination rather than the allegedly equal relations of freely contracting parties.

The economic theory of the firm – at least at the textbook level – has failed to take into account the implications of centralized control. Within the firm the separation of the conception of work from the execution of it has profound consequences. On the one hand, it has resulted in the 'scientific' and bureaucratic management of labour. On the other hand, the reduction of work to monotonous routines has "stifled the human capacity for thought, imagination and skill"

(Murphy, 1993, p. 9) – a danger that Adam Smith was not oblivious of.[8] The point to emphasize is not simply that specialization and the separation of the conception of work from its execution entails a moral and spiritual degradation of workers.[9] It is, rather, that the lack of equal social relations in production is at the root cause of those problems. In other words, the radical point is this: a society of equals cannot take form unless there is political *as well as* economic democracy.

Economic theory has tended to avoid any discussion of power relations within the workplace arguing, instead, that the technical and social division of labour could be justified on efficiency grounds (Coase, 1937). Given the large, indivisible capital requirements for large-scale production, the costs of coordinating activities amongst workers, as well as the costs of constantly renegotiating contracts and of specifying all contingencies in them, the centralized coordination of labour activities, it is argued, makes sound economic sense.

An alternative tradition, however, suggests that efficiency considerations are not at the heart of the story. Marglin (1974, 2001) argues in his 'divide and conquer' thesis that by separating labour from the control and knowledge of the whole labour process (its final ends and the *way* in which something is produced) the power of capitalists rested on their ability to integrate a fragmented labour force. Capitalist control from the inception of industrial capitalism was, therefore, not so much about maximizing efficiency and overall profits; it was more a case of capitalists maximizing *their* unequal share of the profits.

Though Marglin's insights are extremely useful, he fails to note that if private property determines the governance structure of firms then 'private government' ultimately relies on the state, which by defining and enforcing corporate property and employment law, "establishes legal parameters for the constitution of capitalists firms" (Anderson, 2015, p. 50). What this alerts us to is that the claims of economic theory are fundamentally mistaken. Centralized control is not an efficient response to market imperfections coupled with individual characteristics (asymmetries in talent or information). Instead, the structure of dominance in firms is better explained by wider mechanisms of control than inter-personal relations between abstract agents. Social control and domination depend, ultimately, on capital-labour class relations (Palermo, 2016).

On the normative side economic theory has had no unified and consistent principles to evaluate distributions. In fact, as Atkinson (2001) notes, there has been a strange elimination of welfare economics from the textbooks and of welfare principles as a guide to policy/research work. Even when the possibility of equality could be imagined theoretically (as under the Second Fundamental Welfare Theorem) the chances of actually establishing it were acknowledged to be practically very slim (dependent as they are on the possibility of making appropriate lump-sum transfers).

In any case, given that preferences are more often than not thought to be ordinal and non-comparable across individuals the main welfare criterion left to economic theory is Pareto optimality. And as is well understood, the Pareto criterion is insensitive to the issue of distribution. Moreover, as I have argued in previous chapters, 'utility' is increasingly seen in economic theory as a purely formal concept with a tenuous relation to welfare. In some sense, then, equality of formal freedoms has come to be thought of as more important than equality in outcomes (utility/welfare).

This last observation would account for the fact that from the 1970s onwards the only palatable aspect of egalitarianism in our neoliberal era of choice and competition is the idea of equality of opportunities (Le Grand, 2013). Which is another way of saying that of the three central ideas of the French Revolution only liberty really holds our attention. More accurately, the negative liberty of economic agents in the market represents an idea of equality of sorts: an equality of formal freedoms. And this idea dominates equality (egalitarian distributions of outcomes) and fraternity (equal social relations).

So, it appears for the most part that the economics discipline has only a limited interest in analysing the rich and complicated problem of inequality. It largely ignores the multi-dimensional nature of the problem (multiple causes *and* multiple evaluative spaces). It also marginalizes the view that inequality is important primarily because of the way in which it alters our social relations. In other words, it fails to recognize that the distribution of outcomes (in whatever evaluative space) is important to us not in its own right but because of its impact on our social relations.

I'll return to the latter point later on in the chapter (section 4). For the moment, though, I want to say a few more things about what economic analysis of inequality *does* say, rather than about what it misses out on. In particular, if we want to understand inequalities in real-world economies we should turn to the development economics literature since it typically drops the assumption that markets are perfectly competitive.

6.2 Market failures and inequality

Even in a fully functioning market system income inequalities may emerge because of innate differences in talent and because of sheer luck. Globalization (greater trade and financial liberalization) can generate or perpetuate existing inequalities. Changes in technology, a shifting structure of production, differential levels of, and rates of return to, human capital might explain some of the unequal outcomes across occupational groups as wages fail to keep in line with price increases.

Fiscal policy may be able to dampen the severity of income disparities. Conversely, it can also be an important determinant of inequality.[10] For example, the lack of productivity-enhancing egalitarian investments in public health and education and a regressive tax system can have an impact on inequalities and their persistence over time.

It is now increasingly acknowledged, however, that in real-world economies in general, and in developing economies in particular, markets may be absent or weak – and for a whole host of reasons: poor information, weak legal and regulatory systems, imperfect contracts in which goods cannot be fully specified, costly enforcement of transactions, and the existence of low levels of trust. As a result, markets can be in equilibrium and yet many of the poor – those with few physical and financial assets and low nutritional status – are rationed out of labour and credit markets. The result is inequality and inefficiency.

Unequal outcomes are not, therefore, the simple result of individual choices in perfect market conditions or the consequence of an uneven distribution of talent, but follow instead from the fact that broad segments of the population are denied adequate opportunities, some of which may be transmitted over time through inter-generational mechanisms.

The first important thing to learn from this framework of market failures is that there is an economic cost to inequality, from which it follows that egalitarian policies can lead to improvements and growth. In fact, there is significant empirical evidence that there is a negative correlation between inequality and growth (Persson and Tabellini, 1994; Alesina and Rodrik, 1994; UNCTAD, 2012). Birdsall (2006), too, confirms this and notes that the negative correlation is higher in developing countries, where markets are weaker. This is worth stressing because for far too long policy makers have thought there is a trade-off between growth and equity. This point tallies with the often ignored fact that for the most advanced industrial countries there was a positive relation between equality and productivity in the post-World War II period up until the late 1970s.

Under this framework the inefficiency of inequality often stems from market imperfections coupled with unequal distributions of wealth. For example, given market imperfections those with low levels of effective assets/capital (De Soto, 2000) do not have sufficient collateral to obtain credit or credit on reasonable terms. This may affect their occupational choice, their low level of investment in agricultural production (Rosenzweig and Binswanger, 1993), their investment in education, skills, or high risk (high return) projects. As a result it is not surprising that many of the poorest are engaged in low productive activities (Banerjee and Duflo, 2007).

The key point is that given the weakness of formal insurance mechanisms along with credit market imperfections, people with different levels of wealth are likely to end up with different contractual arrangements and this explains levels of income inequality. In addition, recent literature suggests that the poor may also make more myopic decisions so that even if there are potentially beneficial trades open to them they will not take advantage of them (Mullainathan, 2004).

Secondly, in the absence of perfect markets (contracts) ethical codes or trust (social capital) may help resolve the coordination problem (Greif, 1993). But the level of trust in a society itself may itself be a function of ethnic or religious fragmentation. If that is true there may be a virtuous cycle whereby a society of equals generates greater trust and therefore greater growth (Easterly, 2007) and equality. Or, alternatively, it may be that ethnic, religious or linguistic 'fractionalization' lead to worse institutions and lower growth (Alesina, Devleeschauwer, Easterly, Kurlat and Wacziarg, 2003) – and, perhaps, also to a detrimental impact on both the quantity and the type of public goods provided (Alesina, Baqir and Easterly, 1997).

Thirdly, the distribution of wealth may play a role in determining political participation, the distribution of political power in a society and the subsequent optimal set of policies in a political economy framework.

Fourthly, inequalities in opportunities (health, educational and political) may result in lower overall growth and a more unequal society over time. But inequality is 'costly' not just because it can lead to lower growth, higher poverty and lower levels of solidarity; there may be a direct and sometimes significant economic cost of maintaining unequal structures through what is called 'guard labour' – the police, security personnel, army, prisons, etc. (Bowles, 2013).

6.3   The persistence of inequality and elite capture

Focusing on market failures also helps us understand the persistence of inequality over time since the path of income distribution may be influenced by a combination of market failures and initial inequalities in wealth.

Eswaran and Kotwal (1986) show that in the presence of high monitoring costs the initial distribution of wealth (land) can determine occupational choice in an agrarian setting with the result that in equilibrium the occupational groups with low levels of wealth find themselves in low-wage, low productivity activities and others emerge as rich 'capitalists'. Given the difficulty the poor face in accumulating capital it is not difficult to see how these inequalities could be sustained over time.

Banerjee and Newman (1993) show in a dynamic setting how unequal distributions in wealth coupled with credit market constraints determine occupational choice, bequests and therefore future distributions of wealth over time. These, in turn, determine occupational choices (or 'classes') and possibilities for future generations. Again, it is not hard to see how an initial unequal distribution may progressively become worse.

Galor and Zeira (1993) show how inequalities can be perpetuated over time through decisions to invest in human capital. Again, in the presence of credit market imperfections households with initial low levels of wealth may not be able to borrow enough to invest in education and end up as unskilled workers, transmitting less wealth to their children, with the result that *their* children are even less likely to get an education. In contrast, those with enough initial wealth face no such constraints and invest in education. Given the high returns to education it is easy to see how this model generates a divergence between the two groups. More generally, it is quite in line with some of the evidence that those with more human capital are in a better position to exploit the gains from globalization and changes in technology (Stiglitz, 2013; Birdsall, 2006).

There are many other ways in which inequalities may continue in societies with weak markets and/or an unequal distribution of wealth but we will only briefly note them here. Firstly, in the presence of imperfect information social networks may play a key role in the allocation of jobs. Munshi and Rosenzweig (2006) have demonstrated how this may lead to the persistence of inefficient occupational choices.

Secondly, gender inequalities may play a pivotal role in the transmission of inequalities – either directly via differential earnings and status or indirectly through educational choices, human capital accumulation and fertility decisions.

Thirdly, people with low levels of initial wealth may suffer from relatively low nutritional status which then impairs their educational opportunities and health status, resulting in an inequality trap of low status and low wages (Bose, 1997).

Fourthly, specific government policies, its ideological stance and the quality of a country's institutions may play a major role in determining levels of inequality. Governments shape markets and the distribution of income through macro, fiscal and public policies as well as via the quality of governance. The distribution and strength of property rights, information and regulation, taxation, tariffs and subsidies, expenditures on infrastructure and public education/health as well as the enforcement of contracts via the legal system all have an impact on levels of inequality and so it is natural that our discussion turns to structural issues.

Inequality is not simply the result of some *given* market failure but is ultimately driven by deeper structural failures: elite capture. Some part of market failure may in fact be the *result* of weak, inefficient or corrupt governments. The efficacy of markets (and their impact on inequality) is partly determined, then, by government policy and the strength of its institutions. It follows that inequality is *made* and not simply a 'natural' outcome of the markets (Stiglitz, 2013). Acemoglu and Robinson (2015) rightly point out, the evolution of technology, the functioning of markets and the distribution of gains from various economic arrangements depend on a society's institutions.

Nancy Birdsall (2006) shows that economic inequalities may be responsible for government failures and the undermining of good public policy with the subsequent effect of producing lower growth and more inequality. There is now a growing political economy literature on the role of political institutions, corruption and poor governance in preventing societies from becoming prosperous and in generating and maintaining economic inequalities.

If unequal societies are inefficient why don't we see egalitarian, efficiency-producing policies being implemented? There are social gains to be had from adopting better technologies, improving public services, implementing progressive taxation, and social insurance. The fact that societies do not make these changes is a 'coordination failure' that can be explained by the poor governance structures or institutions that determine the incentives and constraints people face, namely: rules of ownership, forms of competition, norms, etc.

These institutions, then, determine a country's long-term growth (Acemoglu, Johnson and Robinson, 2005) and the distribution of resources (inequality). Crucially, however, the institutions can in part themselves be determined by the distribution of wealth and power and are therefore subject to elite capture. Glaeser, Scheinkman and Shleifer (2003) show how the wealthy subvert institutions and policy in their favour. Acemoglu (Acemoglu and Robinson, 2000; Acemoglu, Johnson and Robinson, 2002; Acemoglu, 2012) also demonstrate how an 'extractive elite' – or what others have called a parasitic or vampire elite (Lockwood, 2005) can block technologies, competition, democracy, or public spending on education that lead to social gains. They do so because as a result of these changes they will lose out and cannot be expected to be compensated. The key point is that it may not be in the interest of certain elite actors to promote equity-enhancing, growth-led policies.

The wealthy, the powerful and the relatively educated may, then, have an incentive in influencing policy (Dixit, Grossman and Helpman, 1997) and capturing rents or what Do (2002) calls 'regulatory capture'. Initial structural inequalities (Easterly, 2007) or the initial distribution of factor endowments (Hoff, 2003) may go some way in explaining the formation of those elites and some of the inertia preventing large-scale and effective reforms. They may also go some way in explaining ideologies and expectations that reinforce the likelihood of inequalities persisting. If what is said above is true then greater economic competition and a redistribution of wealth may mean the elites have less to gain by controlling institutions (Acemoglu and Robinson, 2008) and a more egalitarian equilibrium may emerge.

6.4   A society of equals

In the analysis above we have seen that inequality is a complex, multi-dimensional concept and that the causes of inequality and its persistence are also complex and multi-faceted. The focus in development economics, however, still largely rests on the impact of inequalities on economic growth and of growth on income inequalities.

Important as these connections are, I want to argue that we're not primarily interested in inequality because of its functional impact on growth or in the distribution of incomes *per se*. Instead, the distribution of different things (goods, welfare etc.) is important to the extent that they promote egalitarian social, political and personal relationships (Scheffler, 2015). As Miller (1997) notes, equality is not the same thing as distributive justice – except under certain circumstances, such as the uncertainty involved in ascertaining individual contributions to a collectively produced output. Equality is not a rigid, arithmetic and abstract concept but a *social* ideal intimately related to equal respect and regard.

Certainly distributional equality is a relational idea in the limited sense that it is a comparative one. This comparative aspect of egalitarianism is often contrasted to the priority view in which inequality may not matter as long as everyone's absolute needs[11] are met (Parfit, 1997). On the other hand, the notion of distributional equality makes a claim about how good an overall distribution is based on the relative position of individuals in some given evaluative dimension. But the ultimate purpose of thinking about equality is to know whether it fosters egalitarian social relations (a society of equals) in which there is fraternity, solidarity and fairness.

The *moral* ideal of a community of equals may stretch far back into human history, drawing upon religious critiques of hierarchy – from the 17th-century Levelers to earlier radical traditions (Williams, 2004). As Craig Calhoun (2012) helpfully informs us, up until the early 19th century, one strand of this radical tradition of opposition to the elites was founded on a lived sense of equality rooted in tradition, custom and local communities rather than on a republican notion of universal and equal rights of an abstract individual/citizen or on the progressive and utopian hopes of rationally ordering society.

For large parts of the 20th century, this relational notion of equality played a central role in underpinning both the critique of the structures of dominance by radical political thought (Badiou, 2007) as well as the more modest reforms under the auspices of the social welfare state. From the 1970s onwards, however, the currency of egalitarianism has lost some of its value. This is partly the result of the dominance of economic thought in this period since, as was noted above, economic theory is not, in any fundamental sense, concerned with distributional or social equality. This great reversal in the prestige of social equality has been presaged, according to Rosanvallon (2013) by a functional and moral crisis in the institutions of solidarity, changes in the structure of production under late capitalism[12] and a shift in our understanding of individualism from a relational and socially embedded notion to an emphasis on a heightened artistic and dissident idea of individualism: an individualism of singularity.

Since the financial crisis the question of what constitutes a fair society has come to the fore once again (Hutton, 2010). There is a renewed interest in the idea of a society of equals animated by considerations of fairness, a society in which hierarchies and domination are minimized and in which certain distinctions (race, ethnic, religious and gender) do not form the basis for superior social standing.[13] For such a society to come about we need equitable institutions and political equality (a distribution of political power, rights for all and a limit on the influence of any one group). As was said above, equal social and political relations themselves depend on distributional equality. So our story is a complex one because a society of equals is a product of history, political institutions (constitutions), culture and economic equalities.

6.5 Conclusion

In this chapter we have seen that market economies (whether perfectly competitive or not) can lead to substantial inequalities. Given that skewed distributions can profoundly hamper the prospects of egalitarian personal, social and political relationships from taking root in society, we need an economic theory that can adequately represent these concerns.

It was shown, however, that economic theory typically avoids discussions of equality in any meaningful sense – assuming that under perfectly competitive conditions the only morally relevant fact is that economic transactions can be modeled as voluntary exchanges and that because such transactions are conducted by formally equal agents questions of power, coercion and domination are redundant. An economic transaction is really a solved political problem.

The paucity of economic theory as it stands means that it fails to account for why distributional equality is important beyond the idea that it *might* foster economic growth.[14]

The development economics literature usefully explains some of the various causes of inequality and its persistence over time but its focus is too narrowly confined to income inequalities. A richer theory will have to cast its net wider and consider the distribution of capabilities – the inequalities in what people can be and do. Such a move would lead us to acknowledge the importance of the idea of relationality in both our individual lives and our social arrangements.

This in turn would mean going beyond Scheffler's (2015) notion of an egalitarian deliberative constraint in cases of conflicting interests and expanding the notion of deliberation and social equality to reflect mutual reciprocity and the idea of the common good. In other words, social equality is a complex but (necessarily) vague concept. Vague, since it is attached to a lived sense of equal relations that unfold over time; complex, because the idea of relationality can imply, as Rosanvallon (2013) informs us, many things: a relation between fundamentally similar people (an equality of equivalence); relations that are free of subordination (an equality of autonomy); relations that respect difference (an equality of singularity); and relations nurtured in and by communities and guided by the ideas of citizenship and the common good (an equality of participation). Egalitarian social relations are, then, a way of re-invigorating the radical tradition of equality, liberty and fraternity.

Notes

1 This chapter draws on earlier work (Burki, Memon and Mir, 2015).
2 There is now growing evidence of the scale of inequalities across countries as well as over time. See Piketty (2017) and Dorling (2014).
3 On the idea that periods of equality are brought about by exogenous factors such as war, revolution, state failure and pandemics see Scheidel (2017).
4 On the relevance of property to the flourishing of autonomy see Scott (2014).
5 On the historical idea that markets with their emphasis on freedom and interests might support a moral order see Taylor (2007) and Hirschman (1982). That markets might support a political order, see Sahlins (2005). Markets, today, are still believed to be potentially liberating (Fraser, 2013).
6 It is questionable whether all dependencies are hierarchical and asymmetrical and even when they are that that necessarily implies that such associations are oppressive. Impersonal benevolence and gift-giving between those facing equal vulnerabilities also have to be considered, as does the possibility that commercial societies lead to a substitution of a dependence on people to a dependence on things and money (O'Neill, 2015).
7 On the resistance of artisans and other members of society to machine production, see Calhoun (2012).
8 It is not a surprise that if workers have little say in the final ends of the labour activity they will find work to be meaningless or pointless. If skills are transferred to machines and if workers are driven exclusively by the extrinsic rewards of money as a compensation for the disutility of work, it is little wonder that many of them increasingly think of themselves as being engaged in "bullshit jobs" (Graeber, 2013).
9 Of course, it has now been realized that the sapping of morale and the crowding-out of intrinsic motivation might itself be bad for productivity and profits. Market economies and to some limited extent economic theory – human capital theory, for example – take into account these adverse consequences (see chapter 7).
10 This assumes that the state is not weak, lacking in fiscal and legal capacity (Besley and Persson, 2011).
11 Similarly, under the influential Rawlsian view unequal arrangements may be acceptable as long as they work to the benefit of the most disadvantaged.

12 As we will see in the next chapter, there has been an increased emphasis on the importance of human subjectivity (intellectual, creative and affective capacities) as a key factor in production. In a knowledge and service economy personal qualities – individual singularity – are the source of economic value.

13 That is to state things too starkly. As rational dependent animals certain hierarchies may be necessary to our flourishing (MacIntyre, 2011). Also, see footnote 5 above. Furthermore, not all valuable social relationships are based on the idea of 'sameness' – the abstract individual citizen or affiliations based on shared personal characteristics and identities, for example (Badiou, 2012). Equal respect and dignity can also be based on the notion of 'difference': the uniqueness and unknowability of the other (Walker, 2015).

14 In reality economists have often made the counter argument. Inequalities may be fair because they're simply the result of differences in talent and effort. Also, equality may actually dampen the incentives to save, invest or work, thus lowering overall economic growth and/or social welfare. Such arguments, even if empirically true ignore the possibility that inequalities can undermine social solidarity, community and inter-personal relations. See Cohen (1991) for an extended discussion of this point.

Bibliography

Acemoglu, D. (2012). *Why Nations Fail: The Origins of Power, Prosperity and Poverty.* New York, NY: Crown Publishers.

Acemoglu, D., Johnson, S., and Robinson, J. A. (2002). Reversal of Fortune: Geography and Institutions in the Making of the Modern World Income Distribution. *The Quarterly Journal of Economics, 117*(4), 1231–1294. doi:10.1162/003355302320935025

Acemoglu, D., Johnson, S., and Robinson, J. A. (2005). Institutions as the Fundamental Cause of Long-Run Growth. In P. Aghion and S. Durlauf (Eds.), *Handbook of Economic Growth*, 1A. Amsterdam: Elsevier North-Holland. Available at: https://doi.org/10.1016/S1574-0684(05)01006-3

Acemoglu, D., and Robinson, J. A. (2000). Political Losers as a Barrier to Economic Development. *The American Economic Review, 90*(2), 126–130. Retrieved from www.jstor.org/stable/117205

Acemoglu, D., and Robinson, J. A. (2008). Persistence of Power, Elites and Institutions. *American Economic Review, 98*(1), 267–293. doi:10.3386/w12108

Acemoglu, D., and Robinson, J. A. (2015). The Rise and Decline of General Laws of Capitalism. *Journal of Economic Perspectives, 29*(1), 3–28. doi:10.1257/jep.29.1.3

Alesina, A., Baqir, R., and Easterly, W. (1997). Public Goods and Ethnic Divisions. *The Quarterly Journal of Economics, 114*(4), 1243–1284. doi:10.3386/w6009

Alesina, A., Devleeschauwer, A., Easterly, W., Kurlat, S., and Wacziarg, R. (2003). Fractionalization. *Journal of Economic Growth, 8*(2), 155–194. doi:10.3386/w9411

Alesina, A., and Rodrik, D. (1994). Distributive Politics and Economic Growth. *The Quarterly Journal of Economics, 109*(2), 465–490.

Anderson, E. (2015). Equality and Freedom in the Workplace: Recovering Republican Insights. *Social Philosophy and Policy, 31*(2), 48–69. doi:10.1017/s0265052514000259

Anderson, E., and Macedo, S. (2017). *Private Government: How Employers Rule Our Lives (And Why We Don't Talk About It)*. Princeton, NJ: Princeton University Press.

Atkinson, A. B. (1997). Bringing Income Distribution in From the Cold. *Economic Journal, 107*(441), 297–321.

Atkinson, A. B. (2001). The Strange Disappearance of Welfare Economics. *Kyklos, 54*(2 and 3), 193–206. doi:10.1111/1467-6435.00148

Atkinson, A. B. (2015). *Inequality: What Can Be Done?* Cambridge, MA: Harvard University Press.

Badiou, A. (2007). *The Century* (A. Toscano, Trans.). Cambridge: Polity Press.

Badiou, A. (2012). *Ethics: An Essay on the Understanding of Evil* (P. Hallward, Trans.). London: Verso.

Banerjee, A. V., and Duflo, E. (2007). The Economic Lives of the Poor. *Journal of Economic Perspectives, 21*(1), 141–167. doi:10.1257/jep.21.1.141

Banerjee, A. V., and Newman, A. F. (1993). Occupational Choice and the Process of Development. *Journal of Political Economy, 101*(2), 274–298. doi:10.1086/261876

Berger, J. (2008). *Hold Everything Dear: Dispatches on Survival and Resistance.* New York, NY: Vintage International.

Besley, T., and Persson, T. (2011). *Pillars of Prosperity: The Political Economics of Development Clusters.* Princeton, NJ: Princeton University Press.

Birdsall, N. (2006). *The World Is Not Flat: Inequality and Injustice in Our Global Economy.* Helsinki: UNU-WIDER.

Bose, G. (1997). Nutritional Efficiency Wages: A Policy Framework. *Journal of Development Economics, 54*(2), 469–478. doi:10.1016/s0304-3878(97)00052-7

Bowles, S. (2013). *The New Economics of Inequality and Redistribution.* Cambridge: Cambridge University Press.

Burki, A. A., Memon, R., and Mir, K. (2015). *Multiple Inequalities and Policies to Mitigate Inequality Traps in Pakistan.* Report, OXFAM, Oxford.

Calhoun, C. J. (2012). *The Roots of Radicalism: Tradition, the Public Sphere, and Early Nineteenth-Century Social Movements.* Chicago, IL: University of Chicago Press.

Coase, R. (1937). The Nature of the Firm. *Economica, 4*(16), New Series, 386–405. doi:10.2307/2626876

Cohen, G. A. (1991, May 21–23). *Incentives, Inequality, and Community.* Lecture presented at The Tanner Lectures on Human Values in Stanford University, Stanford, CA.

De Soto, H. (2000). *The Mystery of Capital: Why Capitalism Triumphs in the West and Fails Everywhere Else.* New York, NY: Basic Books.

Dixit, A., Grossman, G., and Helpman, E. (1997). Common Agency and Coordination: General Theory and Application to Government Policy Making. *Journal of Political Economy, 105*(4), 752–769. doi:10.1086/262092

Do, Q. T. (2002). *Institutions, Institutional Change, and the Distribution of Wealth* (Tech.). Cambridge, MA: MIT Press.

Dorling, D. (2014). *Inequality and the 1%.* Brooklyn, NY: Verso.

Easterly, W. (2007). Inequality Does Cause Underdevelopment: Insights From a New Instrument. *Journal of Development Economics, 84*(2), 755–776. doi:10.1016/j.jdeveco.2006.11.002

Eswaran, M., and Kotwal, A. (1986). Access to Capital and Agrarian Production Organisation. *The Economic Journal, 96*(382), 482–498. doi:10.2307/2233128

Fraser, N. (2013). A Triple Movement? *New Left Review, 81.* Retrieved from https://newleftreview.org/II/81/nancy-fraser-a-triple-movement

Galor, O., and Zeira, J. (1993). Income Distribution and Macroeconomics. *The Review of Economic Studies, 60*(1), 35–52. doi:10.2307/2297811

Glaeser, E., Scheinkman, J., and Shleifer, A. (2003). The Injustice of Inequality. *Journal of Monetary Economics, 50*(1), 199–222.

Graeber, D. (2013, August). On the Phenomenon of Bullshit Jobs: A Work Rant by David Graeber. *Strike! Magazine.* Retrieved from https://strikemag.org/bullshit-jobs

Greif, A. (1993). Contract Enforceability and Economic Institutions in Early Trade: The Maghribi Traders' Coalition. *The American Economic Review, 83*(3), 525–548. Retrieved from www.jstor.org/stable/2117532

Hardoon, D. (2017). *An Economy for the 99%: It's Time to Build a Human Economy that Benefits Everyone, Not Just the Privileged Few.* Oxfam Briefing Paper. Oxford: Oxfam International. Available at: https://www.oxfam.org/en/research/economy-99

Hirschman, A. O. (1982). Rival Interpretations of Market Society: Civilizing, Destructive, or Feeble? *Journal of Economic Literature, 20*(4), 1463–1484. Retrieved from www.jstor.org/stable/2724829

Hoff, K. (2003). Paths of Institutional Development: A View From Economic History. *The World Bank Research Observer, 18*(2), 205–226. doi:10.1093/wbro/lkg006

Hutton, W. (2010). *Them and Us: Politics, Greed and Inequality Why We Need a Fair Society.* London: Little, Brown.

Le Grand, J. (2013). *Motivation, Agency, and Public Policy of Knights and Knaves, Pawns and Queens.* Oxford: Oxford University Press.

Lerner, A. (1972). The Economics and Politics of Consumer Sovereignty. *The American Economic Review, 62*(1/2), 258–266. Retrieved from www.jstor.org/stable/1821551

Lockwood, M. (2005, November 20). States of Development. *Prospect Magazine.* Retrieved from www.prospectmagazine.co.uk/magazine/statesofdevelopment

Lucas, R. E., Jr. (2004). The Industrial Revolution: Past and Future. *Economic Education Journal, 44*(8), 5–20.

MacIntyre, A. C. (2011). *Dependent Rational Animals: Why Human Beings Need the Virtues.* Chicago, IL: Open Court.

Marglin, S. A. (1974). What Do Bosses Do? *Review of Radical Political Economics, 6*(2), 60–112. doi:10.1177/048661347400600206

Marglin, S. A. (2001). Losing Touch: The Cultural Conditions of Worker Accommodation and Resistance. In F. A. Apffel-Marglin and S. A. Marglin (Eds.), *Dominating Knowledge: Development, Culture, and Resistance.* Oxford: Clarendon Press.

Miller, D. (1997). Equality and Justice. *Ratio, 10*(3), 222–237. doi:10.1111/1467-9329.00042

Mullainathan, S. (2004). *Development Economics Through the Lens of Psychology.* Working Paper No. 28974, Vol. 1, The World Bank. Retrieved from http://documents.worldbank.org/curated/en/415731468779687162/Development-economics-through-the-lens-of-psychology

Munshi, K., and Rosenzweig, M. (2006). Traditional Institutions Meet the Modern World: Caste, Gender, and Schooling Choice in a Globalizing Economy. *The American Economic Review, 96*(4), 1225–1252. Retrieved from www.jstor.org/stable/30034337

Murphy, J. B. (1993). *The Moral Economy of Labor: Aristotelian Themes in Economic Theory.* New Haven, CT: Yale University Press.

Norman, R. (1997). The Social Basis of Equality. *Ratio, 10*(3), 238–252. doi:10.1111/1467-9329.00043

O'Neill, J. (2015). Equality, Vulnerability and Independence. In A. Bielskis and K. Knight (Eds.), *Virtue and Economy: Essays on Morality and Markets.* Surrey: Ashgate.

Palermo, G. (2016). *Economics and Power: A Marxist Critique.* New York, NY: Routledge.

Parfit, D. (1997). Equality and Priority. *Ratio, 10*(3), 202–221. doi:10.1111/1467-9329.00041

Persson, T., and Tabellini, G. (1994). Is Inequality Harmful for Growth? *The American Economic Review, 84*(3), 600–621. Retrieved from www.jstor.org/stable/2118070

Piketty, T. (2017). *Capital in The Twenty-First Century* (A. Goldhammer, Trans.). Cambridge, MA: Belknap Press of Harvard University Press.

Rosanvallon, P. (2013). *The Society of Equals.* Cambridge, MA: Harvard University Press.

Rosenzweig, M., and Binswanger, H. (1993). Wealth, Weather Risk and the Composition and Profitability of Agricultural Investments. *The Economic Journal, 103*(416), 56–78. doi:10.2307/2234337

Sahlins, M. D. (2005, November 4). *Hierarchy, Equality, and the Sublimation of Anarchy The Western Illusion of Human Nature.* Lecture presented in The University of Michigan, Ann Arbor, MI. Retrieved from https://tannerlectures.utah.edu/lecture-library.php

Sandmo, A. (2014). The Principal Problem in Political Economy. In A. B. Atkinson (Ed.), *Handbook of Income Distribution.* Oxford: Elsevier Science & Technology Books.

Scheffler, S. (2015). The Practice of Equality. In C. Fourie, F. Schuppert, and I. Wallimann-Helmer (Eds.), *Social Equality: On What It Means to Be Equals.* New York, NY: Oxford University Press.

Scheidel, W. (2017). *The Great Leveler: Violence and the History of Inequality From the Stone Age to the Twenty-First Century.* Princeton, NJ: Princeton University Press.

Scott, J. C. (2014). *Two Cheers for Anarchism: Six Easy Pieces on Autonomy, Dignity, and Meaningful Work and Play.* Princeton, NJ: Princeton University Press.

Sen, A. K. (1979, May 22). *Equality of What?* Lecture presented at The Tanner Lectures on Human Values in Stanford University, Stanford, CA. Retrieved from https://tannerlectures.utah.edu/_documents/a-to-z/s/sen80.pdf

Stiglitz, J. E. (2013). *The Price of Inequality: How Today's Divided Society Endangers Our Future.* New York, NY: W.W. Norton & Company.

Taylor, C. (2007). *Modern Social Imaginaries.* Durham, NC: Duke University Press.

UNCTAD. (2012). *Trade and Development Report, 2012 – Policies for Inclusive and Balanced Growth.* Report, United Nations, New York, NY. Retrieved from http://unctad.org/en/PublicationsLibrary/tdr2012_en.pdf

Walker, H., Dr. (2015, May 28). *Equality Without Equivalence: An Anthropology of the Common.* Lecture presented at Malinowski Memorial Lecture in LSE, London.

Walzer, M. (2010). *Spheres of Justice: A Defense of Pluralism and Equality.* New York, NY: Basic Books.

Wilkinson, R., and Pickett, K. (2009). *The Spirit Level: Why More Equal Societies Almost Always Do Better.* London: Allen Lane.

Williams, R. (2004). *Anglican Identities.* London: Darton, Longman and Todd.

7 Do markets crowd out ethics?

He who owes his good fortune to the numbers abides in them.

(Crouch, 2015, p. 66)

The task of an educator is to stand against a current which will in fact probably overwhelm him.

(MacIntyre and Dunne, 2002, p. 1)

7.0 Introduction

In previous chapters we have seen that what undergirds mainstream economic models of behaviour are the structuring assumptions of rationality, self-interest and individuality. Only in recent years has this view been dented somewhat and it admitted that markets are the result of both the interactions of individuals as well as *social* features of society (trust, goodwill, (moral) norms, culture and institutions). In other words, a flourishing market economy is best understood not simply as a spontaneous order that miraculously emerges from the actions of isolated and amoral rational self-interested individuals. If that is true then economic theory quite obviously has to take sociality and ethics seriously.

For some authors the statements above imply that markets and market behaviour are not necessarily devoid of ethics. For others, though, they just go to reinforce the notion that the success of markets (capitalism) has been dependent on their (its) ability to free-ride on pre-modern social capital and moral values. In other words, the flourishing of market economies is dependent on areas of social and political life that escape the frontiers of the market. Accumulation and economic growth, then, are reliant on the existence of non-commoditized capacities, practices and dispositions such as female labour, ethical behaviour, cognitive abilities and natural 'resources'.

In this chapter we take the latter perspective seriously and examine the implications of such a view. Is it the case, we might ask, that the expansion of market behaviour (purportedly based purely on the interactions between rational, self-interested individuals) leads to a diminishing of social capital and/or ethical values? And if so, does such a process also result in an undermining of the economy itself?

I have already broached these question in the previous chapter but it is a large and unwieldy one. So, in this chapter I will try and look at it from a slightly different and narrower angle by asking whether market ideology, practices, policies and reforms have undermined not just the public sector but the public sector ethos (or 'the public'). I take this ethos to encompass a wide set of attitudes, values, motivations and institutional practices but we'll come to definitions later.

To try and get a grip on this vitally important question, one that is at the heart of many current policy debates, it is necessary to first introduce what is meant by 'the public' (section 1). From there I look at the rise and decline of the public in a historical context (sections 2 and 3). Can we even talk about 'the public' as a category of experience that transcends empirical and historical realities? In the following two sections (4 and 5) I then turn to briefly look at the impact of the growing pervasiveness of market mechanisms ('quasi-market reforms') such as performance related pay on the public ethos. In section 6, I look at the specific example of the university in an era of neoliberalism as a way of understanding how the extension of market practices and mentalities in higher education can crowd out important values. This is just another way of stating the main thesis of this book: unadulterated markets, and the structuring assumptions of an economic theory that supports them, can have important ramifications for the way in which we understand ourselves as well as our relation to other people and objects of value.

7.1   What or who is the public?

Later on in this chapter I will be looking specifically at motivations in the public sector (a wide array of attitudes and values that constitute, in our shorthand, the public sector ethos) and whether they can be crowded out by the introduction of market-type policies. But in order to place a discussion of the various ways in which 'the public' is understood in some context I think it is necessary to first of all set out what is meant by 'the public' and why its possible decline is so important.

At the outset we are faced with the problem that the utopian and normative vision of 'the public' has often been at odds with the historical record. But any coming to terms with the tension between the ideal and historical reality entails acknowledging the role of pluralism. Let me try and explain that.

First, the term 'the public' is used to describe a vast number of distinct values, attitudes, practices and institutions. For instance, we are by now used to discussions about: public accountability, public spaces and accessibility to them (libraries, parks, etc.), public goods (goods that are non-rival and non-excludable), the public sector and public service, public intellectuals, publicity, public opinion and public reason. And tied up with those discussions are questions about equality, freedom, motivations and solidarity. Given those diverse meanings of the term it has to be asked whether it is profitable to continue to think of an overarching abstraction, 'the public'.

The second way in which pluralism is important is that we need to think of 'the public' sphere as a historically conditioned formation rather than a universal category of experience. By doing so we can conceive the different trajectories of 'the public' across different countries and also examine how the very notion of 'the public' changes with background economic conditions and technological possibilities. Pluralism, therefore, would entail thinking about the possible differences in character of, on the one hand, the public realm in classical times, and the bourgeois public sphere and the subsequent welfare state on the other. It follows that the 'decline' we are interested in, then, is that of a *particular* historical understanding of 'the public' rather than a universal category. It is not surprising, therefore, that already academics are asking whether a new model of publicity is emerging (transnational publics, the internet) from the loss of the older forms (Fraser and Nash, 2014; Dean, 2003).

A third reason why pluralism is important is that the idealized construction, 'the public', has often in practice been exclusionary. Central to the ideal of the public sphere are notions of equality, openness and participation. But as has been frequently noted, publicness in reality has gone hand in hand with the marginalization and exclusion of certain groups – in classical times women and slaves; in the bourgeois public sphere we can think of exclusion in terms of gender, ethnicity and class (Fraser, 1990). Far from being a simple failure to live up to the utopian emancipatory possibilities embodied in the concept of 'the public', some have argued the exclusions are a manifestation of the hegemonic power of a particular class.

The argument above is an important one. In the ideal public sphere a specific subjectivity is assumed, a particular way of relating to other people (perhaps impersonally but always on an equal footing), and an understanding that through free and open (rational) discourse a political community will come to a common understanding of its common interests. But the criticism of this ideal from a pluralistic perspective throws into relief the reality that the underlying socio-economic inequalities in society have in practice barred women, the property-less and the working classes from the public realm.

Even when they have not been formally excluded certain communities may still be disadvantaged – through a lack of education or 'voice' – because built into the idea of public discourse is a particular style of reasoning that is not shared by everyone. And, related to that, concentrations of power may mean that access to information and available knowledge puts professional and middle classes at a relative advantage over working classes, making effective public discourse less likely. Furthermore, the exclusion of the latter group – whether by subtle or blunt methods – can mean that issues related to production and the encroachment of the market are not genuinely publicly debated.

Given these criticisms pluralists argue for the crucial importance of counter-publics as a counterweight to a hegemonic and monolithic public that is supposedly neutral but that in reality has been effectively co-opted by the market or the state. Since the main focus of this chapter is on the first of those processes – how private interests can undermine the public spirit ethos – let me just say a few words about the second, the relation between the public and the state (or the political).

In the oldest meaning of the word 'public' we can see the idea of common interests or a common world. For thinkers like Arendt (1998) the original, classical notion of 'the public' was, in addition to being a common world that at once united and separated individuals, also a space of appearances, a place where through individual words, deeds and collective memory a relatively stable world would endure. The *polis* or the *republic* was, then, a space in which the moral virtues of the good life were expressed: equality, pluralism, openness and freedom. And freedom was conceived in terms of an independence from the idiocy of a solely private life, from natural associations, from the needs of the body, from the life process and from the laboring activity.

Inherent in that idea of freedom was the understanding that the self could only speak and act against the background of a relatively stable world. In other chapters I have been arguing that in economic theory and in actual real-world economies the individual has all but disappeared and that time has been whittled down to the present moment. Both of these 'disappearances' – that of the individual and that of narrative time – can now readily be understood to be inextricably bound with the undermining of the public/political realm, or 'worldlessness'.

Perhaps this 'worldlessness' is not so different from a sense of 'homelessness',[1] which elsewhere I have associated with the rise of liquid modernity and which finds expression in both our lack of affection for local places and our sense of attachment to specific people, objects and traditions[2] (O'Donovan and O'Donovan, 2004).

And so to surmise, the depletion of 'the public' can be thought of as the simultaneous loss of spatial and temporal matrices by which we understand our experiences. A loss, as we will see in chapter 9, that is understandable given the predominance of market economies and economic theory's neglect of institutions, history and lived time.

But how did such a situation arise? For Arendt it was a long-drawn out series of historical changes by which the life process became a central concern to the public realm. Politics, in the modern era, is increasingly thought of as biopower or the biopolitical: the management and production of the body and its desires (Juvin, 2010). Another way of saying that is we are now living in a laboring or, equivalently for Arendt, a consumer society.

This emancipation of the body and its desires from any notion of natural limits is what Arendt (1998) terms the unnatural growth of the natural. We tend to think of this emancipation as simply a product of the rise of commerce and money in the modern era. But that is to miss the fact that for modernity the life process, previously hidden or shielded by the household, has become the subject of political discourse and techniques of management.[3]

Of course, the rise of a consumer society was seen by some as being ultimately antithetical to an older, classical notion of the political[4] (including republican virtues). But for our purposes I want to briefly mention two points. Firstly, under this view 'the public' is already assimilated to the political rather than being a space that is independent of it (see below). And, secondly, in the modern era the state and the market are not necessarily opposed to one another (though both may be to 'the public').

What emerges from our discussion is that the older notion of 'the public' as a realm independent and critical of the political has come under increasing pressure not just because of the rise of the market (which we explore in section 4). We also have to acknowledge that 'the public' has, to some extent, been assimilated to the state – the biopolitical state and the welfare state with its centralized, administrative and bureaucratic structures of power (Graeber, 2015).

The erosion of 'the public', then, may be a more complicated matter. To talk of state capitalism or political economy is to recognize the role both market *and* state have played in undermining a genuine, critical public realm from forming. For the remaining part of the chapter, however, I concentrate on how economic theory and market economies may be undermining the public realm.

In economic theory and in the world created by markets we lack the public models and standards of excellence that a previous generation would employ to judge action. To the questions: Who am I and what do I *really* want? economic theory has little to say. Moreover, the dominance of markets, by undermining the public spirit ethos (public discussion on ultimate ends, non-self-interested motivations, and a long-term perspective), has meant that the forums in which such questions could be asked – and answered – have been depleted.

One further caveat. It has also been argued that the erosion of 'the public' has been furthered in recent times by the forms of our media and communications technologies. Unlike the older print media which probably encouraged 'slow thinking' and reflection (Haldane, 2015), the current modes of communication actually encourage distraction, the banalization of experience and 'artificial frenzies' (Mills, 2008, p. 114). In a remarkably prescient essay, Gunther Anders (2016) argued that with the advent of technology the world would become a phantom-world, a pseudo-world whose images would hold us spellbound and transfixed.

7.2   The rise of the public

In this section, I want to briefly outline the rise of 'the public' as a historical formation and indicate why its demise, despite all the shortcomings highlighted above (its various exclusions, its discounting of competing interests and of socio-economic inequalities), is of significant importance. In the next section I will narrow the focus of our lens and concentrate specifically on public sector motivations, or the public spirit ethos. But for now let's return to the abstract notion of 'the public' that was instantiated in numerous and various practices, agencies and institutions from the 18th century onwards.

A large number of authors have noted that the bourgeois public sphere was in fact understood by its members to be both a space of discussion about the common good as well as a way of interacting with one's peers. 'The public' (somewhat questionably) was seen as an amalgamation of various publics and associations, a realm that was crucially an extra-political and secular sphere of life (Taylor, 1997). The public sphere, in other words, was deemed to be distinct from the state (the political), the market, the private world of intimacy, and from natural communities. And by being orthogonal to the state it played a vital role, it was argued, in ensuring political accountability, thus furthering the quality of democratic governance.[5]

Of course, it has been questioned, as we have seen above, whether a *bourgeois* public sphere could be a genuine public realm – and for several reasons. First, the exclusions of women and the working class might justifiably be seen as legitimating the dominance of the bourgeois class rather than the public sphere. Second, as Charles Taylor (1997) has argued, a bourgeois society, one that was peaceful, rational and productive, formed the backdrop to the rise of the public sphere. Under such circumstances it is questionable whether there could be a genuine public discussion about each of those three background assumptions/ components. For instance, could questions about the underlying violence involved in primary accumulation or colonialism be included? Or: if society is productive, then to what ultimate end?

So, we must continue to posit that the relation between the public sphere and capitalism is problematic. This tension is not dissipated in the modern period when the state and 'the public' increasingly become conflated with one another. For, as we shall see in section 5 below, the state and the market are deeply intertwined with one another in the era of neoliberalism.

Third, to the extent that the public realm, an arena of free and open discussion, stands apart from the political it is also questionable whether it can ever be an effective check on either the market or the state. This is another way of raising the question: in a world dominated by powerful market and state institutions, how efficacious are the texts, discussions and culture of the public realm?

Having said that, in the remaining part of this chapter I want to argue that 'the public', both as an ideal and as a set of practices, values and attitudes (an ethos), *has* provided a way of organizing social experience that has opposed both the dominance of markets and the wide acceptance of the assumptions underlying economic theory.

From the 18th century, Richard Sennett (1977) informs us, the public world envisaged social encounters, subjectivity and a form of relationality beyond the frame of reference of the isolated and boundless self that came to form the bedrock of economic theory. Commitment to and reflection on the common good, civility, "action at a distance from the self" (Sennett, 1977, p. 87), and the idea that genuinely meaningful and expressive speech and acts depended on artifice, social conventions, and rules all placed a limit on the growth of natural appetites, intimacy and authenticity.

Public behaviour, reason and speech, active civic engagement (positive liberty), and acting in character, then, worked as a restraint on the development of private fantasies and an unbridled self-interest. Of course – and we will come to this presently – to a later and more individualistic generation public life and public institutions would seem arbitrary, shallow, restrictive and drained of meaning – a meaning that could be more readily found in the personal and private realms of experience. To paraphrase Rousseau: 'I feel, therefore I am'. Sennett (1977) is correct, therefore, to state, "The public world put a limitation on the principle of happiness as a full definition of reality" (p. 98).

The public world stands opposed to the dominance of the economy and the assumptions of economic theory in other ways too. First, the public sphere is a space of substantive equality (as opposed to the market which, at best, could be said to embody formal equality). Also, as we have seen in the previous chapter, economic theory is usually not concerned about equality as an ethical ideal in its own right.

Second, as Arendt (1998) emphasized, although the public world is a place of openness ('natality') it is also a *given* world into which everyone is born. Such a view involves thinking of the existence of a social world, culture, collective interests and public language over and beyond the individual (Taylor, 1997). And that notion is diametrically at odds with both the methodological individualism at the heart of economics and the lack of importance economies and economic theory afford concepts such as durability and the narrative self.

Third – and this is something we return to in section 4 below – the public world, and the public sector in particular, can be the site of a number of attitudes, values, motivations and norms that question the over-riding emphasis economic theory places on self-interest. Individual behaviour in the public sector has to, on any reasonable account, take into consideration a public sector ethos that encompasses the role professionalism, trust, duty, commitment, social responsibility, disinterested benevolence and altruism.

At the heart of 'the public', then, we find an ideal rooted in civic virtue and ethical motivations, in ideas of citizenship, equity and service. These moral and ideological commitments, David Marquand (2005) informs us, formed part of what Polanyi called the 'counter-movement' to the commodification of land, labour and money.[6] In practice, throughout the 19th century and up until the early 20th century, the emergence of an independent civil service and professional class, the growth in civic pride, charitable associations and the strengthening of both the regulatory state and trade union power militated against the complete dominance of market economies, hedonism and egoism.

Even well into the 20th century, when 'the public' became increasingly equated with public sector institutions and the state, these ideals continued to animate the quality of social life. The existence of social democracies – or whatever we want to call it: the welfare state, the social market, the Keynesian consensus – lent a certain 'moralized quality' to public policy debates (Judt, 2011).[7] Up until the 1970s we could still, just talk about the public sphere as a site that fostered shared purposes, common goals, other-regarding motivations and trust in public authorities/experts. But all of that was about to change, and I want to now try and trace some of the reasons for our shifting involvement away from the public to the private realm.

7.3 The world we have lost

From the 1970s onwards the decline in the idea of the public man as well as scepticism towards the public sector institutions[8] and the people who worked in them ushered in a return to the cult of the private. The reasons why this happened are complex and manifold; they include changes in structural features of the economy, culture, technology, demographics and political ideology.

Well, with a greying population it was certainly envisaged that the financing of the welfare state would, in purely pragmatic terms, become more difficult over time as the ratio of net beneficiaries of public services to suppliers of tax funds declined. And a greying population was also likely to put upward pressure on the demand for those services. This increasing demand was likely to be compounded by the growing realization that education (or 'human capital') was a fundamental component of growth and something that, therefore, needed to be promoted. And with the looming threat of lower productivity and economic growth, the question of whether the fiscal capacity of the state would be able to meet the rising tide of demands and 'entitlements' was a pressing one.

It should be added, however, that such views already presupposed the idea that the central aim of public policy and the public sector is to enhance economic growth and the competitiveness of the economy.

So, the first major shift in thinking about 'the public' can be thought of as a departure from the older notion of the 'ends' of 'the public'. Those older goals of equality, accountability and solidarity – couched in a political language of shared rights – needed to be gradually displaced and replaced by 'efficiency', 'competitiveness' and 'growth' (the language of the market).

The second major change also involved the resurgence of the market as an ideal. For various reasons the public sector came to be viewed as a highly bureaucratic institution that was inefficient, wasteful and unresponsive to the demands of the people dependent on it. And how could that not be the case when it was reasserted time and again that markets were in fact the best processors of information? Worse, or so it was argued, the system of highly centralized decisions, command-and-control, destroyed personal autonomy – the kind of freedom (negative liberty) that was fundamental to the functioning of markets.

The third major factor in the decline of 'the public' was what we might call heterogeneity, the fragmentation of value, and the rise of interest-group politics. From the 1970s onwards there was a growing belief that what mattered was the individual and his or her private interests. This resurgence of the emphasis on the private self could, of course, always have been expected given it formed the core of the liberal tradition and was part and parcel of what might be called 'the century of the self'. But this rebellion against (public) authority and bureaucratic control was played out with particular force in the western world thanks to the cultural loosening up of the 1960s (Bell, 1978).

If what counted was instant gratification, the eclipse of distance from the self, authenticity based on one's private feelings and freedom from authority then it is not hard to see that the values and attitudes enshrined in the public realm must have appeared to be at best artificial, and at worst inimical to the full development of the individual. Can there be any principles, acknowledged public or customary standards of appropriate action, or shared meanings and purposes over and beyond the legitimacy of individual desires – whether the latter are idiosyncratic and frivolous or not? And if the answer to that question is 'no', would we be led to a 'world' in which only subjective states of the mind were of importance, with the result that "Humanity becomes an inner state.

Freedom, goodness and beauty become spiritual qualities. . . . The inner state is to be the source of action that does not come into conflict with the given order"? (Marcuse, 2009, p. 76).

Given this emphasis on the isolated individual and self-interest (an emphasis that we will argue in the next section is central to economic theory) it is not hard to see why beliefs in collective goals, belonging, solidarity, culturally sustained norms of behaviour and the public interest would come to seem anachronistic. We will presently come back to the role of economic theory and the New Public Management in presaging these shifting perceptions of 'the public'. But it is worth mentioning that the fracturing of the self – which mirrors the fracturing of the social body – has other important ramifications. One symptom of that fracturing is that it becomes increasingly questionable whether a heterogeneous population of individuals, each with their own private interests, would be willing to fund or even believe in the public good (Alesina, Baqir and Easterly, 1997; Alesina, Glaesar and Sacerdote, 2001).

Given what was just said it might be thought that the main determinants of heterogeneity revolved around ethnicity, religion, gender, or just individual differences. But a related reason for the decline in the support for the values of public sector institutions is something we have already mentioned in an earlier section: inequality.

Not only might societies be becoming too diverse to sustain a functioning public sector; they may also be becoming too unequal. Growing inequalities (see previous chapter) put an additional stress on the viability of the public sphere. In an age given over to calculation, monetary values and narrow self-interest, why should the rich be willing to contribute through taxes to those who are net beneficiaries of the services when they don't belong to their class?

In some sense, then, it seems that the welfare state in the post-World War II era was largely endorsed, political speaking, because of the existence of a fairly substantial middle class and low levels of inequality.[9] Whether the legitimacy of the public sector and its ideals can be sustained in the face of growing inequalities remains to be seen. But well might we ask whether a world of highly stratified private affluence is also inevitably a world of public squalor?[10]

A final reason for the demise of 'the public' has to do with a growing scepticism towards experts[11]/authority, and a decline in trust[12] (Merrifield, 2017). In the welfare state it had been previously assumed that those who were on the 'supply side' of public service delivery (professionals, managers, planners and bureaucrats) were essentially 'knights' (Le Grand, 2013). These knights were widely believed to be guided by a public spirit ethos: a set of values and attitudes that included, amongst other things: professionalism, impartial benevolence, and a sense of duty. In summary, they were supposed to know what was in the public interest *and* to want to work to that interest being achieved. Both of these claims were, from the late 1970s onwards, widely disputed and scepticism towards them, therefore, contributed to the clamour for public sector reform.

On the other hand, those on the demand side, the recipients of public services, were assumed to be largely passive and trustworthy. A combination of asymmetries in knowledge and class deference resulted in them trusting the advice and prescriptions of the professionals. Nanny knows best!

It goes without saying that this notion of the individual is strikingly at odds with the supposedly 'active' market participant. If markets were to be unimpeded something would have to be done about these notions of agency for the true potential of the individual and the market to be unleashed. In a word, economic agents should be 'queens' rather than passive 'pawns' (Le Grand, 2013). But if that was to come about all that should ideally stand between individuals was the contract and cash payment – a choosing[13] 'self' torn out of the web of social relations that actually sustain individuality – and not the public world of obligation and shared memory. But, it might be asked, without the public world, as Milton claimed, would we only have "the forced and outward union of cold, and neutral, and inwardly divided minds"? (as cited in Marquand, 2015, p. 157).

The positive narrative in economic theory that pictures individual economic agents as being free and rational fits neatly with the triumphant rise of the market over the last 30 years. An alternative and disconcerting reading of our recent history holds that the loss of the public world, the social fabric of public life – which was mainly, but not exactly, equivalent to the decline of the public sector in the late 20th century – might usher in a 'society' of individuals who were, as Burke said, "disconnected into the dust and powder of individuality" (as cited in Rothschild, 2013, p. 29). A return to a Hobbesian 'war of all against all', perhaps? And worryingly, as we will see in section 5 below, the rootless and self-made man of the market economy and economic theory did not escape the clutches of power but, instead, became the subject enmeshed in a new form of it that we name neoliberal power: the administration of men and things; of men as if they *were* things.

7.4   Motivations and public policy

Economists, by and large, continue to assume that economic actors are solely driven by self-interest. In real-world economies, where there is an ever-greater division of labour and specialization, this creates problems because economic interactions take place in contexts of incomplete contracts and imperfect information. With asymmetric information and monitoring costs the problem of incentives and motivation comes to the fore. For why should economic actors, solely motivated by their own self-interest, put in the required effort when it is costly for the principal to supervise their work and/or verify the link between effort and outcomes?

In development economics we are used to thinking about how the incentive problem in various markets (land, labour and credit) are compounded by a whole host of other problems.[14] Far from being an isolated problem I want to suggest that the incentive problem, the selection problem (how do you get the right kind of people), and the enforceability of contract problem are difficulties that are endemic to many real-world markets in developing and developed economies alike.

The problem of purely self-interest agents coupled with the existence of incomplete contracts, then, is also a feature of modern economies (think: regulators, firm managers, bankers). In particular, in the public sector of any advanced economy we can expect incompleteness to be of significant importance. In addition to poor, asymmetric and costly information contracts may be irremediably incomplete because it is not possible to define beforehand what, exactly, is required. For example, how can one stipulate in a contract, with any degree of specificity, the kind and quality of care that should be provided to an elderly patient in a hospice?

Furthermore, in the health and education sectors there are usually multiple goals (since education and health are almost by definition multi-dimensional concepts). In such cases one has to be aware that incentives to enhance one objective may quite plausibly lead to the neglect of another. But there is also another kind of complexity that has to be taken into account. With complex 'goods' such as health and education it is not easy to always attribute a given outcome to *individual* effort, thus making the problem of setting appropriate individual incentives all the more difficult.

If that catalogue of complicating factors wasn't enough we also have to remember that any system of incentives ought to recognize the heterogeneity of agents as well as the lack of long-term relations between principal and agent. In cases where there is an extended relation over time one would imagine there would be less incentive to cheat or shirk for the simple economic reason: a threat of losing potential future contracts with the principal.

And, finally, even if one could write a contract in a precise language for each contingency and put a price on each required action, it might still be the case that it is too expensive to do so. Writing out specific and detailed contracts may actually be counter-productive and demotivate people because they believe their autonomy and ability to exercise judgement is being curtailed.

This latter point about autonomy underlies my main considerations in this section: what if economic agents are not in reality motivated exclusively by pecuniary gain or, more generally, by their own interests?

The standard economic model, and public policy thinking since the 1980s, assumes that in reality people are 'knaves' rather than 'knights' (Le Grand, 2013). Or at least they ought to be. This supposedly more realistic picture of individual motivated by self-interest and little else formed the intellectual underpinning of public policy reforms in the neoliberal era – roughly from the late 1970s onwards.

If economic agents are solely concerned with their own interests (producers with profits, consumers with their own utility/happiness/welfare) then, logically speaking, public sector institutions and the value systems they embodied ought to be overhauled. This could be brought about by wholesale privatization (a popular choice in the 1980s), by the introduction of greater choice and competition in public services, the introduction of performance related pay (PRP) and other various market-like mechanisms (vouchers, say), as well as by the widespread adoption of market proxies (targets, audits).[15]

As already hinted at above, though, economists are now gradually realizing that economic agents in the wider economy and more specifically those in the public sector or with a public sector role – judges, doctors, soldiers, teachers, nurses, care workers – can be motivated by a whole raft of factors which for convenience sake I will subsume under the catch-all term 'intrinsic motivation' (Besley and Ghatak, 2005).

But before we press on it is important to say a bit more about this term. Intrinsic motivation, as I understand it, can comprise not only a concern for autonomous decision-making but can encompass creativity, reputation and identity as well. The latter is linked to loyalty to a particular organization and/or an identification with its mission/goals; also to fidelity to a particular type of work (as in the old sense of the word 'vocation') and the expression of other-regarding preferences (an altruistic concern for the welfare of others), a sense of professional obligation or duty[16] as well as the sheer pleasure of doing a good day's job.

Given the prevalence[17] of intrinsic motivation in the public sector we are faced with the unsettling possibility that the introduction of markets or market-like mechanisms (as described above) may lead to its crowding-out. In other words, the assumptions we are handed down in economic theory can, if reflected in public policies, have profound implications for the quality of public service delivery.

So, we are led back to our familiar theme. The expansion of markets and economic thinking into areas of social life that were previously largely independent of them can fundamentally alter the picture we form of ourselves as moral agents, the way in which we relate to other people and how we understand the narrative structure of our lives. In general, the increasing reliance on incentives to enhance productivity and contribute to more efficient outcomes ignores the impact on equality and the community spirit. In fact, as G.A. Cohen (2008) has argued, the incentive argument rests on us taking "as given unequal structures and/or inequality-endorsing attitudes" (p. 33).

More specifically, the problem in the case of the public sector, it is argued, is that the implementation of market-like policy reforms (which rely on extrinsic motivation) can undermine or crowd out the motivations that are intrinsic or internal to practices in the sector.

If what has just been said is true then economics' traditional emphasis on the separability between ethical motivations, social norms and moral codes on the one hand, and self-interested (or pecuniary) ones on the other, is misguided. If economic agents are only in part self-interested then policies and incentives geared to mobilize those particular aspects of their make-up may crowd out ethical/intrinsic motivations.

This point is worth spelling out in a bit more detail. For what is lost in the crowding-out process is not just the loss of a public spirit ethos, which is an important way of relating to other people and of understanding ourselves as moral beings. In addition, the cannibalization of intrinsic motivation at the hands of narrow self-regard can be bad for the economy as well (I return to the efficiency implications below).

The idea that the 'lower' motives of monetary gain and pure self-interest cannot always be harnessed to generate the social good stands in stark opposition to the trajectory of much of modern economic thinking. Acknowledging this fact would require us to think more seriously about the relations both between material sentiments and ethical motivations, and between individuality and sociality. But why, exactly, does crowding-out occur?

7.5 Crowding-out or crowding-in?

As has already been stated, intrinsic motivation refers to a wide array of possible reasons to act but for the sake of convenience in the following discussion I will largely focus on one aspect of it, namely: altruism.

We can think about the crowding-out and crowding-in of intrinsic motivation in the following way. At certain low levels of extrinsic rewards individuals' effort levels may actually *increase* with the level of rewards. This may be because the extrinsic rewards (performance-related pay or bonuses) are at first seen as a recognition of one's desire to do a good job for its own sake (i.e. intrinsic motivation).

However, as external intervention increases – which may involve in addition to monetary incentives, deadlines, threats, auditing of performance, more explicit contracts, or surveillance – there is a crowding-out effect as intrinsic motivation declines. This is another way of saying that the traditional 'carrots and sticks' approach may have perverse consequences. Essentially, the greater reliance on extrinsic factors to motivate individuals crowds-out intrinsic motivation because individuals perceive them as leading to a diminishing of their autonomy, self-esteem or ability to behave as act-relevant[18] altruists (Le Grand, 2013).

The idea that greater monetary rewards might not have the desired effect of improving the quantity and quality of work effort is deeply troubling to economists. But from history we know that such reactions are not so surprising. People who worked on the land may have had 'satisficing preferences' and not been persuaded to work in factories by the mere existence of higher earnings. The possibility of crowding-out, however, is even more problematic since it suggests economic agents may actually *reduce* their effort levels. How can that be?

The monistic view of economists has in general denied the existence of knightly behaviour in market settings. Moral philosophers have, of course, recognized that there isn't always a strict 'separability' between ethical and economic motivations and that at least one part of our nature – if we can still talk of nature in academic circles – is concerned with principles of action that revolve around particular affections towards particular external objects (Rogers, 1997).

That altruistic motivations exist in the public sector is hardly in dispute.[19] Perhaps the most well-known exponent of the crowding-out hypothesis is Richard Titmuss (1997). In this seminal work Titmuss argued that the introduction of cash payments for blood would reduce the quantity (and perhaps quality, too) of blood that was provided compared to the previous system of voluntary donations.

Thus on efficiency grounds alone a market for blood was a dubious intervention.[20] But there was more: extrinsic motivations, it was argued, might be exploitative (given the poor were more likely to sell blood) and monetary incentives might in some sense actually *reduce* individuals' autonomy (a remarkable claim, since markets are supposed to enhance freedom!). This might happen for the simple reason that if the altruistic inclination to give freely is part of human nature then any policy that makes altruism less likely in effect restricts some of the choices open to us.[21]

Before turning to our discussion of the university in the neoliberal era I want to introduce one small caveat to the discussion so far about crowding-out. While it is undoubtedly true that mainstream economic theory has generally ignored the existence and role of intrinsic motivation/social preferences in labour markets (whether in the private or public sector) the same cannot be said for actual real-world economies. In this regard, Tim Besley's question is an intriguing one: can intrinsic motivation be 'cultivated and expanded' (Besley and Ghatak, 2014, p. 14) to produce better outcomes? We might, in addition to that question, ask why so much effort is being expended on generating effort in the first place?

The two questions are not unrelated. Perhaps we now live in a world in which there is an abundance of commodities (which no one is sure they really need), a shrinking of long-term time horizons and an emphasis on growth without end (i.e. scarcity). Those features of modern society have produced a growing unease with the lack of any purpose – shared or individual – to our activities.

In short, a sense of demotivation prevails: fatigue, *ennui* and *acedia*, none of which can easily be rectified by the extended use of purely external incentives. It seems that capitalism has in fact understood this to be the case. The inefficacy of external motivation requires capitalist firms to cultivate and harness intrinsic motivation to its own ends (profit maximization). The limits to capitalism's ability to maintain forward momentum are, therefore, located in human subjectivity.

What must be produced in the neoliberal era, then, is not just the erosion of ethical and social perspectives and principles – what in this chapter I have called a public spirit ethos.[22] Of equal importance, it is now recognized that a more sophisticated organizational mechanism must turn away from relying on extrinsic motivations, 'scientific management' and external discipline to extract surplus value. Instead, the perpetuation of economic growth depends on individuals themselves becoming 'entrepreneurs' and on organizations harnessing/capturing their intrinsic motivations. Those motivations, which include the surplus from individuals' 'innate' capacities and energies, their creativity, risk-taking propensities, initiative, team-playing (or leadership) potential, as well as their commitment, loyalty and altruistic tendencies (Paoli, 2013) must all be made into capital or put to work[23] for capital.

The new mode of governing, then, is not so much about the control of the body and its desires as it is about their liberation (as we have seen in a previous chapter). The expansion of markets depends on exploiting the inner resources of the subject – the attitudes, values, intrinsic motivations and feelings of our inner world (Kluge and Negt, 2014). In other words, capitalism's new focus is on subjectivity and living capital. One aspect of that is the human capital dimension, and it is to that to which I now turn.

7.6 The neoliberal university

In the strict sense of the term, as employed by economists, school or university education is not necessarily a public good. But it is, however, certainly quite justifiable to talk about a public sector ethos when discussing them because of the personal attitudes, professionalism and commitment of the people who work in such institutions. Moreover, there is a strong sense that knowledge is a common good and that at least one part of the whole point of the university is to strengthen citizenship and thus the *demos* (Calhoun, 2006). Given the central importance of intrinsic motivation and the nature of the 'good' of education, then, it is reasonable to consider the university as forming a core element of 'the public'. And if so much is granted, the question of the crowding-out of the public ethos in the university, as market mentalities and practices rapidly encroach on it, needs to be addressed.

This is a vast and complex topic involving a whole array of issues and a number of distinct but related fields of inquiry. Of the various overlapping analytical approaches and critical conceptual frames needed to understand the current predicament of the university we could name: an intellectual history of the university[24]; fictitious commodification (Polanyi, 2014); cultural capitalism and 'immaterial knowledge' (Gorz, 2010); local particularities and global trends, (Burawoy, 2011); privatization; and 'knowledge corruption' (Crouch, 2015).

I will say a bit about each in what follows but I think the best way of grappling with the multi-dimensional problems facing the university is to think about the overarching term 'neoliberalism'. The rise of academic capitalism and the knowledge economy in the last third of the last century was also a time when economic theory was discovering the importance of human and social capital for economic growth. The growing influence of neoclassical economics in academic circles, then, needs to be looked at in conjunction with the rise of neoliberalism

Neoliberalism – and I'll try and define it presently – represents a new attack on an institution whose central ideas, concepts and values have, for the last 800 years, remained remarkably resilient to attempts by state, religion and industrial capitalism to co-opt them for their own purposes.[25] I say 'new', but it is possible to see some of the current debates and concerns about the future of the university[26] mirrored in previous times.

Arguably, the relation between knowledge and citizenship has been important since classical times – the order of the soul homologous to the order of the city – so that the corruption of knowledge has profound ramifications for the viability of the public/political world. And the corruption of knowledge that resulted from its commercialization (Hénaff, 2010), is not too dissimilar to contemporary debates about the role of consultancy and contract research (Castree, 2010).

Closer to our own times, Nietzsche's 1872 brilliant and enigmatic lectures, *Anti-Education*, took place against the background of a growing unease with consumerism, academic specialization, distraction and the simplification brought about by mass journalism (Nietzsche, 2016).[27] Throughout the lectures we hear Nietzsche railing against the formation of students as a mere means to serve a bureaucratic system or the ends of the market. Education, as an exposure to and engagement with the best of human thought, stands radically opposed to a utilitarian perspective and is in that sense truly 'useless', as Russell (2004) reminds us. To contemplate that a university education might once have been thought of to have been quintessentially about the risky endeavor of spiritual, meaningful learning rather than the "more certain rewards of specialized and routine research" (Ringer, 1990, p. 13) is to be made aware of the distance separating the past from our present moment.

We should also note that in the 1930s concerns about the fragmentation of knowledge, the growing importance of science and specialized studies, as well as the shifting focus towards research led to an emphasis on Great Books, general education and the liberal arts to stem the tide (Wellmon, 2017). For some thinkers, however, it was too late, and in the post-war generation the idea that there was a crisis of education began to take root (Arendt, 2006).

And then there was the great intellectual insurgent, C. Wright Mills, who warned us of the dangers that academics, becoming bereft of intellectual puzzlement and devoid of responsibility to wider publics would, driven by a narrow set of values, techniques, self-esteem or careerism, focus on arbitrary or trivial research projects (Mills, 2008). If theory is de-politicized and decontextualized, and if intelligence is separated from one's personality (a process that opens the door for the commodification of knowledge) then maybe it would be better, as he insisted, to remain a "wobbly professor", and be "both simultaneously inside and outside of the whale" (Mills, 2001), a kind of amateur who resists incorporation into the system of 'knowledge production'.[28]

The university is, then, eminently the site of all kinds of public goods. Thinking and writing about ideas for their own sake, the engagement in conversations across disciplines and generations, the personal autonomy involved in the free pursuit of knowledge, the critical reflection on the nature of our desires and goals, and the attempt to understand the historical and political contexts of our concepts all militate against the subsumption of knowledge to the ends of the economy. In a similar vein, economic theory's emphasis on human capital is a gross deformation of what is really meant by education. Both market economies and economic theory can, therefore, crowd out intrinsic motivation and the 'good' of education. But how, exactly, they do so remains to be spelt out.

The best way to understand that process is, I suggest, by thinking of neoliberalism. Neoliberalism has a complex and varied history but for the sake of analytical convenience we can, following Wendy Brown (2015) and Philip Mirowski (2014), highlight a few of its essential features.

First, departing from a central tenet of classical liberalism, we have to be cognizant of the fact that states, institutions and bureaucracies fabricate the subjectivities, social relations and representations required for the extension of markets. That means we have to think carefully about how the language,[29] rhetoric, values, mentalities and practices associated with the markets are constructed. In addition, we need to think seriously about power: what is the structure of governance within universities; are there exclusions based on gender and class (Graeber,

2014); and who is pushing for market-led reforms: teachers, bureaucrats, administrators or businessmen?[30]

A second and related feature of neoliberalism revolves around the strategies employed – and not just the identity of those who exercise power – to establish the ideal market in higher education. Amongst the strategies privatization and enhanced competition have been much commented upon. I think it is more useful to focus on techno-managerial governance which employs various techniques, most of which come from the business world: an emphasis on quantification and measurement, on performance (metrics, targets), standardization, objectivity, auditing, accountability and transparency.

Third, as was said above, neoliberalism is fundamentally geared to constructing subjectivities. Students must be made into consumers and customers or, more pro-actively, into entrepreneurs who are constantly updating their skills; and faculty must put to one side their old-fashioned ideas about learning and intrinsic value and both understand and accept that they and the economy can capitalize on their creativity and commitment. Under this view, the best way of transforming education into human capital is not to rely on external rewards and constraints but, as we have already seen in the previous section of this chapter, to somehow, if possible, marshal the inner resources of individuals themselves.

A fourth feature, one that I can only mention in passing, is the role of 'financialization' and debt in higher education. Some of the key issues here centre on student fees, value for money, inequalities in salaries, low-paid casual and precarious work, and the role of consultancy work on the integrity of the profession (both in terms of teaching and research).

In a moment I will conclude this section by saying a bit more about the third feature just mentioned, subjectivity and immaterial knowledge, but before that let me just touch on the second, the rise of an audit culture.

The audit culture may in many respects seem like a recent phenomenon but it is important to see it in its historical context. In fact, it could, with some justification, be claimed that statistical knowledge (Hacking, 2010; Foucault, 1991), quantification and standardization have always gone hand in hand with the calculative practices, bureaucratic control and governmentality associated with capitalistic development (Thompson, 1993; Scott, 2008).[31]

The emergence of what might be called a political economy of measurement has, therefore, deep historical roots. In more recent times, the idea that it was entirely possible (and desirable) that "the individual becomes routinely knowable and accountable" (Miller and O'Leary, 1987, p. 253) has had wide implications for the scientific management of different areas of social life.

More specifically, from the 1980s onwards a broad process that we can call 'auditing' was taking shape. This process involves classification, counting and measurement in many different organizational settings (firms, health, education and finance). This institutional demand for numbers, simplification, representation, abstraction, aggregation and analysis has spurned a whole growth industry in expert knowledge[32] (Power, 2004). And, crucially, it would appear, its main aim has been "the modification of behaviour in the interests of control" (Power,

2004, p. 776) rather than that of increasing efficiency and accountability.[33] In higher education (as elsewhere) it could be argued that this "ideological system for disciplining" (Power, 2000, p. 114) has had disastrous effects.

As has been argued throughout this chapter, the imposition of external motivations and constraints is of severely limited use when we are considering the public sector ethos and complex goods such as education-complex because education is not a uniform product that can be priced but a multi-dimensional 'good' with immaterial, qualitative, subjective, non-quantifiable and non-measurable features.

As Colin Crouch (2015) has amply demonstrated, the emphasis on performance measures, targets and league tables[34] can lead to the neglect of the intangible aspects of education. Equally, they can lead, over and beyond this neglect, to moral corruption: a reduction in, a crowding-out of, autonomy and intrinsic motivation (Miller and Power, 2013), the distortion of agents' perceptions and the meanings they attach to education. These distortions may take the form of a greater allocation of time and energy towards commercialized research and policy work (at the expense of independent scholarly endeavor); they may involve a completely instrumental notion of education and the gaming of indicators[35]; they can crowd out discussions of what a good education consists of and what kind of person the university wants to see flourish (Biesta, 2008); and, finally, they can have a deleterious effect on human subjectivity (Morrish, 2015).

So, let's turn to the impact of market reforms on human subjectivities in the higher education sector. It is posited that in the neoliberal era the ultimate source of value in the economy depends on the mental and affective capacities of labour: intelligence, creativity, imagination, openness, emotional maturity, commitment or intrinsic motivation. These traits and dispositions are formed via the culture, social relations and habits of everyday life (i.e. in the non-market institutions outside of the sphere of market relations). But that means there is a problem of how to appropriate that value without destroying it.

Some authors have argued that this problem of subjectivity is indeed a contradiction of late capitalism but that it can be averted either by limiting free access to knowledge or by externalizing knowledge beyond labour by relying on robots and artificial intelligence. But putting these arguments to one side, the problem of appropriation is a hugely significant one.[36]

Throughout this chapter I have been arguing that certain modes of being are of intrinsic value – modes that we have alternately tied to terms such as a 'public spirit ethos' and 'intrinsic motivation' and whose loss is in itself is of great relevance. In addition, it is increasingly recognized that those very same motivations, ways of self-understanding and relating to other people help the economy flourish. But we also now understand that a greater reliance on market incentives and external monitoring can lead to intrinsic motivation being crowded out.

So, can market societies create knowledge economies? It is hard to see how there can be a successful internal colonization whereby values are converted into economic value. If both teachers and students identify in a wholesale fashion with the production of 'useful' knowledge and the ceaseless 'updating' of skills for the market then the essence of the university is distorted. But equally, markets and bureaucracies cannot tap into that essence since a lot of the core values and subjectivities associated with the university are antithetical to the progress of capitalism (Brown, 2015)!

The life of the mind is not the whole of life.[37] But it is important nevertheless, and the university gives shape to that life by encouraging a certain relation to texts (Reitter and Wellmon, 2015). The university is, more than anything else, a place where the exalted silence of the book (Steiner, 1998) reigns. And that 'bookishness' involves 'slow thinking', attentiveness, conversations across disciplines and generations, critical, ethically reflective and contextualized thinking. It also requires time and space for hesitation, imagination, wandering, as well as a role for both analysis and for memory amongst countless other things. My main contention is that not only are markets incapable of transforming the kind of subjectivity nurtured by the university into capital; more pointedly, that very same subjectivity provides intellectual and moral resources which can be – and often are – used to critique the expansion of market mentalities and practices.

7.7   Conclusion

In previous chapters we have seen how capitalism's current focus is on the body and/or on machine intelligence (Gorz, 2010) – the formalized and algorithmic knowledge, disentangled from the human subject, which continues the process of the 'mathematization' of nature. Given these trends, economic theory's traditional image of agents as being rational, self-interested individuals seems woefully out of tune with our times.

In this chapter we have seen how market incentives and policies have furthered the hollowing out of individuality by leading to the dismantling of public sector institutions and the crowding-out of a public sector ethos (or intrinsic motivation).

I then argued that in the neoliberal era there has been a conscious attempt by an administrative mode of power to manage and capture the 'wealth' represented by intrinsic motivation. This is done partly by a reliance on auditing but also by creating a particular kind of entrepreneurial subject whose sole focus is on competitiveness and self-investments that enhance their human capital. Crucially, in our liquid modernity this kind of power must rely less on constraints and more on the participation and identification of the individuals themselves in the process of wealth creation. Life, it *must* be admitted, is little else than a business. But this, paradoxically, leads to what some call a "compulsory individuality" (Gill, 2016) and others a "voluntary servitude" (Paoli, 2013).

Finally, I looked at the university as a prime example of the eclipse of the public sector ethos. Here, as well as more generally in society, it appears that we have "lost a recognition of ourselves held together by literatures, images, religions, histories, myths, ideas, forms of reason [and] languages" (Brown, 2015, p. 188). There is no denying that the dominant trajectory of neoliberalism is indeed leading us to an anti-social sociality and to an undermining of relationality. But although the university is the site of capital's attempt to subsume human subjectivity to its own logic it is also, I contend, a site of contestations and obstinacy. We are, in the end, faced with the choice of two notions of value: on the one hand the economist's concept of human capital; on the other, Ruskin's profound understanding that "life is wealth" (1967).

Notes

1 Others might argue that the two are in fact opposed to one another since 'the world' is a distinct realm of experience from 'the home'.

2 In a later chapter, I will argue that the loss of affection and sense of specific attachments is intimately related to the decline of relationality – with profound implications for our ability (and desire) to care for both non-human beings and future generations. The loss of a sense of place is also, I think, deeply intertwined with the feeling that human beings (and other species) are almost out of time (Merton, 1977).

3 This is not to say that the older forms of power based on discipline and 'subtraction' have disappeared. It is just to note that the new form of power is much more interested in generating, multiplying, optimizing and administering the desires and energies of individuals and the population. In the current, neoliberal version of biopower there is a shift in emphasis. Individuals, as micro-entrepreneurs, must care for their own self and be responsible for their own investments in the prolongation and expansion of life's energies; and, secondly, the meaning of life in 'the managing of life' extends beyond the concept of 'bare life' (labour, bodily desires, life expectancy) since it now includes our affective and cognitive capacities as well (see section 5 below).

4 See Ignatieff (1994).

5 Such ideas continue to reverberate in our times where it is often argued that civil society plays a major role in promoting effective democratic institutions.

6 See chapter 3 for a discussion of Polanyi's idea of a 'counter-movement'.

7 This assertion needs to be tempered by Cohen's (2000) claim that for the left there was a lack of a moral dimension to politics.

8 This plays out, no doubt, against older modes of scepticism towards institutions (in general) in both liberal and romantic traditions.

9 There is, of course, a question of cause and effect here since lower inequalities in the period of 1945–75 were most likely to have been, at least in part, a consequence of social democracy.

10 A related question pertains to whether empathy and sympathy can take root in a society that is so riven with inequalities. It is important to remember that the public realm is also a site of care and sympathy, and not just a realm of cold reason and impartial rules.

11 Also see Illich (1978) for a discussion of the increasing professionalized administration of our (commoditized) needs.

12 See O'Neill (2010) for a brilliant discussion of the displacement of older forms of accountability and trust, a theme I return to in section 5.

13 Williams (2000), writes of how the act of choice as presented in economics, the choice of an abstract will at a single moment in time, is not necessarily the best way of thinking about genuinely free and intelligent decisions. The picture of the isolated individual bereft of social relations and obligations, someone who faces unlimited choice, fantasy driven, with little or no capacity (or desire) to reflect on his or her responsibilities, is in some senses a childish depiction of choice.

14 For example, it is widely understood that the ability to apply effort in a project financed by a debt contract can depend on the ability of the principal (the landlord) to acquire the borrower's collateral in case of default. If the borrower faces

limited liability in the case of default why should she put in so much effort (Ray, Ghosh and Mookherjee, 2000)? In rural labour markets the principal (landlord) may want to 'incentivize' workers to provide effort by tying good and bad outcomes to large wage differentials but he has to take into consideration that risk-averse workers do not like such differentials.

15 I look at some of these mechanisms in more detail in the following section.

16 'Duty', in the abstract, can often sound like a joyless reason for action. It should be noted that we can derive a deep sense of pleasure and meaning from acting in conformity with our professional duties.

17 For experimental evidence, see Bowles (2017).

18 Act-relevant altruists are motivated to help other people out of a sense of social recognition, duty or obligation. Unlike act-irrelevant altruists it is important that they themselves play a role in providing assistance to someone in need.

19 See Janet Steele cited in Le Grand (2013). Wright (2001) provides evidence for the existence of generosity and charitable instincts. For brief comments on the history of 'charity' see Williams (2000). Although the system of gift and counter-gift is not quite the same thing as altruism, it too is understood to be fairly widespread in society, see Godbout and Caille (2014). In the economy, too, economic transactions are not always devoid of a gift element, see Solow (1980) and Akerlof (1982).

20 However, more generally it could also be quite possible that in the long-run there are efficiency gains (better outcomes) from an increasing use of monetary incentives despite the decline in altruistic behaviour and intrinsic motivation that such use brings about. See Le Grand (2001).

21 This argument is repeated by Graeber (2007) in *Army of Altruists: On the Alienated Right to do Good.*

22 The public spirit ethos and the public realm (a space of critical reflection) might plausibly help us order our desires and thus put a brake on the seemingly infinite process of accumulating ever-more abstract wealth. The contradiction of capitalism is that it also requires the public sector and a public sector ethos to flourish.

23 In chapter 8, I briefly look at the idea that nature (which includes human nature) must be put to work.

24 Of the vast literature Minogue's (2005) *Concept of a University* remains essential reading. For recent work that also draws us to an older historical understanding of the university and the difficulty of reconciling Newman's idea of a university to our modern fragmented times see Macintyre's illuminating discussion with Dunne (Macintyre and Dunne, 2002). The medieval ideas of the university as a place of leisure as understood in terms of 'slowness' and 'passivity' by Pieper (2009), and of a kind of 'reading' that encourages an ethical transformation is explored in Illich's (1996) wonderful *The Vineyard of the Text.*

25 The belief in an ahistorical idea of the university is, of course, highly problematic. But see Oakeshott (2002) and Illich's (1991) "Text and the University".

26 See Deresiewicz (2015) for a nice summary.

27 The latter seems to be an important phenomenon around this time well into the early 20th century as well (Kraus 2013). On distraction much has been written. See Crawford (2015) for an excellent overview of what is at stake. More specifically related to education, Turkle's (2008) remains indispensable. Illich (1995), as always, was there before anyone else; see his 'Guarding the Eye in the Age of Show'

28 This notion of 'smallness' or marginality is an important and recurrent theme in literature (one thinks of Robert Walser, Pessoa, and Nescio's wonderful *Amsterdam Stories*). In academic circles, it may be more difficult to disentangle oneself from the ever-tightening grip of the frenzied demands for greater 'productivity'. But against the neoliberal idea of the production of the self the ability to situate

oneself on the margins (Said, 1994), the capacity to say "I prefer not to", still remains an alluring and vital possibility.

29 An increasingly typical (and depressing) example: "Where the key selling point of a course is that it provides improved employability, is charge [fee] will become an indicator of its ability to deliver" (UK Govt, 2010, p. 31). Also, see Collini (2011, 2003).

30 For the role of business in the formulation of policy in the UK, see Collini (2011). On the lack of freedom and intellectual integrity in the modern university, see Bauman and Donskis (2013).

31 As was pointed out earlier, commodification and the market – the locus of the exchange of equivalents – require the establishment of a 'common currency'. On the importance of standardization for the realization of value see de Soto (2000).

32 It is tempting to see a link between the increasing importance of quantification and abstraction in actual real-world economies and economic theory in this period.

33 On the alliance between precision and control see Fowles' (1979) stimulating *The Tree*.

34 League tables and rankings can "encourage universities to take superficial actions to improve their positions rather than engaging in the more challenging task of enhancing teaching and student learning" (Foley and Goldstein, 2012, p. 42).

35 The problems here are manifold: the excessive use of student evaluations to assess quality; the emphasis on citations and impact factor; data manipulation; the incentive to publish articles and in 'hot' topics rather than books on 'unfashionable' topics in order to boost one's credibility or 'visibility'.

36 For example, the production of a book exhausts political economy's ideas of production, consumption and ownership (Lazzarato, 2004).

37 "No genuinely radical living for truth is possible in a university" (Nietzsche cited in MacIntyre, 1994, p. 35).

Bibliography

Akerlof, G. A. (1982). Labor Contracts as Partial Gift Exchange. *The Quarterly Journal of Economics*, *97*(4), 543–569. Retrieved from http://www.jstor.org/stable/1885099

Alesina, A., Baqir, R., and Easterly, W. (1997). Public Goods and Ethnic Divisions. *The Quarterly Journal of Economics*, *114*(4), 1243–1284. doi:10.3386/w6009

Alesina, A., Glaesar, E., and Sacerdote, B. (2001, October). *Why Doesn't the U.S. Have a Welfare State?*(Working paper No. 8524). Retrieved October 15, 2017, from NBER Working Paper Series. http://www.nber.org/papers/w8524

Anders, G. (2016). *Prometheanism: Technology, Digital Culture, and Human Obsolescence*(C. J. Müller, Trans.). London: Rowman & Littlefield International.

Arendt, H. (1998). *The Human Condition*. Chicago, IL: University of Chicago Press.

Arendt, H. (2006). *Between Past and Future: Eight Exercises in Political Thought*. New York: Penguin Books.

Bauman, Z., and Donskis, L. (2013). Consuming University: The New Sense of Meaninglessness and the Loss of Criteria. In *Moral Blindness: The Loss of Sensitivity in Liquid Modernity*. Cambridge, UK: Polity Press.

Bell, D. (1978). *The Cultural Contradictions of Capitalism*. New York: Basic Books.

Besley, T. J., and Ghatak, M. (2005). Competition and Incentives with Motivated Agents. *American Economic Review*, *95*(3), 616–636. doi:10.1257/0002828054201413

Besley, T. J., and Ghatak, M. (2014). *Solving Agency Problems: Intrinsic Motivation, Incentives, and Productivity*. Background paper for the World Development Report

2015. Retrieved from https://thred.devecon.org/papers/2014/2014-001_Ghatak_Solving_Agency_Problems.pdf

Biesta, G. (2008). Good Education in an Age of Measurement: On the Need to Reconnect with the Question of Purpose in Education. *Educational Assessment, Evaluation and Accountability, 21*(1), 33–46. doi:10.1007/s11092-008-9064-9

Bowles, S. (2017). *The Moral Economy: Why Good Incentives Are No Substitute for Good Citizens.* New Haven, CT: Yale University Press.

Brown, W. (2015). *Undoing the Demos: Neoliberalism's Stealth Revolution.* New York: MIT Press.

Burawoy, M. (2011, August 5). *Redefining the Public University: Developing an Analytical Framework* (Publication). Retrieved from http://publicsphere.ssrc.org/burawoy-redefining-the-public-university/

Calhoun, C. (2006). The University and the Public Good. *Thesis Eleven, 84*(1), 7–43. doi:10.1177/0725513606060516

Castree, N. (2010). Contract Research, Universities and the 'Knowledge Society': Back to the Future. In R. Imrie and C. Allen (Eds.), *The Knowledge Business: The Commodification of Urban and Housing Research* (pp. 221–240). Farnham, UK: Ashgate Publishing.

Cohen, G. A. (1991, May 21–23). *Incentives, Inequality, and Community.* Lecture presented at The Tanner Lectures on Human Values in Stanford University, Stanford.

Cohen, G. A. (2000). If You're an Egalitarian, How Come You're so Rich? *The Journal of Ethics, 4*(1/2), 1–26. Retrieved from http://www.jstor.org/stable/25115633

Cohen, G. A. (2008). *Rescuing Justice and Equality.* Cambridge, MA: Harvard University Press.

Collini, S. (2003, November 6). HiEdBiz. *London Review of Books, 25*(21), 3–9. Retrieved from https://www.lrb.co.uk/v25/n21/stefan-collini/hiedbiz.

Collini, S. (2011). From Robbins to McKinsey: The Dismantling of the Universities. *London Review of Books, 33*(16), 9–14.

Crawford, M. B. (2015). *The World Beyond Your Head: On Becoming an Individual in an Age of Distraction.* London: Penguin Books.

Crouch, C. (2015). The Wire. In C. Crouch (Ed.), *The Knowledge Corrupters: Hidden Consequences of the Financial Takeover of Public Life.* Cambridge, UK: Polity Press.

De Soto, H. (2000). *The Mystery of Capital: Why Capitalism Triumphs in the West and Fails Everywhere Else.* New York: Basic Books.

Dean, J. (2003). Why the Net is not a Public Sphere. *Constellations, 10*(1), 95–112. doi:10.1111/1467-8675.00315

Deresiewicz, W. (2015, September). The Neoliberal Arts: How College Sold its Soul to the Market. *Harper's Magazine.*

Foley, B., and Goldstein, H. (2012). *Measuring Success: League Tables in the Public Sector* (Rep.). London: The British Academy.

Foucault, M. (1991). Governmentality. In G. Burchell, C. Gordon, and P. Miller (Eds.), *The (Michel) Foucault Effect. Studies in Governmentality. With 2 Lectures by and An Interview with Michel Foucault.* London: Harvester Wheatsheaf.

Fowles, J. (1979). *The Tree.* Boston: Little, Brown.

Fraser, N. (1990). Rethinking the Public Sphere: A Contribution to the Critique of Actually Existing Democracy. *Social Text,* (25/26), 56–80. doi:10.2307/466240

Fraser, N., and Nash, K. (2014). *Transnationalizing the Public Sphere.* Cambridge, UK: Polity Press.

Gill, R. (2016). Breaking the Silence: The Hidden Injuries of Neo-Liberal Academia. *Feministische Studien, 34*(1), 39–55. doi:10.1515/fs-2016-0105

Godbout, J. T., and Caille, A. (2014). *The World of the Gift*. Montréal: McGill-Queens University Press.

Gorz, A. (2010). *The Immaterial: Knowledge, Value and Capital* (C. Turner, Trans.). London: Seagull Books.

Graeber, D. (2007, January 1). Army of Altruists: On the Alienated Right to Do Good. *Harpers Magazine.*

Graeber, D. (2014). Anthropology and the Rise of the Professional-managerial Class. *HAU: Journal of Ethnographic Theory, 4*(3), 73–88. doi:10.14318/hau4.3.007

Graeber, D. (2015). *The Utopia of Rules: On Technology, Stupidity, and the Secret Joys of Bureaucracy*. Brooklyn: Melville House.

Hacking, I. (2010). *The Taming of Chance*. Cambridge, UK: Cambridge University Press.

Haldane, A. G. (2015, February 17). *Growing, Fast and Slow*. Speech presented in University of East Anglia, Norwich.

Hénaff, M. (2010). *The Price of Truth, Gift, Money and Philosophy* (J. Morhange and A. Feenberg-Dibon, Trans.). Stanford, CA: Stanford University Press.

Ignatieff, M. (1994). *The Needs of Strangers*. London: Vintage.

Illich, I. (1978). *Toward a History of Needs*. New York: Pantheon Books

Illich, I. (1991, September 23). *Text and University – On the Idea and History of a Unique Institution*. Address presented at Twentieth Anniversary of the Founding of the University of Bremen in Bremen City Hall, Bremen. Available at: http://www.davidtinapple.com/illich/1991_text_and_university.PDF

Illich, I. (1995). Guarding the Eye in the Age of Show. *RES: Anthropology and Aesthetics, (28)*, 47–61. Retrieved from http://www.jstor.org/stable/20166929

Illich, I. (1996). *In the Vineyard of the Text: A Commentary to Hughs Didascalicon*. Chicago, IL: University of Chicago Press.

Judt, T. (2011). *Ill Fares the Land: A Treatise on our Present Discontents*. London: Penguin.

Juvin, H. (2010). *The Coming of the Body*. London: Verso.

Kluge, A., and Negt, O. (2014). *History and obstinacy* (D. Fore, Ed.; R. Langston, Trans.). New York: Zone Books.

Kraus, K. (2013). *The Kraus Project: Essays by Karl Kraus* (J. Franzen, Trans.). London: Fourth Estate.

Lazzarato, M. (2004). European Cultural Tradition and the New Forms of Production and Circulation of Knowledge. *Multitudes : une revue trimestrielle, politique, artistique et culturelle*, n. 16 Jan.

Le Grand, J. (2001). *The Provision of Health Care: Is the Public Sector Ethically Superior to the Private Sector?* London: LSE Health and Social Care, London School of Economics and Political Science.

Le Grand, J. (2013). *Motivation, Agency, and Public Policy: Of Knights and Knaves, Pawns and Queens*. Oxford: Oxford University Press.

MacIntyre, A. C. (1994). *Three Rival Versions of Moral Enquiry: Encyclopaedia, Genealogy, and Tradition*. Notre Dame, IN: University of Notre Dame Press.

MacIntyre, A. C., and Dunne, J. (2002). Alasdair MacIntyre on Education: In Dialogue with Joseph Dunne. *Journal of the Philosophy of Education, 36*(1), 1–19. doi:10.1111/1467-9752.00256

Marcuse, H. (2009). The Affirmative Character of Culture. In J. J. Shapiro (Trans.), *Negations: Essays in Critical Theory*. London: MayFlyBooks.

Marquand, D. (2005). *Decline of the Public: The Hollowing-out of Citizenship*. Cambridge, UK: Polity Press.

Marquand, D. (2015). *Mammon's Kingdom: An Essay on Britain, Now*. London, UK: Penguin Books Limited.

Merrifield, A. (2017). *Amateur: The Pleasures of Doing What you Love*. London: Verso.

Merton, T. (1977). *Raids on the Unspeakable*. London: Burns & Oates.

Miller, P., and O'Leary, T. (1987). Accounting and the Construction of the Governable Person. *Accounting, the Social and the Political, 12*(3), 235–265.

Miller, P., and Power, M. (2013). Accounting, Organizing, and Economizing: Connecting Accounting Research and Organization Theory. *The Academy of Management Annals, 7*(1), 557–605. doi:10.1080/19416520.2013.783668

Mills, C. W. (2001). *Letters and Autobiographical Writings* (P. Mills and K. Mills, Eds.). Berkeley, CA: University of California Press.

Mills, C. W. (2008). *The Politics of Truth: Selected Writings of C. Wright Mills* (J. H. Summers, Ed.). Oxford: Oxford University Press.

Minogue, K. (2005). *The Concept of a University*. New Brunswick, NJ: Transaction.

Mirowski, P. (2014). *Never Let a Serious Crisis go to Waste: How Neoliberalism Survived the Financial Meltdown*. London: Verso.

Morrish, L. (2015, November 26). *Raising the Bar: The Metric Tide That Sinks All Boats*. Retrieved October 16, 2017, from https://academicirregularities.wordpress.com/2015/11/26/raising-the-bar-the-metric-tide-that-sinks-all-boats/

Nietzsche, F. W. (2016). *Anti-education: On the Future of our Educational Institutions*. New York: New York Review Books.

Oakeshott, M. J. (2002). The Idea of a University. In *The Voice of Liberal Learning*. Indianapolis, IN: Liberty Fund.

O'Donovan, O., and O'Donovan, J. L. (2004). The Loss of a Sense of Place. In *Bonds of Imperfection: Christian Politics, Past and Present*. Grand Rapids, MI: Eerdmans.

O'Neill, O. (2010). *A Question of Trust*. Cambridge, UK: Cambridge University Press.

Paoli, G. (2013). *Demotivational Training* (V. Stone, Trans.). LBC Books.

Pieper, J. (2009). *Leisure: The Basis of Culture*. San Francisco, CA: Ignatius Press.

Polanyi, K. (2014). *The Great Transformation: The Political and Economic Origins of Our Time*. Boston: Beacon Press.

Power, M. (2000). The Audit Society – Second Thoughts. *International Journal of Auditing, 4*(1), 111–119. doi:10.1111/1099-1123.00306

Power, M. (2004). Counting, Control and Calculation: Reflections on Measuring and Management. *Human Relations, 57*(6), 765–783. doi:10.1177/0018726704044955

Ray, D., Ghosh, P., and Mookherjee, D. (2000). Credit Rationing in Developing Countries: An Overview of the Theory. In D. Mookherjee and D. Ray (Eds.), *A Reader in Development Economics* (pp. 283–301). London: Blackwell.

Reitter, P., and Wellmon, C. (2015). How the Philologist Became a Physician of Modernity: Nietzsches Lectures on German Education. *Representations, 131*(1), 68–104. doi:10.1525/rep.2015.131.1.68

Ringer, F. K. (1990). *The Decline of the German Mandarins: The German Academic Community, 1890–1933*. Hanover: University Press of New England.

Rogers, K. (Ed.). (1997). Early Modern Era. In *Self-interest: An Anthology of Philosophical Perspectives*. New York: Routledge.

Rothschild, E. (2013). *Economic Sentiments Adam Smith, Condorcet, and the Enlightenment*. Cumberland: Harvard University Press.

Ruskin, J. (1967). *"Unto This Last"*: *Four Essays on the First Principles of Political Economy*. Lincoln: University of Nebraska Press.

Russell, B. (2004). *In Praise of Idleness and Other Essays*. London: Routledge.

Said, E. W. (1994). *Representations of the Intellectual: the 1993 Reith Lectures*. London: Vintage.

Scott, J. C. (2008). *Seeing Like a State: How Certain Schemes to Improve the Human Condition have Failed*. New Haven, CT: Yale University Press.

Sennett, R. (1977). *The Fall of Public Man*. Cambridge, UK: Cambridge University Press.

Solow, R. (1980). On Theories of Unemployment. *American Economic Review*, *70*(1), 1–11.

Steiner, G. (1998). *Errata: An Examined Life*. New Haven, CT: Yale University Press.

Taylor, C. (1997). *Philosophical Arguments*. Cambridge, MA: Harvard University Press.

Taylor, C. (2007). *Modern Social Imaginaries*. Durham: Duke University Press.

Thompson, E. P. (1993). *Customs in Common*. London: Penguin.

Titmuss, R. M. (1997). *The Gift Relationship: From Human Blood to Social Policy* (A. Oakley, Ed.). New York: The New Press.

Turkle, S. (2008). Always-On/Always-On-You: The Tethered Self. In J. E. Katz (Ed.), *Handbook of Mobile Communication Studies*. Cambridge, MA: MIT Press.

UK Govt. (2010). *Securing a Sustainable Future for Higher Education* (Rep.). UK Govt. Retrieved from http://www.educationengland.org.uk/documents/pdfs/2010-browne-report.pdf

Wellmon, C. (2017). Whatever Happened to General Education? *The Hedgehog Review: Critical Reflections on Contemporary Culture*, *19*(1). Retrieved October 15, 2017, from http://iasc-culture.org/THR/THR_article_2017_Spring_Wellmon.php

Williams, R. (2000). *Lost Icons: Reflections on Cultural Bereavement*. London: T & T Clark.

Wright, K. (2001). Generosity vs. Altruism: Philanthropy and Charity in the United States and United Kingdom. *Voluntas: International Journal of Voluntary and Nonprofit Organizations*, *12*(4), 399–416.

8 Climate change and ethics[1]

All the fine winds gone
And this sweet world is so much older
Animals pull the night around their shoulders
Flowers fall to their naked knees.

(Cave, 2016)

Time is the essential ingredient but in the modern world there is no time.

(Carson, 2002, p. 6)

8.0 Introduction

We live in a world beset by a number of inter-related problems, contradictions and crises: from financial and economic crises to the crisis of the environment and the university; from problems related to work and meaning to problems relating to the decline of the public sector ethos and the hollowing out of individuality. The main thesis of this book is that underlying those features of our world is the problem of the social or relationality. Market economies and economic theory work in tandem to undermine the possibility of a relational perspective.

In this chapter I want to focus on what is arguably the most important of these crises, the imminent threat posed by climate change. Of course, the problem is in many crucial respects related to the other topics analysed in this book. Climate change is intimately connected to a contrived scarcity and the imperative of growth; to commodification and to our understanding of time. Climate change is the result of global inequalities[2]; and its consequences will impact people unequally. It is inextricably bound to the false idea of the autonomous individual whose own nature is utterly distinct from that of Nature. In fact, the externalization of 'Nature' is precisely what has allowed us to quantify, measure, domesticate, rationally control and commoditize it without realizing that because we are in fact part of nature our destructive habits will ultimately impact our own lives and those of future generations.

From the outset we are faced with the great difficulty of how we are to think and talk about climate change since there are obviously technological, political, legal, economic, scientific and ethical dimensions to the problem. What kind of language[3] *is* available to us, then? It is hard *not* to talk in terms of an irreversible loss, a great 'thinning out' (McCarthy, 2015), homelessness,[4] and possible catastrophe.[5] Our language is haunted not just by the sense of absences and disappearances, but also by the foreboding that we are irrevocably hurtling towards an unprecedented future, a broken world.

If we are nearing a point of rupture, a fundamental break in human history, are there any modes of thought that would allow us to come to terms with the end of nature?[6] Later on in this chapter I will suggest that in addition to recovering a sense of the joy, wonder, beauty and abundance of nature (McCarthy, 2015) a more relational understanding of "our complex entanglements with collective life, history and the universe" (Scranton, 2015, p. 94) might point us to a way forward.

Before that, however, I briefly summarize the magnitude of the problem we're facing (section 1) since the scientific facts establish the horizons within which ethical, economic and political thinking takes place. In the following section I briefly discuss some of the ways in which we think about the problem of climate change. Section 3 then looks at the standard economic evaluative approach to the problem (i.e. utilitarianism) and its limitations. Taking on board those limitations I next explore the idea that the recovery of a relational perspective offers the prospect of a more sophisticated approach to climate change (section 4). A key part of that relational approach includes thinking about our interactions with future generations in an appropriate way and so I briefly touch upon this theme as well. Section 5 concludes with some final thoughts about the possible intertwining of ecological and capitalist crises.

8.1   The scale of the problem

It is now widely recognized that the degradation of the environment represents a potentially severe threat to human and non-human life. Its manifestations are manifold: the depletion of the ozone layer, global warming, the acidification of the oceans, air pollution, soil erosion,[7] the shrinking of Arctic sea ice, a reduction in biodiversity[8] and the contamination of ground water supplies by toxic pollutants. It is also now abundantly clear that accelerated economic activity (industrial production, urbanization and intensive farming) are the major causes of these changes.

For the purposes of this chapter I am only focusing on the global warming aspect of the looming environmental crisis, though in reality the other, interrelated issues are of crucial importance as well.

The change in temperature itself depends on, amongst other things, the level of greenhouse gasses (GHGs) in the atmosphere (in particular, carbon dioxide) and those levels, in turn, depend on both how much is released into the atmosphere and how much is absorbed (by forests and the seas).[9] In reality we face a cascade of uncertainties when it comes to climate change since we are not sure how fast emissions will increase under the various projected scenarios of economic and technological development or what, precisely, changes in the level of emissions mean for changes in temperature. Furthermore, there is some uncertainty about the extent to which those temperature changes generate 'damages'.[10]

If we look at trends in world CO_2 concentration levels we see that they were at 280 ppm (parts per million) in 1769 and just over 400 ppm now. That represents a level of concentration that has probably not been witnessed for at least 800,000 years (and possibly for three million years). Equally alarming, CO_2 emissions over that period have not risen by more than 30 ppm over any thousand-year period. In our own lifetime we have seen them rise by that much in just seventeen years (Weitzman, 2009). The figures for methane, a more powerful GHG, are as worrying.

If we look more generally to GHGs – which include CO_2 but also nitrous oxide and methane amongst others – and factor them in our evaluation, then the current CO_2 level can be thought to be equivalent to 440 ppm. It is worth noting that global emissions have been increasing at the rate of 2.6 percent every year over the last century *despite* reductions in carbon intensity (i.e. 'decarbonization') of 1.1 percent per year over the same period (Nordhaus, 2015). Which is another way of saying that efficiency gains are not coming at a quick enough pace.

If CO_2 stabilizes at 450 ppm temperatures are expected to rise, on average, anywhere between 1 and 3.8 degrees Celsius, with 90 percent confidence.[11] It is worth emphasizing that these are average figures with the reality for different communities/countries likely to be a lot more varied. Also, since this is an *average* figure, and because the oceans are cooler than the land, we should expect land temperatures to be around one degree warmer than the average figure cited.

If we take 'moderate' steps to curtail emissions temperatures may still rise by two to three degrees Celsius. Even then, there is the possibility that things will turn out to be significantly worse. The Intergovernmental Panel on Climate Change (IPCC, 2008) also states that there is a five per cent chance that temperatures will increase by more than 8 degrees and a 1 to 2 percentage chance that they will do so by more than 10 degrees Celsius.[12]

These figures highlight the fact that we're not even sure of the magnitude of changes in temperature because our estimates are based on observed data and extrapolation, not on the occurrence of rare events. There may be feedback loops that lead to non-linearity. Or 'thresholds', which mean that the impact is only linear in temperature increases over some range. In that case extrapolation is not justified.

If we stabilize at 550ppm then temperatures are likely to rise by anywhere in the region of 1.5–5.2 degrees Celsius (again, with 90 percent confidence). The bad news is that if current trends persist (BAU-business as usual) we can expect levels of up to 750 ppm by 2100[13] (with mean temperatures rising by at least 2.2 degrees, and possibly by up to 6 degrees). CO_2 emissions, unlike methane, can remain in the air, on average, for 50–100 years, so even a drastic reduction now means we'd still see increases on our current levels. The real question, then, is not whether levels will go beyond 430 ppm but by *how much* and how quickly.

To highlight just how late we might already be the following estimates should be noted: if emissions fall by 70 percent (or by the greater amount, 85 percent) by 2050 then there's still a 16–43 percent chance (or a 9–26 percent chance for the greater reductions) that world average temperatures will rise by more than 2 degrees Celsius with significant impacts on our lives (Mackay, 2013). The bleak prospects for transition is reaffirmed by Anderson and Bows (2010) who state that even with global annual reductions of 10 percent each year (over the period 2020–2040) there will still be a 50 percent chance that temperatures will increase by 2 degrees – a figure now considered to be dangerous/extremely dangerous. Given we may be locked into some emissions over this period (because of deforestation and the demands on food production) we may actually need a *global* reduction in energy-related emissions of 10–20 percent every year for the next two decades.

Climate change, then, is a hugely complex phenomenon. What makes it such a difficult issue to grapple with stems, in part, from the science underlying it. The sheer scale of its effects, and the uncertainty associated with many of them, means tackling the problem requires collective rather than individual decisions-making. Furthermore, since climate change involves externalities with respect to both current and future generations it is hard to see how decentralized decisions (the market) can provide a solution. And finally, climate change will lead to the deaths of large numbers of human and non-human beings and not just economic damage. Again, it is not clear that markets are particularly good at valuing lives (Aldred, 2010).

Overall, then, the scientific facts coupled with the fact that we may be economically and technologically locked into a high-carbon infrastructure for some time yet[14] point to the unlikelihood of us avoiding significant or even catastrophic damage from climate change. Market economies, with their short-term perspective and their reliance on cheap fossil fuels, have been at the heart of the problem. But if that's true, are there any alternative approaches to understanding climate change (beyond economics) and any alternative ways to prevent disastrous climate change (beyond market economies)? In the following two sections I try and answer those questions.

8.2 Ways of approaching

At the very heart of the environmental problem is, I contend, a degree of confusion over exactly what *type* of problem it is. That confusion results, in its turn, in us being drawn to different types of solutions. For example, if technology (and in particular, the technologies of producing energy) is at the root of the problem then maybe we need a technological fix: geoengineering or more efficient technologies; or an understanding of technology and design not as "challenging nature" (Heidegger, 2008), but, rather, as a way of maintaining and taking care of it. It follows that a move to electricity generated by using low-carbon technologies or fuels rather than coal can have significant benefits (Nordhaus, 2015).

Alternatively, it might be put forward that politics is the central component of any binding solution. The problem, in this reading, is political: the lack of well-defined property rights[15] or supra-national legal institutions to enforce policies. Ultimately, the uneven global distribution of political power can determine the distribution and control of energy and, therefore, the likely extent of future emissions and climate change.

Economists, of course, tend to think that the main issue is that there is a colossal economic failure – an externality that leads to an inefficient allocation of resources. However, if market economies are self-correcting, as many of its advocates maintain them to be, then the problem will be solved on its own, via prices and incentives and the impetus they give to discovery, innovation, improvements in efficiency, and substitutability. Here, it would seem, the only scope for policy intervention is the strengthening of market forces through carbon taxes or cap-and-trade.

Climate policy is often explicitly guided by the notion that through cost-benefit analysis (CBA) we can determine the efficient level of pollution, the point at which the marginal costs of abatement are just equal to the marginal 'damages' caused by it. Policies such as 'cap and trade' or 'carbon taxes' then act as an incentive to consumers and producers to get us to the desired, efficient level. But built into that approach are a number of highly contested assumptions – shared by Utilitarianism (see below) – that make us question whether climate policy is based on firm foundations.

Firstly, it assumes we can put a value to the various kinds of disparate 'damages' (namely: to health, life,[16] and the erosion of eco-systems and biodiversity). Prices, unreasonably, reduce all particular values to one abstract, monetary value when in fact 'goods' may not be substitutable because "they meet quite distinct dimensions of human well-being" (O'Neill, 2007, p. 105).

Secondly, the approach assumes away radical uncertainty[17] and the possibility that economic agents have less than perfect information about the damages (Hodgson, 2013). Prices only reflect marginal values under perfect market conditions. How, though, do people value environmental goods if there is no market for them? One way out of this quandary is to directly ask people how much they actually value the environmental good (such as clean air, the aesthetic value of woodlands etc.). Such an approach may not be very helpful, though, because in actual surveys individuals typically refuse to put a price on nature. It doesn't get us very far in resolving the often very profound dilemmas and trade-offs involved in our choices (Nussbaum, 2000). Furthermore, since climate policy/change is likely to result in *non-marginal* changes it is not clear if market prices are what we are after.

Thirdly, the approach assumes we can aggregate these values across individuals for any one generation. This is equivalent to determining the distribution of costs and benefits or, in other words, the distribution of emission permits in a 'cap and trade policy', across countries and firms. Fourthly, it assumes we have a sound way of discounting the 'damages' inflicted on future generations. Prices, including the discount rate are, however, only a reflection of the way in which *we*, the current generation, relatively value things.

Fifthly, even if we could accurately assess damages/costs and work out a fair basis for allocating carbon credits, we'd still be left with the political problem of whether an international[18] regime exists to enforce the policies.

Given what was said above, market economies (and prices) do not provide a good way of thinking about value when it comes to climate change. They distort the way in which we ought to relate to other human and non-human beings, to beauty and to diversity; they can ignore considerations of long-term (and non-marginal) import; and there is no market contract with future generations that might result in efficient exchanges since future generations do not, quite obviously, currently exist.

In summary, climate change and climate change policies will impact the shape of the world we live in, the quality or goodness of our lives, and the distribution of that goodness across populations and over time. Market economies only address questions of goodness and its distribution – if at all – in a particularly narrow fashion.

Individuals, through their self-interested actions, cause serious harm to others with relatively little benefit to others (even though if not intended) when an alternative course of action was possible. This suggests that they have a responsibility not to harm others. Alternatively, it could mean they have a private duty to promote overall goodness (which is a rough definition of utilitarianism). More realistically, it might be thought they are under an obligation to endorse their government's public duty to promote overall goodness (Broome, 2012).

The standard (ideal) approach to evaluating the impact of projects and climate change policy is usually some version of utilitarianism – or a derivative of it (such as CBA). In fact, if we had good information in the case of the former we might be tempted to dismiss CBA altogether, problematic as it is, and simply rely on the ideal approach, utilitarianism. In what follows, however, I suggest that utilitarianism is equally problematic – and for similar reasons.

8.3   Utilitarianism

Utilitarianism, it has often been said, is the dominant framework guiding public policy (Wiggins, 2009). Although it has undergone some modifications over time (notably in terms of what is meant by utility) the fundamental structure, if not the content, of the doctrine remains intact. Following Amartya Sen (1979) we can factor utilitarianism into three components for analytical convenience: consequentialism, welfarism and sum-ranking.

Consequentialism requires that the impact of an act/project/policy should be assessed in terms of its consequences (and only its consequences). Its intuitive appeal seems to rest on the apparent irrationality of not wanting the best overall state of affairs to attain. However, it is countered that we can and often do have particular duties and not just the impersonal duty to bring about the best state of affairs (see section 4). The maximization of overall 'goodness' can, therefore, have a place in morality even though it is not the whole of morality. Giving weight to considerations of justice – not to harm anyone, for example – or to fairness can undercut the "spellbinding force" (Foot, 1983, p. 274) of consequentialism. Consequentialism unreasonably rules out us paying attention both to things we think are 'intrinsically' right as well as to values, processes and relations that we have reason to value independently of their consequences.[19] In some (but not all) circumstances the right action does not necessarily have to maximize overall goodness (Smart and Williams, 2008).

Welfarism places further restrictions on our evaluative stance by requiring that the only consequences of any relevance are those associated with welfare. To use Sen's terminology: utility/welfare is the relevant 'evaluative space' (or the 'informational basis' for our theory)

The criticism of this view are well known (Sen and Williams, 2010). First, why should non-welfare information be excluded when doing so might result in us ignoring important features of a situation, such as the infringements of a person's rights (Sen, 1979)? Furthermore, to maintain that welfare is the informational foundation of our evaluations is to ignore agency issues, our ability to form goals (Sen, 1985). Welfare assessments focus on what we actually achieve neglecting the important consideration of our freedom to achieve. Agency freedom cannot be reduced to welfare, even though it might indeed contribute to our welfare.[20]

Second, even if we accept utility/welfare as the only basis of our evaluative judgements we might still be left wondering what, precisely, we mean by that word, 'utility'. For example, is utility happiness or pleasure (and are these of one or many kinds?)? Is it a mental state or does it denote something more objective, such as a determinate ethical way of life?

Or is it, as economic theory suggests, actually only a formal and not a substantive concept? If so, utility is a mere numerical representation of an individual's underlying preferences (Broome, 1999) and isn't, therefore, of much use in making *evaluative* judgements. Utility gets uncoupled from substantive notions of goodness and welfare.

Third, under the utilitarian viewpoint the different arguments in a utility function are, ultimately, commensurate with one another. Put in other words, any individual can aggregate across various 'goods' by comparing them to get to some overall level of utility. This, however, ignores that some values may be incommensurable with one another and that there are differing views on the appropriate way to value different things, depending on our ideals, social relations and identity, our sense of solidarity, the context of our choices and our conceptions of the self (Beckerman and Pasek, 1997). Relying exclusively on an abstract notion of welfare rules out pluralistic modes of evaluation.

Fourth, do individuals truly understand or appreciate the value of the environment?[21] If our notion of utility is the subjective one of desire-satisfaction (rather than an objective-list notion) then it could be argued that a policy that leads to the satisfaction of someone's desires – no matter what they are – should count as an enhancement of their well-being. But that seems deeply problematic. What if *everyone* values economic growth and the lifestyle of high-consumption more than the environmental costs of it? It is not obvious under utilitarianism that such preferences are necessarily irrational or that they should be rejected, since the satisfaction of those preferences might be consistent with the maximization of overall goodness.

It seems that utilitarianism does not adequately take account of our values, such as freedom, beauty, or respect for the environment. It was argued that because the utilitarian view relies on desire-satisfaction it may fail to give due consideration to these values and to what they mean in the context of a good human life. Our relation to the world around us and how we value our relationships to human and non-human beings cannot be reduced to an abstract notion such as 'welfare' or 'utility'. Ultimately, even an informed-desire account of utility is more focused on the intensity of preferences and says, therefore, little about the reasons for our preferences or our judgements of value (Keat, 1997).

The third component of utilitarianism, the principle of sum-ranking, maintains that the right action/policy is one that maximize the sum of utilities since the best overall outcome or state of affairs is one in which the aggregate level of utility/welfare is maximized.

This feature of utilitarianism is no less problematic than the other two.[22] The first thing to note is that in any attempt to aggregate across individuals we have to assume that individual levels of well-being *can*, in fact, be compared. And that, itself, assumes that the policy maker (the social planner) knows in advance what individuals' preferences are. However, in the case of climate change (an inter-generational problem) we may only have a rough idea of how many people will exist in the future, let alone what the shape of their preference functions might be!

The main criticism of sum-ranking revolves around its serious neglect of distributional concerns. To try and elaborate upon this consider Larry Summers' infamous memo (Hausman and McPherson, 2010). In the memo he argues that people in rich, advanced countries value clean air more than additional units of money (compared to the relative valuations of those in poor, less-developed countries). The costs of marginal increases in pollution (in terms of foregone wages due to ill-health) are relatively low in the latter as well. According to economic logic a shift of 'dirty industries' from the rich to the poorer countries would lead to a Pareto improvement since at least one party (country) is made better-off without the other being made any worse-off. The Pareto principle is an aggregating principle that is not fundamentally concerned about the distribution of welfare, the inequality between people (or in this case, countries).

The utilitarian aggregating principle, sum-ranking, is even more oblivious of distributional concerns. If resources or production are reallocated in such a way that the rich countries (already at a high level of welfare) are made a *lot* better off at the expense of the poor (those at a low level of welfare) then utilitarianism would endorse such a change if the *overall* level of welfare is increased. The welfare or rights of certain groups (the poor) can be sacrificed if it serves the greater good.

The standard utilitarian approach, it has to be said, deals with these complexities in an unsatisfactory way, which is to say that it does so by ignoring them! (Roemer, 2010). The approach typically assumes that each generation is represented by a single agent.[23] This at once cuts off all discussions over the very real and significant intra-temporal conflicts between individuals in any given country as well as over questions about distribution between countries.

Climate change and climate change policy will have impacts not just on those people who are alive now but also on future generations. Seen in this light the aggregation problem is how to maximize inter-temporal social welfare and that involves an assessment of whether (and to what extent) we should discount the utility of future generations.[24]

The choice of the discount rate cannot be made simply on technical grounds. It is perfectly understandable that *individuals* would want to discount future welfare, just as it is that society should discount future *commodities*, but the idea that society should discount future welfare is highly problematic (Beckerman and Hepburn, 2007). In fact, Frank Ramsey (1978), the distinguished economist, wrote: "Discounting is a practice which is ethically indefensible and arises merely from weakness of the imagination" (p. 261). Furthermore, in his influential review of climate change Stern (2006) explicitly states that ethics and value judgements play a role in evaluating not only the aggregation of utilities across individuals at any one given point in time, but also in the aggregation of them across generations.

Stern tends to favour a discount rate which is close to 1, which means that in effect people in the future are not discriminated against in our policy analysis simply because they are born much later. However, having said that, it should be noted that questions surrounding the discount rate continue to be a point of fierce contention between economists and philosophers.

How we aggregate welfare, weigh up lives, is a matter of choice, reflection and ethical judgement. For example, we could quite conceivably argue that instead of unreservedly trying to maximize overall inter-temporal welfare we should try and maximize it subject to the constraint that no single generation slips below some adequately defined cut-off level of welfare. Such an ethic, a max/min strategy, can justifiably be called a 'sustainable' approach to the environment problem (Anand and Sen, 2000). Sustainability offers a particular critique of utilitarianism on the grounds of its relentless pursuit of maximizing overall goodness. Other critiques (addressed in chapter 9) focus on the fact that the utilitarian approach assumes we relate to other people in an impartial way. In section 4, I'll return to the drawbacks of doing so. But for now I want to return to another difficulty associated with the utilitarian approach to climate change.

As a result of our current choices of technology, projects, consumption and lifestyles some people in the future will exist who otherwise wouldn't have existed and, conversely, some people who might have existed will not. The distinction between this point and the ones made above is this: there our concern was over the relative weights (discount rates) assigned to members in a *given* series. The point being raised now, on the other hand, is that there may not be a given series.[25]

The question that John Broome (2005) raises, then, is this: should we take into account the well-being of such people in our evaluation of policies/technologies? There may be technical reasons that incline us to think that we shouldn't, namely, the sheer degree of complexity added to our standard utilitarian approach in doing so.[26] But even if we can second-guess in this regard, should we, *ought* we to, include the well-being of such people in our utilitarian evaluation of states of affairs? Broome argues, plausibly, that we ought to be concerned about extreme levels of well-being but beyond that we should be neutral to a whole range of individual well-being when it comes to such future people.

If the weak and strong intuitions of neutrality are not valid, however, we are left with an unpalatable conclusion (Broome, 2016). Global warming will result in the deaths and suffering of many people and we all agree that that is an unequivocally bad thing. But Broome's point is that though these deaths will directly affect the world's population they will not alter the *timeless* population.

Global warming will *indirectly* alter the timeless population: some people who otherwise would have existed in the future will now not do so as a result of climate change (for example, if a couple is killed as a result of global warming the kids they might have had (and all the possible progeny across the generations) will not exist). Similarly, some people will exist in the future who otherwise wouldn't have. Should we take into account the 'value of population', by which is meant the taking into consideration of all these additions and subtractions to the population in the evaluation of a states of affairs? If we are not neutral and we do in fact do so, it is quite conceivable that this value outweighs the disvalue of all the killing that results from climate change. The perverse conclusion of that train of thought is that global warming is, overall, not necessarily a bad thing, even though it may lead to the killing of millions of people!

8.4   Taking care and partiality

In the first part of this chapter I claimed that we stand in a unique relation to future generations and to the environment. Never before have our choices had such an immense potential for altering the future. In fact, over the last two centuries our choices of technology, lifestyles and values have led to the very real possibility that the future of human and non-human life is threatened, or at least seriously impaired. If so much is true, we need a radically new form of ethical thinking since the older versions never countenanced this enlarged scope for human action[27] (Jonas, 1985).

But does the mere awareness of the potentially disastrous consequences of our actions ground our responsibilities (to other people and to nature)? Why should we, the current generation, sacrifice our welfare for people we do not know or who may not even exist in the future? 'We owe it to them', we might say, even though we don't know who the 'them' is, how many of them there will be or, indeed, what their desires and goals will be; and even though they have never done anything for us!

So, is the utilitarian approach psychologically plausible?[28] Why should we *care* about the welfare of other people (current or future generations)? Utilitarianism depends on an abstract notion of welfare and on us taking or endorsing an impersonal, impartial approach to the welfare of other people. For both of those reasons it is unlikely to motivate us to taking appropriate actions – especially when most of our life is structured by the relentless pursuit of self-interest in our economic interactions.

Are there alternative ways, then, of thinking of this problem? Can we think, perhaps, of future generations having rights (to clean air, say) and does that translate into a set of corresponding obligations on our behalf? I'm not sure if we can meaningfully talk about people's rights or of contractual relations with them when they're not around to make claims on us. It is not easy to imagine what type of political arrangements we might conceive to ensure that they have some form of current representation.

I think we need to shift our focus by thinking more seriously about values and a relational view of ethics, as well as the set of supporting institutions and culture that make that possible (Keat, 1994). To ask what grounds our obligations to future generations is not the same as asking the difficult question of the precise *extent* of those obligations. It is, instead, to ask whether we have, at the very minimum, the *fundamental* obligation to ensure that there will be people around like us, with the same responsibilities to people who represent *their* future generations

I said 'at the very minimum' for a reason. It is appealing to believe that we have an obligation to ensure that future generations have, like us, the right to form their own goals and preferences. It is important to realize that those future people cannot do that if they do not exist in the first place or if there is nothing left of the environment for *them* to pass on. But this takes us back to an abstract or 'thin' notion of relationality since what is valued is the abstract freedom/right to form goals when what we want is the continuation of specific things of value (nature, art) and *particular* human ways of relating to the world and to other human and non-human beings.

A genuinely relational view, which is neither purely subjective or objective (impartial) would, therefore, recognize that we have specific attachments to identities, practices, projects, values and ways of being that cannot be subsumed under abstract categories such as 'the good' or 'welfare' (Wolf, 1999). We are not committed, therefore, to maximizing some abstract, universal value ('the good',[29] say). Instead, we can be moved to conserve the *particular thing* (art object, nature) that bears value rather than to maximize abstract 'value' *per se*. Alternatively, I can reasonably value something (a specific place, object or person) because of its special relation to me. That 'something' is inextricably woven into the social, cultural and intellectual *habitus* to which we[30] belong (Cohen, 2013).

Unlike the impartial, bureaucratic (and 'timeless') utilitarian view this partial but reasonable view of morality entails "patterns of engagement, and forms of mutual familiarity, attachment and regard developed over time" (Scheffler, 2012, p. 59).[31] We have specific obligations (to particular people, places and things) depending on who or what they are. This non-reductive and non-calculative deontic approach is deeply embedded, therefore, in a relational structure and stands in stark contrast to utilitarianism (Wallace, 2012, 2013).

One way out of the impasse, then, would be to imagine ourselves as part of a continuous moral community (Baier, 2012). Here we are, part of the human chain, our lives lived between the past and the future. We stand in an asymmetric relation to future generations, a relation in which they are dependent on us just as we, too, were and are dependent on others before us.

Perhaps it is this system of inter-relations, of mutual dependencies, that offers the way forward. Instead of thinking of ourselves as autonomous, self-interested utility maximizers (a view that is fostered by market economies) or as impersonal, impartial agents (as the utilitarian view demands) it would make more sense to think of ourselves as 'rational dependent animals' (MacIntyre, 2011) who form and are formed by diverse relations of care. This would entail thinking of our relation to the environment and to future generations in terms of stewardship (Arrow, 2004): an obligation to preserve, regenerate and renew that which we didn't ourselves generate, but simply inherited.

To do so would also mean thinking about language again, about what we mean when we use words like 'resource' (Berry, 2010) and how, therefore, a particular understanding (or lack of understanding) of nature is *produced*. It would also mean an acute awareness of the fact that we're nearly out of time to act.

8.5   Conclusion

In this chapter we have seen that both the theory economists typically use to assess climate change (utilitarianism) and market economies do not adequately address the looming environmental crisis. In both cases these inadequacies largely stem from a distortion of our relationships to places, people and other living beings.

In recent times some economists have argued that the environmental problem is actually a result of markets not working properly and that an extension of them (and/or market norms) would therefore be greatly beneficial (Smith, 2007). It follows that well-defined property rights over environmental goods (or the establishment of consumers' willingness to pay for them) and cap-and-trade policies are a big part of the solution.

As we have seen, however, this ignores the reality of distributional concerns (if the rich are more willing to pay for clean air is that morally acceptable?); it ignores that future generations and non-human beings cannot express their 'preferences' through a price mechanism (O'Neill, 2017a). More generally, individuals may not deliberate over how important environmental goods are and even if they do it is questionable whether they have good information on the consequences of their actions – particularly given the role of uncertainty in climate change dynamics. Even then, individual behaviour in markets may suffer from myopia. But even if it doesn't, there is the distinct possibility that all economic agents may simply prefer material wealth and high-energy consumption to environmental goods.

Part of the problem, I would argue, is that we continue to fail to make the distinction between 'market economies' (whose description is modeled as the exchange of commodities in economic theory) and actually existing markets under capitalism.[32] In the former there is little account of history/time, power relations, debt, culture, ideology or uncertainty (Hutton, 2001).

Seen in this light the problem of climate change is best understood not as a result of market failures but of the consequence of the historically specific ways in which capitalism 'produces nature' (i.e. putting human and non-human natures to work). Part of this process[33] involves an 'externalization' or objectification of 'Nature' that allows for its measurement and commodification – and it is impossible to get to grips with that process unless one factors in the role of the law, capitalist notions of property, surveying, mapping and a dualistic[34] worldview in the production of nature.

Since the 1980s, as already stated, there has been an intensification of the subsumption of nature to capital with the commodification, marketization and financialization of ecosystem services. And perhaps the latest stage of this accumulation[35] strategy will involve the eradication of the very idea of an 'external' nature as we produce[36] artificial[37] natures ourselves (Smith, 2007).

In the final analysis it is worth remembering Pope Francis's profoundly wise thoughts about the need for an integral ecology that recognizes that the green and the red, the ecological and the social, are deeply implicated with one another. "Being in tune[38] with and respecting the possibilities offered by the things themselves" (Francis, 2015, "The Globalization of the Technocratic Paradigm") would require us to think seriously about our relation to other people, to places, and to other beings. And to consider relationality in this way would also entail thinking about solidarity and the common good.[39]

Notes

1 This chapter draws upon Mir (2015).
2 It is estimated that three countries – America, Russia and China – are responsible for approximately half of all current carbon dioxide emissions (Scranton, 2015). On a per capita basis developed countries are currently responsible for up to 10 to 50 times the emissions of low income countries (*People and the Planet*, 2012). For the historical record, see MacKay (2013).
3 For a brilliant discussion of why literature has typically avoided the topic of climate change see Ghosh (2016). The need for fresh perceptions, new, non-habitual forms of representation so that we might re-learn our way to be human is explored by Williams (2014). For economists nature either provides inputs to the growth process or is thought of as capital (providing a stream of ecosystem services). As with the term 'social capital', 'natural capital' implies a distorted understanding of relationships.
4 To paraphrase Merton (1977), at the end of time there is no place: a time of no room (and a time when there is no time itself). For recent work on the way in which 'homelessness' (an internal displacement) can lead to unease, distress and the lack of solace, see Albrecht et al. (2007). The meaninglessness that can result in a loss of attachment to the land is brilliantly depicted in Lear (2008).
5 Kolbert (2015) provides an urgent and invaluable series of snapshots of the fragility and vulnerability of the ecosystem. For an economic analysis of the startling dangers we face see Wagner and Weitzman (2016).
6 See Ronda (2013). It may be that poets (such as W.S. Merwin) are in a better position than both economics and fiction to describe the extinction of species and our role in that process. Religious voices, too, can offer profound insights (see conclusion).
7 The alarming rate of soil erosion and the decline in productivity on cropland is spelt out in The Global Land Outlook (2017).
8 According to Kolbert (2015) a quarter of all mammals, a fifth of all reptiles and a sixth of all birds are headed towards extinction.

9 It is reasonable to expect that with deforestation and the acidification of the oceans the earth's absorptive capacity will decline over time.

10 A wide canvassing term that has to include damage to the economy but also, more problematically, to human and non-human life.

11 The data in this and the next few paragraphs come from Roemer (2010), unless otherwise stated.

12 Wagner and Weitzman (2016) suggests that structural uncertainty is a central feature of climate change. Since there is uncertainty they claim there is 'roughly' a 1 percent chance that we'll see extreme temperatures which are up to 10 degrees hotter than those in pre-industrial times.

13 Stern (2016) thinks that a figure of 750 ppm (Carbon equivalent) by the end of the century means there will be a 20–60 percent chance we will see average global temperatures of over 4 degrees hotter than pre-industrial times. That represents a temperature not seen on earth for possibly 10 million years.

14 The growth of population and of urban populations in particular has important implications for land use as well as for the demand for food and energy. Economic development – a transition to a burgeoning middle class – will obviously add to those pressures. Our decisions about transport and infrastructure – and technology, more generally – may lock us into patterns of energy use that will be harder to reverse later on.

15 An alternative understanding to a purely economistic regime of property rights, however, is far more important: the *common* rights to subsistence, a "reasonable frugality" (Wiggins, 2011) based on use values and particular understandings of human flourishing, human needs, as well as the rights *of* nature. In that sense what is needed is an extended Charter of the Forest (Linebaugh, 2008).

16 For the difficulties associated with putting a monetary value on the value of a life (or a statistical life), see Aldred (2010).

17 Most of the damages are likely to arise from extreme (uncertain) events rather than changes in *average* temperatures (Jamieson, 2014).

18 The difficulty of individuals and nation states taking up a global perspective is at the heart of the problem with the utilitarian approach (see section 3).

19 Broome (2004) argues that in some cases a broader notion of 'consequences' that includes the act itself may mitigate some of these objections.

20 In addition, as was pointed out in chapter 5, we can think of morality in terms of our ability to make counter-preferential choices (i.e. decisions that drive a wedge between choice and welfare).

21 It is also possible that individuals have adaptive preferences so that over time we tend to value economic growth over a clean environment (Qizilbash, 2014).

22 As O'Neill writes (2002), not all dimensions of social choice can be reflected in preferences or prices; and there are no algorithmic rules for aggregating.

23 Hands (2017) suggests that the *assumption* of the representative agent (in macroeconomics and microeconomics) over the last 30 years is partly about analytical convenience and partly about the need to avoid distributional questions. It is also related to the earlier discussion of the disappearance of the individual (see chapter 4) since in behavioural economics various anomalies throw into question the idea of the rational utility maximizing individual. With a representative agent we can, therefore, disregard specific individuals (and their anomalies) and focus instead on the market, as a whole, being rational.

24 I return to this topic in more detail in chapter 9. For now I only highlight some of the relevant issues.

25 In addition to problems stemming from the dependency of the number and welfare of future people on our current actions there is the distinct problem of the *identity* of those future people.

26 For example, how does the existence of those possible future people affect *our* welfare?

27 It is not just that our actions now have far-reaching, possibly irreversible and unintended consequences; further, by acting in nature we may be unleashing processes that we barely understand. Radical uncertainty, then, may at least in part be our own doing (Dupuy, 2013).

28 Birnbacher (2012) argues that in practice the possibility of solidarity with (distant) future generations is limited – especially given uncertainty and our pre-occupation with our own, short-term interests. A more reliable and psychologically plausible approach, along the lines of Scruton (2012), is to focus on what he calls 'indirect motivations': the generation and maintenance of 'goods' for the present and near future generations will indirectly lead to those 'goods' being conserved for (distant) future generations.

29 This is another way of saying that we have *de re* rather than *de dicto* valuations and attitudes (O'Neill, 2017b). Our relationship to specific places, landscapes or habitats may in part be socially and historically determined. Crucially, our valuing of them is non-instrumental; they constitute what we mean by a good life and are not merely vehicles to achieving an independently defined abstract 'value' such as 'the good' or 'welfare'.

30 I say 'we' to emphasize the social dimension to our attachments and to counter the idea that a 'special relation to me' is necessarily a purely individualistic or personal relation. This is not to deny the way in which specific objects of value can be tied to my own personal history (Waal, 2011).

31 Unlike Scheffler, I believe (along with Scruton, 2012) that a partial (or local) viewpoint *can* form the basis of a sustainable response to climate change. Scruton argues for piety, gratitude, restraint and a sense of love for particular places, settlements, as an antidote to the technology, abstraction and consumerism that have been such a central feature of the climate change problem. We can only tackle the unknown if we start from what we already intimately know, and that is always close at hand.

32 For example, economic theory typically elides questions of power and imagines formally equal agents (such as Adam Smith's baker and brewer) contracting with one another under perfect market conditions. See chapter 6.1 for a fuller discussion of this point. In some sense one can think of the history of capitalism as the gradual extension of capital's hold on both market economies and everyday life (Braudel, 1990).

33 This process depends on material practices as well as ideology, culture, technology, science and power (Empire). The reduction of nature to a mathematical abstraction, the representation of time and space as homogenous categories, facilitates the universalization of exchange (Moore, 2017b; De Soto, 2000).

34 Isolation, fragmentation and simplification, "capitalism's governing abstractions" when it comes to "Nature" (Moore, 2017a, p. 603) are, unsurprisingly, also a feature of economic theory. In the former the creation of value depends on the idea that "the web of life can be fragmented, that its moments can be valued through calculations of price and value" (Moore, 2015, p. 63).

35 I have used the word 'accumulation' here but a central theme of the work of Moore (2015) is that the success of capitalism depends on enhancing labour productivity through the *appropriation* of 'Cheap Natures', the unpaid work/energy of nature. As was mentioned in chapter 1, capitalism needs its frontiers: a realm of value outside of the commodity system. The appropriation of 'uncapitalized nature', therefore, serves the accumulation process.

36 Arendt (1998) presciently remarks that we now have the possibility of acting 'into' nature, and not just 'on' a given (external) nature.

37 In some sense this trajectory of capitalism's changing relation to nature is mirrored by its changing relation to labour. Through organization and technology in the workplace the body's energy/power is set to work. Labour power is a mere 'input' into the production process. This is followed in the 1980s by an intensified commodification as even intellectual and affective capacities are understood to contribute to 'value'; perhaps in the final stage both the life of the body and the life

of the mind (roughly what was called *zoon* and *bios* in chapter 7) can be dispensed with and replaced by automatons and artificial intelligence. This organization of human and non-human life I have called elsewhere the 'biopolitical'.
38 On the concept of 'attunement', see Morton (2018).
39 I return to this topic in chapter 10.

Bibliography

Albrecht, G., Sartore, G., Connor, L., Higginbotham, N., Freeman, S., Kelly, B., . . . Pollard, G. (2007). Solastalgia: The Distress Caused By Environmental Change. *Australasian Psychiatry, 15*(1 Suppl). doi:10.1080/10398560701701288

Aldred, J. (2010). *The Skeptical Economist: Revealing the Ethics Inside Economics.* London: Earthscan.

Anand, S., and Sen, A. K. (2000). Human Development and Economic Sustainability. *World Development, 28*(12), 2029–2049. doi:10.1016/s0305-750x(00)00071-1

Anderson, K., and Bows, A. (2010). Beyond 'Dangerous' Climate Change: Emission Scenarios for a New World. *Philosophical Transactions of the Royal Society A: Mathematical, Physical and Engineering Sciences, 369*(1934), 20–44. doi:10.1098/rsta.2010.0290

Arendt, H. (1998). *The Human Condition.* Chicago, IL: University of Chicago Press.

Arrow, K. J. (2004, April and May). *Speaking For Children and For the Future.* Lecture presented at Tenth Plenary Session of the Pontifical Academy of Social Sciences, Vatican City.

Baier, A. C. (2012). *Reflections on How We Live.* Oxford: Oxford University Press.

Beckerman, W., and Hepburn, C. (2007). Ethics of the Discount Rate in the Stern Review on the Economics of Climate Change. *World Economics, 8*(1), 187–210.

Beckerman, W., and Pasek, J. (1997). Plural Values and Environmental Valuation. *Environmental Values, 6*(1), 65–86. doi:10.3197/096327197776679202

Berry, W. (2010). *What Matters?: Economics for a Renewed Commonwealth.* Berkeley, CA: Counterpoint.

Birnbacher, D. (2012). What Motivates Us to Care for the (Distant) Future? In L. H. Meyer and A. Gosseries (Eds.), *Intergenerational Justice.* Aldershot: Ashgate.

Braudel, F. (1990). *Afterthoughts on Material Civilization and Capitalism* (P. M. Ranum, Trans.). Baltimore, MD: Hopkins University Press.

Broome, J. (1999). Utility. In *Ethics Out of Economics.* Cambridge: Cambridge University Press.

Broome, J. (2004). *Weighing Lives.* Oxford: Oxford University Press.

Broome, J. (2005). Should We Value Population? *Journal of Political Philosophy, 13*(4), 399–413. doi:10.1111/j.1467-9760.2005.00230.x

Broome, J. (2012). *Climate Matters: Ethics in a Warming World.* New York, NY: W.W. Norton & Company.

Broome, J. (2016). The Wellbeing of Future Generations. In M. D. Adler and M. Fleurbaey (Eds.), *The Oxford Handbook of Well Being and Public Policy.* New York, NY: Oxford University Press.

Carson, R. (2002). *Silent Spring* (1st ed., Mariner Books). New York, NY: Houghton Mifflin Harcourt.

Cave, N. (2016). *Anthrocene.* On *Skeleton Tree.* Retreat Recording Studios, Air Studios & La Frette Studios: Nick Cave, Warren Ellis & Nick Launay. Retrieved from www.youtube.com/watch?v=14O_HOQXSEM

Cohen, G. A. (2013). Rescuing Conservatism: A Defense of Existing Value. In M. Otsuka (Ed.), *Finding Oneself in the Other*. Princeton, NJ: Princeton University Press.

De Soto, H. (2000). *The Mystery of Capital: Why Capitalism Triumphs in the West and Fails Everywhere Else*. New York, NY: Basic Books.

Dupuy, J. P. (2013). *The Mark of the Sacred* (M. B. DeBevoise, Trans.). Stanford, CA: Stanford University Press.

Foot, P. (1983). Utilitarianism and the Virtues. *Proceedings and Addresses of the American Philosophical Association, 57*(2), 273–283. doi: 10.2307/3131701.

Francis, P. (2015). The Globalization of the Technocratic Paradigm. In *Laudato Si – On Care for Our Common Home*. IN: Our Sunday Visitor.

Ghosh, A. (2016). *The Great Derangement: Climate Change and the Unthinkable*. Chicago, IL: University of Chicago Press.

Hands, D. W. (2017). Conundrums of the Representative Agent. *Cambridge Journal of Economics, 41*(6), 1685–1704. doi:10.1093/cje/bex016

Hausman, D. M., and McPherson, M. S. (2010). *Economic Analysis, Moral Philosophy and Public Policy*. Cambridge: Cambridge University Press.

Heidegger, M. (2008). *Basic Writings From Being and Time (1927) to The Task of Thinking (1964)*(D. F. Krell, Ed.). London: Harper Perennial.

Hodgson, G. M. (2013). *From Pleasure Machines to Moral Communities: An Evolutionary Economics Without Homo Economicus*. Chicago, IL: University of Chicago Press.

Hutton, W. (2001). *The Revolution that Never Was: An Assessment of Keynesian Economics*. London: Vintage.

IPCC. (2008). *Climate Change 2007: Synthesis Report* (Core Writing Team, R. K. Pachauri, and A. Reisinger Eds.). Geneva, Switzerland: Intergovernmental Panel on Climate Change.

Jamieson, D. (2014). *Reason in a Dark Time: Why the Struggle Against Climate Change Failed – And What It Means for Our Future*. New York, NY: Oxford University Press.

Jonas, H. (1985). *The Imperative of Responsibility: In Search of an Ethics for the Technological Age*. Chicago, IL: University of Chicago Press.

Keat, R. (1994). Citizens, Consumers and the Environment: Reflections on 'The Economy of the Earth'. *Environmental Values, 3*(4), 333–349. Retrieved from www.jstor.org/stable/30301497

Keat, R. (1997). Values and Preferences in Neo-Classical Environmental Economics. In J. Foster (Ed.), *Valuing Nature?: Economics, Ethics and Environment*. London: Routledge.

Kolbert, E. (2015). *The Sixth Extinction: An Unnatural History*. New York, NY: Henry Holt.

Lear, J. (2008). *Radical Hope: Ethics in the Face of Cultural Devastation*. Cambridge, MA: Harvard University Press.

Linebaugh, P. (2008). *The Magna Carta Manifesto: Liberties and Commons for All*. Berkeley, CA: University of California Press.

MacIntyre, A. C. (2011). *Dependent Rational Animals: Why Human Beings Need the Virtues*. Chicago, IL: Open Court.

MacKay, D. J. (2013). *Sustainable Energy – Without the Hot Air* (Vol. 2, Without the Hot Air Series). Cambridge: UIT Cambridge.

McCarthy, M. (2015). *The Moth Snowstorm: Nature and Joy*. London: John Murray.

Merton, T. (1977). *Raids on the Unspeakable*. London: Burns & Oates.

Mir, K. (2015). Ethics, Economics and the Environment. In C. Murphy, P. Gardoni, H. Bashir, J. C. Harris, and E. Masad (Eds.), *Engineering Ethics for a Globalized World* (pp. 127–142). Cham, Switzerland: Springer International Publishing.

Moore, J. W. (2015). *Capitalism in the Web of Life: Ecology and the Accumulation of Capital*. London: Verso.

Moore, J. W. (2017a). The Capitalocene, Part I: On the Nature and Origins of Our Ecological Crisis. *The Journal of Peasant Studies*, *44*(3), 594–630. doi:10.1080/03066150.2016.1235036

Moore, J. W. (2017b). The Capitalocene Part II: Accumulation By Appropriation and the Centrality of Unpaid Work/Energy. *The Journal of Peasant Studies*, *45*(2), 237–279. doi:10.1080/03066150.2016.1272587

Morton, T. (2018). *Being Ecological*. UK: Pelican.

Nordhaus, W. D. (2015). *The Climate Casino: Risk, Uncertainty, and Economics for a Warming World*. New Haven, CT: Yale University Press.

Nussbaum, M. (2000). The Costs of Tragedy: Some Moral Limits of Cost-Benefit Analysis. *The Journal of Legal Studies*, *29*(S2), 1005–1036. doi:10.1086/468103

O'Neill, J. (2002). Socialist Calculation and Environmental Valuation: Money, Markets and Ecology. *Science and Society*, *66*, 137–151.

O'Neill, J. (2007). *Markets, Deliberation and Environment*. New York, NY: Routledge.

O'Neill, J. (2017a). Markets, Ethics, and Environment. In S. M. Gardiner and A. Thompson (Eds.), *The Oxford Handbook of Environmental Ethics*. New York, NY: Oxford University Press.

O'Neill, J. (2017b, October). *Life Beyond Capital*. Retrieved cusp.ac.uk/essay/m1-6

Royal Society (2012). *People and the Planet*. The Royal Society Science Policy Centre Report, 01/12. London: The Royal Society. Available at: http://royalsociety.org/policy/projects/people-planet/report

Qizilbash, M. (2014). Utilitarianism, 'Adaptation' and Paternalism. In D. A. Clark (Ed.), *Adaptation, Poverty and Development: The Dynamics of Subjective Well-Being*. New York, NY: Palgrave Macmillan.

Ramsey, F. P. (1978). *Foundations: Essays in Philosophy, Logic, Mathematics and Economics* (D. H. Mellor, Ed.). London: Routledge & Kegan Paul.

Roemer, J. E. (2010). The Ethics of Intertemporal Distribution in a Warming Planet. *Environmental and Resource Economics*, *48*(3), 363–390. doi:10.1007/s10640-010-9414-1

Ronda, M. (2013, June 10). *Mourning and Melancholia in the Anthropocene*. Retrieved from http://post45.research.yale.edu/2013/06/mourning-and-melancholia-in-the-anthropocene/

Scheffler, S. (2012). *Equality and Tradition: Questions of Value in Moral and Political Theory*. New York, NY: Oxford University Press.

Scranton, R. (2015). *Learning to Die in the Anthropocene: Reflections on the End of a Civilization*. San Francisco, CA: City Lights.

Scruton, R. (2012). *Green Philosophy: How to Think Seriously About the Planet*. London: Atlantic.

Sen, A. K. (1979). Utilitarianism and Welfarism. *The Journal of Philosophy*, *76*(9), 463–489. doi:10.2307/2025934

Sen, A. K. (1985). Well-Being, Agency and Freedom: The Dewey Lectures 1984. *The Journal of Philosophy*, *82*(4), 169–221. doi:10.2307/2026184

Sen, A. K., and Williams, B. (2010). *Utilitarianism and Beyond*. Cambridge: Cambridge University Press.

Smart, J. J., and Williams, B. (2008). *Utilitarianism: For and Against.* New York, NY: Cambridge University Press.

Smith, N. (2007). Nature as Accumulation Strategy. *Socialist Register, 43,* 16–36.

Stern, N. H. (2006). *Stern Review: The Economics of Climate Change.* Report, Government of the United Kingdom.

Stern, N. H. (2016). *Why Are We Waiting?: The Logic, Urgency, and Promise of Tackling Climate Change.* Cambridge, MA: MIT Press.

UNCCD. (2017). *The Global Land Outlook* (Publication). New York, NY: United Nations. Retrieved from www.unccd.int/actions/global-land-outlook-glo.

Waal, E. D. (2011). *The Hare With Amber Eyes: A Hidden Inheritance.* New York, NY: Picador.

Wagner, G., and Weitzman, M. L. (2016). *Climate Shock: The Economic Consequences of a Hotter Planet.* Princeton, NJ: Princeton University Press.

Wallace, R. J. (2012). Duties of Love. *Aristotelian Society Supplementary Volume, 86*(1), 175–198. doi:10.1111/j.1467-8349.2012.00213.x

Wallace, R. J. (2013). The Deontic Structure of Morality. In D. Bakhurst, M. O. Little, and B. Hooker (Eds.), *Thinking About Reasons: Themes From the Philosophy of Jonathan Dancy.* Oxford: Oxford University Press.

Weitzman, M. L. (2009). *Some Basic Economics of Extreme Climate Change.* Discussion Paper 2009–2010. Harvard Environmental Economics Program, Cambridge, MA.

Wiggins, D. (2009). *Ethics: Twelve Lectures on the Philosophy of Morality.* Cambridge, MA: Harvard University Press.

Wiggins, D. (2011). A Reasonable Frugality. *Royal Institute of Philosophy Supplement, 69,* 175–200. doi:10.1017/s1358246111000270

Williams, R. (2014). *The Edge of Words: God and the Habits of Language.* London: Bloomsbury Publishing Plc.

Wolf, S. R. (1999). Morality and the View From Here. *The Journal of Ethics, 3*(3), 203–223. Retrieved from www.jstor.org/stable/25115614

9 Time and economics

Our relationship to time reflects our relationship to others.

(Mulgan, 2015, p. 229)

By correct fulfillment of the present, the past and the future will take care of themselves.

(Zerzan, 2002, p. 74)

9.0 Introduction

Peter Brown (1989), the great historian of Late Antiquity, once wrote of how every civilized society has to negotiate the tension between continuity and rootedness on the one hand, and the desire or need for openness and new experiences on the other. It is this 'double capacity' to at one and the same time seek familiarity and what lies beyond us that defines the human condition (Heaney, 2002). We are in a sense always between the past and the future, aware that reason and imagination can often pull us in a different direction from reflection and memory. Arendt (2006) re-iterates the importance of the dependence of the future on the past when she writes:

> Without testament, . . . without tradition – which selects and names, which hands down and preserves, . . . there seems to be no willed continuity at time and hence, humanly speaking, neither past nor future, only sempiternal change of the world and the biological cycle of living creatures in it.
>
> (p. 5)

Arendt (1998), drawing on Adam Smith, also warns of the dangers of being 'dazzled' by an economic system that is effectively an unending process with no *telos*. On the other hand, at the political level, it could be that democracies are, despite appearances, quite stable. This is not because they are grounded in some original, ideal template of appropriate action, but because they accept contingency, are open to the future, and are constantly experimenting with different ways to meet contemporary challenges. In the memorable words of Runciman (2014), democracies have time and space to undo mistakes.

We are, therefore, deeply ambivalent when it comes to the future. On the one hand we have, from time out of mind, devised institutions, rituals and social artifacts to tame chance and prevent randomness, the unscripted, from irrupting into our lives; on the other hand we recognize that the luck, creativity, fragility and freedom associated with uncertainty are central to our most prized self-conceptions. Our relation to time and our understanding of it, then, is crucial to many aspects of our individual, social and political[1] lives – and our economic ones, too.

As a result of the economic crisis the ability of economists and economic theory to predict the future has come into question. In recent years there has been a return to the central insight of Keynes and Knight that real-world markets are more dynamic and unpredictable than the picture of the economy as depicted in the mechanical models that economists typically employ. I look at these issues in the first two sections of the present chapter.

In section 1, I briefly look at the understanding of time in economic theory. Moving away from theoretical considerations, it is often remarked that in actual market societies both the economy and the wider culture may be altering our relation to time, generating greater myopia and more uncertainty (while our economic models remain wedded to a static, abstract and uniform representation of time). I look at this in sections 2 and 4. Why this is happening is briefly hinted at in section 3.

Nowhere is the divergence between theoretical approaches and real-world economies starker than in the economic analysis of climate change. I look at this in sections 5 and 6 before concluding with some final thoughts.

9.1 Time in economic theory

On reflection it turns out that a number of economic decisions incorporate our relative evaluations over different time periods. Arrow (1972) is perhaps right to say "Virtually every commercial transaction has within itself an element of trust, certainly any transaction conducted over a period of time" (p. 357). We allocate resources, effort and consumption over time, assessing the trade-offs between present and future values based on the assumption that we have a good idea of the possible outcomes and their likelihood of occurring. Investments in education, the decision to save, retire, or borrow all depend to some degree or the other on time, as do our work/leisure trade-offs. In fact, Marshall (2009) wrote of how the element of time "is the centre of the chief difficulty of almost every economic problem" (p. vii). It is somewhat surprising, then, that economists pay such little explicit attention to how we understand time in economic theory.

But what, exactly, is the problem Marshall is alluding to? In the standard economic framework (the neoclassical model) economic agents have perfect information (or can acquire it in a costless way), perfect foresight, and they act in environments characterized by certainty and effective legal systems that ensure the enforcement of well-defined contractual arrangements. Given those background assumptions it is difficult to imagine time having any intrinsic importance and the discipline of economics, by and large, carries on as if it doesn't.

If there is certainty or if *all* future contingencies can be specified costlessly in a contract then a known and complete set of relative prices exists that accurately reflects our underlying relative values. In effect, the standard model is a timeless one and it is little surprise that there isn't much room for anything but little surprises: random and short-lived deviations.

Theorizing in economics, then, tends to take place in a timeless world. In that world time is abstract, empty, uniform and continuous, something that can be quantified and, ultimately, exchanged for money. If economic theory is to be grounded on the facts of experience then deterministic and mechanical models which stress equilibrium and timeless laws are not that useful. Such an approach tends to neglect the historical, cultural and institutional specificities of different markets in any one society or across societies. In addition, it also ignores the historical process of change (Streeck, 2015) and fails to account for unpredictability. As Streeck and Mitchell (2009) observe, social reality is formed by "highly contingent, context-sensitive, emergent complex systems" (p. 4). Finally, economic theory underplays the role of freedom and imagination in human agency.

Because economic theory is so closely wedded to a style of thinking that is more at home in engineering and physics we tend to think of transactions occurring 'out' of historical time and lived experience. Whether this tendency towards ahistorical, universal theorizing is similar to aesthetic or religious impulses is something I do not explore in this chapter. But it is reasonable to believe that some of the most interesting challenges to the standard approach to economic modelling will rely on a different conception of time. That new conception will rest on the understanding that models are better served if structured around biological metaphors rather than mechanical ones, since societies (and economies) are more akin to open-ended, organic and interdependent systems (Bronk, 2009). This means thinking of the economy as more dynamic and innovative than the static models allow for: preferences, technologies, ideas and motivations are not simply 'given' but may change over time. To paraphrase Wagner (2013), the self and the world interact *through* time whereas the standard approach has been both asocial and ahistorical.

In economic thinking our models and our outlook are generally forward-looking and so the past doesn't really count.[2] Most of what has happened in the past is viewed as a 'sunk cost' and so to look back in regret at our choices if often irrational since bygones are bygones. More generally, the devaluation of the past results in it not being held up as a standard by which to judge our current actions, pleasures or ways of living. Instead, it is trivialized or packaged for consumption as mere nostalgia or a pastime by the heritage industry. The past in this view is an accumulation of indecipherable ruins, unable to open a space for understanding future possibilities (Agamben, 1999). If that characterization of our attitude to the past is correct then perhaps Wallace Stevens is right to wonder if, looking back, "it is an illusion that we were ever alive" (Gray, 2011, p. 7).

In another sense, though, because the past is dead it casts a deterministic shadow over the future, which is its mere continuation. But the conjunction of such a deterministic world with the assumption of perfect foresight raises the question of how the economy can ever be off-equilibrium. And yet we know from history that economies slump and financial sectors undergo periodic crises. The problem of time, particularly acute for macroeconomists, arises because for much of macroeconomic theory time is 'spatialized', such that economic agents can supposedly perfectly foresee the future – the shape of future preferences and technology.

If the past doesn't matter then the previous levels and quality of our welfare are also by and large not supposed to feature in our current evaluation of it.[3] The standard economic evaluative approach is utilitarianism. But utilitarianism encourages a very peculiar understanding of time. At the individual level the assumption of 'additive separability', which is to say that the utility I have is independent of the order or sequence of utilities, tends to break down the notion of a narrative unity to our lives. Human life is simply a "temporal sequence of person-moments" (Broome, 1999, p. 13). My relation to future utilities, that is, encourages the view that I relate to the bearers of these future utilities as if they were almost autonomous, 'time-slices' of me.

The philosopher John O'Neill (1993) elaborates upon this point with the following example: imagine couple '1' on their honeymoon. They argue for the first four days and experience unhappiness but on the fifth day they make-up and are happy. Let's assume their lives end at that point. Now compare their lives with couple '2' who are happy for the first four days but quarrel bitterly on the final day. Which couple has the 'better' life? If we give credence to the notion of additive separability then we would tot up all the amounts of happiness and unhappiness as experienced on each day and conclude that couple '2' were the happier (this point is reinforced if we include discounting since couple '1's' happiness is achieved much later). But if we were to reasonably see their lives as two stories then it is plausible to conclude that couple '1' have a better life.

In some sense, then, a final event can redeem (or sour) the past. It does so not just because of its timing – that it comes along later in one's life – but, more importantly, because of the meaning, the retrospective significance, it imparts to the overall value and understanding of one's whole life. In this view a good life, even if thought of somewhat narrowly in terms of well-being, is not the mere summation (weighted or otherwise) of momentary well-being (Velleman, 1991). 'Peak events' or special moments can colour how we see and evaluate other related events in our lives (Kahneman, Wakker and Sarin, 1997).

Our actions and behaviour, then, may only be intelligible against both a personal narrative and our ability to situate ourselves within a wider historical and contextual narrative (MacIntyre, 2003). This view of our lives forming an organic unity seems to have been shared by Keynes (Skidelsky, 2009), but is radically at odds with the methodological individualism which lies at the heart of economic theory.

9.2   Uncertainty in real-world markets

Of course, it is now widely recognized that *actual* markets may differ from this theoretical construct in significant ways and that they are in fact shot through with various types of imperfections and incompleteness. Perhaps the 'chief difficulty'

Marshall was hinting at, then, is the possibility that in the absence of perfect conditions actual markets may have to rely on non-economic factors to coordinate actions, namely: norms, conventions, emotions, power and ethics. The difficulty arises not only because information may be incomplete at any point in time but, more radically, because agents may face 'ontological uncertainty' (Bronk, 2011) or 'imperfect knowledge' (Frydman and Goldberg, 2008). There may be some things that we simply *cannot* know beforehand.

In recent years there has been a growing interest in a central insight of economists like Keynes and Knight:[4] we can and ought to distinguish between risk and radical uncertainty.[5] For Knight, markets were much more creative and innovative than what standard economic theory suggested. Under that standard view markets are valuable because they result in people optimally satisfying their *given* preferences. But for Knight and other thinkers like him the real importance of markets was their ability to create new products, new ways of doing things, and to realize new opportunities that couldn't have been previously foreseen. Knight's understanding of markets suggests a much more open view of time than found in our closed and mechanical models with their emphasis on both a pre-determined notion of behaviour and a *given* equilibrium.[6]

An older generation[7] of economists, then, recognized the importance of having a better account of time in particular, of the need for an account in which time is experienced as both throwing up unpredictable futures as well as being irreversible. Both of these features sit uncomfortably with the mechanical and static view of time in the neoclassical framework. It is not surprising, given that, that economists like Hicks (Boland, 2005) could write of the need for an economics *in* time, as well as an economics *of* time.

In recent years some attempts have been made to incorporate a more realistic understanding of time into economic theory. Early on Nelson (1970) recognized the existence of 'experience goods' – goods such as education and health services, whose quality we can't assess until we've actually 'consumed' them. More recently, Hart, Shleifer and Vishny (1997) have suggested that not all contracts are complete in the sense of economic agents being able to perfectly foresee or specify all future contingencies. In such cases it may not be possible to imagine a world of perfect contracts across different time periods.

In behavioural economics, too, there is evidence to suggest that we don't always rationally optimize over time in the way implied by our models and may instead have 'satisficing' preferences (Camerer, Babcock, Loewenstein and Thaler, 1997). This may be because we don't always know what we want since at any point in time we only have a partial understanding of our identity and our values. The future is another country.[8]

Summarizing our discussion, we can say that our neoclassical model represent a timeless world. It is increasingly understood that actual market behaviour takes place *in* time and sometimes under conditions of uncertainty, thus rendering the model problematic. Furthermore, actual market societies may be *generating* greater uncertainty. Of course, it would be mistaken to conclude that markets on their own are the cause of greater uncertainty. Valéry (1989) may well be right to note that unpredictability is an outgrowth of the tremendous enhancement of scientific power, a view re-iterated by Arendt's astute observation that our ability to act *in* nature (rather than 'on' it) may lead to the unleashing of forces we barely comprehend (Arendt, 1998).

One of the possible effects of greater uncertainty about the future is that it undermines our capacity for visualizing our long-term prospects and for taking actions in line with them. Market economies, that is, may be making us more myopic.[9]

We have seen above that in economic theory our relation to our past and future does not take the shape of a narrative; the past is generally ignored and because time is spatialized' the future is in some sense just a repetition of our present circumstances. Furthermore, a genuine narrative structure is undermined because we relate to our future selves/states in an abstract and fragmentary fashion, a telling point when we come to consider our relation to future generations in the looming environmental crisis.

In the following section I ask *how* market economies (and not just economic theory) contribute to this disjointed view of time.

9.3 A brief history of time

So far there has been little explicit discussion as to the way in which socio-economic conditions influence how either time is theorized in economics or thought about in daily life; but it is clear that we cannot isolate our perceptions of time, and the meaning we give to it, from the prevailing social conditions. These include, amongst other things, religious and cultural ideas, as well as the customs and material practices associated with them. As Harvey (1989) observes, "Every social relation contains its own sense of time" (p. 223). If that is true we should not be surprised to find different ways of relating to the past and the future both within and across societies.

The way in which we understand, value and give meaning to time varies with underlying socio-economic background conditions. To say this is not, however, to suggest a form of determinism. Older ways of understanding time (cyclical time, for example) may to some extent co-exist with newer modes of comprehension; and there can always be resistance to any dominant perspective. In the remaining part of this subsection I try to briefly outline some of the salient changes in our perspectives of time, along with the causes and implications of those changes.

In a seminal analysis of time-work discipline E.P. Thompson (1993) explained how during the early stages of industrial capitalism certain external practices – the division and supervision of labour, money incentives, inventions (notably, clocks) and the spread of attitudes fostered by schools and churches helped create a new time-work discipline. In the early modern period Barbara Adam (2003) writes of how the increased 'rationalization' of work practices, an intensification in the working hour (what Marx called 'the degree of density'), competition and innovation all effectively translated into the commodification and quantification of labour and the veneration of speed and efficiency.

It is worth laboring the point that under such a temporality time is a scarce resource and if it is not utilized is wasted. It follows that leisure itself is not valued independently of labour-time since its value is, in fact, just measured by foregone wages. Furthermore, those who work and live according to different temporal rhythms and for whom labour-time cannot easily be measured (artists, carers, teachers, the young, elderly and disabled) – are likely to see their way of relating to time come under severe pressure as capitalism advances. In some sense this pressure is just another manifestation of the conflict between use values and exchange values, between lived experience and the abstract time of capital. The dominance of commoditized time leads to the exclusion or devaluing of ways of being in the world that involve us in sharing, giving, recognizing and caring for the lives of others. In other words, markets 'crowd out' the kinds of temporality that reflect a more relational and social way of being in the world.

For some thinkers the last 30 years of the 20th century marked the beginning of a new phase in the disruption of temporal rhythms. The continued acceleration of time in this period is brought about by what some call a shift from 'solid modernity' to 'liquid modernity' (Bauman, 2000) or what others call a transition from modernism to post-modernism. I think it is best to think of these changes, however we label them, as being the product of cultural *and* economic changes. Daniel Bell (1978) stresses the former by highlighting the emergence of a culture of self-expression and unbound experience. That culture manifests itself in a valorization of speed, simultaneity, ephemerality, 'happenings', spectacles, surfaces and 'depthlessness'. Harvey (1989) adds to this picture of time-space compression by relating the new culture to shifts in the economic system (acceleration in exchange, consumption, production turnover times and quicker flows of information flows).

Both authors recognize the continuities between 'solid' and 'light' modernity, between modernity and post-modernity. However, the key difference is that in late capitalism the transient, fleeting, contingent and fragmentary nature of the world is embraced (Jameson, 2015). We have come to accept, almost with a blasé mental attitude (Simmel, 1961), that our own lives are full of ambiguities and that they lack the coherence or narrative structure of a former age. In the following section, I elaborate upon this point.

9.4   Myopia and discontinuity

Market societies can be distinguished by their breathtaking speed of change as well as by the sheer abundance, immediacy and variety of choices they offer us. The result is that in market societies novelty trumps prudence and we are committed to thinking that the 'shock of the new' is the only way forward. Market expansion and intensification[10] may mean that, ultimately, 'liquidity' is more important than durability, continuity, and 'customary expectations' (Thompson, 1993).

It is likely, therefore, that the lack of permanence in late capitalism and the culture associated with it is contributing to a thinning out of our associations with particular places. Globalization and changes in technology mean that we are unlikely to live and work in one place for the whole of our lives. Also, in late capitalism the flexibility of labour (a greater reliance on temporary contracts and the rapid changes in skill or knowledge-requirements) means that work is more precarious and less likely to be defined by a single profession over a person's career. The net result is that the solid markers (work, place) against which we once took stock of our lives are evaporating before us. It is not any great surprise, therefore, that the self has come to seem less substantial as well.[11] This hollowing out character leads to anxieties and the "specter of uselessness" (Sennett, 2007, p. 83), with profound impacts on our well-being.

In a rapidly changing, shape-shifting world, then, a coherent notion of the self persisting over time may be undermined (Scheffler, 2010). This is one of the reasons, I believe, that the idea of acting in character finds such little traction in economic thinking. To act in character suggests that we can order our desires (ethically) and forego our interests to the degree that we have a determinate notion of 'the good' and a relatively stable character. We can, that is, only make sense of our actions against the background of an "ongoing narrative, consistent with a certain self-conception" (Baier, 2008, p. 17).

Market societies (and not just economic theory), however, do not allow for such stable formations. All that is solid melts into air, Marx wrote many years ago. Some would say prophetically so. Our inability to picture the *longue durée* (Armitage and Guldi, 2015), a consciousness that is dazzled by the spectacular,[12] and the demise of cultural and institutional 'commitment devices' that place limits on instant gratification may be responsible for the prevalence of myopic choices in developed and developing countries alike.

So far I have mainly been talking about the economic and cultural causes of our changing perception of time. But what of its consequences?

One way of thinking about the damages of short-termism to the economy and to the tenor of social life is to recall Daniel Bell's (1978) notion of a 'cultural contradiction of capitalism'. The value we ascribe to things that are durable and beautiful – assuming the latter is non-instrumental and therefore less transient – may be diminished (Scruton, 2012). If valuation depends on something persisting over time then it is possible that pleasure – which was once understood as being fundamentally an "intensified awareness of reality" (Arendt, 1995, p. 6) – loses its worldly character and is transformed into a series of hedonistic and disconnected episodes in our entertainment or fantasies. More generally, if we view our own lives and the world as a mere flash in the pan, it may very well be that our desire to work, save and pass on legacies to the next generation is dimmed, with serious repercussions to the economy.

In this regard it is worth paying attention to recent warnings that an excessive focus on the short-term ('Quarterly Capitalism') may lead to lower growth. Haldane (2015), in a broad and sweeping survey of economic history claims that one of the deep sources of economic growth over the centuries has been patience, the ability to defer one's present consumption/happiness in order to invest in the various forms of capital – physical, social, institutional and intellectual – that promote growth and flourishing. But, as Haldane and others (Offer, 2006) suggest, with growing affluence it may be that developed countries are becoming more impatient with profound implications for education, the acquirement of skills and innovation as individuals and companies fail to invest in long-term projects.[13]

Thanks to the expansion and intensification of market behaviour myopia may well be a central feature of western institutions in every sector, from politics to business to the media (Barton, 2011). The 'crowding-out' of longer-term perspectives is also intimately linked to the decline of the public sector. It is fairly well established that in late capitalism there has been a serious attack on both the public sector and its very ethos (see chapter 8). This is worrying because it is in the public realm where short-term perspectives and interests are set aside in favour of long-term objectives. One indication of this is the different discount rates government set when investing in education, defence or infrastructure (Mulgan, 2015). If thinking in the public realm is more likely to be influenced by moral obligations and attitudes of stewardship then it is not unreasonable to expect different rates of time preference to those under market conditions where short-term private interests dominate.

One further point worth noting – though largely speculative – is related to technology. Haldane (2015) cautiously suggests that in previous time periods technology may have fostered the habits of 'slow thinking' (books are a good example) that went hand in hand with patient attitudes. It may be, however, that technology is now not just producing more and more innovations; it may also be contributing to increasing levels of distraction and impatience (Crawford, 2015). Slow and longer-term thinking are unlikely to emerge under such conditions.

In summary, we have seen that developments in both the economy and culture may be leading to a restructuring of temporality with a devaluing of long-term perspectives and continuity at the individual level. We have also examined how short-termism and discontinuity may have deleterious consequences for both the economy and for the quality of social life (as our relation to place, work, things of value and notions of a stable, coherent self are undermined).

But the biggest challenge to the standard way in which time is incorporated into our economic models is the looming environmental crisis and it is to this that I now turn. We have seen above that the standard approach to time in economic theory devalues the past and tends to ignore the uncertainty of the future. Both of these failings are pertinent to discussions about climate change. In addition, we only relate to our 'future selves' in a peculiarly abstract way since our theoretical approach doesn't incline us to think of our lives on the whole, as a continuous narrative. In the following sections we will be asking if the standard theoretical approach used to understand climate change in economics fails in the same way when 'future selves' applies to future generations and not just to our own lives in the future.

9.5   Climate change and future generations

Some greenhouse gasses can stay in the atmosphere for hundreds of years. This makes climate change an inter-generational problem. In response to the problem our theoretical perspective is often understood to centre on the question: how does an impartial social planner weigh up the welfare or interests of current generations against future ones? One answer is to throw one's weight behind an inter-generational view of justice with the notion of 'harm' at its core. A more typical response is to rely on utilitarianism. Both are problematic because we are not sure of the existence, number or identity of future generations. But even in the absence of uncertainty, I argue, utilitarianism is still problematic.

It could be argued that, at least in some respects, utilitarianism does take into account the importance of time in the inter-generational problem by explicitly allowing for the discounting of *known* future streams of utility. But this itself is highly contested with some academics such as Knight and Pigou maintaining that the 'pure discounting' of utility is ethically indefensible (Stern, 2014). Why, after all, should the fact that utility occurs at a later date and to a future person/generation matter less to an *impartial* social planner? That seems unfair and even though it might make some sense to discount because of the positive probability that future generations will be extinct, the other arguments for doing so are not so convincing.

First, individuals may exhibit impatience or pure time preference but it doesn't follow that that an impersonal planner should (Schelling, 1995). Second, we may plausibly discount, *at the margin*, future utility if future generations are better off. However, though future generations may be richer we cannot simply assume they will necessarily be better off overall – especially in the face of significant climate damage (Broome, 2012). Third, if we ignore the impersonal perspective in favour of an agent-relative one it may follow that we ought to discount future utilities. However, it still remains true that the extent to which we do say can be lessened in direct proportion to the strength of our associations with an inter-generational 'we'. In a similar vein, when it comes to long-term investments in health, education and defence governments typically see themselves as trustees for unborn generations. Since they're stewards (rather than rational, self-interested individuals) they subsequently discount at a lower rate than the market. Fourth, while additional *marginal* units of utility might plausibly be discounted it is not clear why, from an impersonal point of view, the overall *level* of utility should be.

Some economists suggest that *commodities* (rather than utility *per se*) can and ought to be discounted but this, to me, seems to be really an argument for taking inequalities seriously. If future generations are richer (have more commodities) then on the margin commodities will not be as valuable to them as they are to current generations and optimization would require giving more importance to the current generation. Discounting is not in this sense really about time *per se* and it is dependent on assumptions about future growth and the elasticity of the marginal utility with respect to consumption (Beckerman and Hepburn, 2007).

Also, it is clear that there are some commodities that should not be discounted. Non-renewable or scarce resources shouldn't be discounted because they are not naturally productive and therefore do not 'grow'. Moreover, even though some commodities such as 'life-saving' can be produced (through investments in health services, say), it may be that they yield constant well-being and should not be discounted (Broome, 1999).

Summarizing the above discussion: to discriminate against someone simply based on the date at which they live seems unfair on philosophical grounds. But if we take the opposite view and hold that future generations should be given roughly the same weight in our calculations as current ones then this could impose huge sacrifices on current generations given the sheer number of expected future people. It seems unrealistic to expect such a view to be widely endorsed, especially if future generation are richer than us (Arrow, 1996). Utilitarianism, it turns out, is either too demanding and unrealistic, or unfair.

In addition, when it comes to climate change policies it is likely that the shape of the future world is actually – in a non-marginal way – endogenous to those policies and therefore it is questionable whether market prices accurately reflect relative values. Even if we ignore this complication and the possibility that not all 'goods' can or should be priced (such as the loss of life), we are still left with a thorny problem. It is not only that markets are very frequently imperfect; in addition, market prices (such as interest rates) do not and cannot reflect future generations' relative values since they do not currently exist. The market interest rate only reflects how the *present* generation values future commodities.

The standard utilitarian approach to climate change, then, is problematic – and this ultimately stems, I would argue, from a number of distinct issues relating to time. First, given that climate change and climate change policies will have non-marginal impacts we cannot take the development of future technology or population dynamics as given. Prices and probabilities over events cannot be taken as being independent of policy.

Second, even in a fully deterministic and known world the question of whether and to what extent we discount the future is an open question – largely because it relies on a mixture of ethical reflection and economic analysis.

Third, while the two points alluded to above indicate a significant degree of complexity in any evaluation of climate change, there is the further problem of uncertainty. It is now widely acknowledged that one of the striking features of climate change is the sheer level of uncertainty surrounding it. We cannot be sure how technologies and economies will evolve or what the underlying processes governing climate change are. So, when it comes to the impact of economic activity on emissions, the relation between those emissions and temperature increases, or the impact of those temperature changes on economic activity and well-being we are faced with a "cascade of uncertainty" (IPCC, 2001, p. 79). In fact, for some economists – like Weitzman (2011) – uncertainty is the fundamental characteristic of climate change. Given that, along with the complexities deriving from the existence of 'tipping points', 'thresholds' and feedback effects it is not clear exactly how useful our standard economic approaches are when it comes to assessing the likely net damage from climate change.

Fourth, the approach encourages us to believe that we can only relate to future generations as strangers. The ethical demand to give these people equal weight in our considerations is based on the impartial stance of reason and is therefore psychologically implausible. Let me elaborate on this point.

Utilitarianism, we have concluded, is unlikely to generate a psychologically realistic set of motivations. To see this remember that at the individual level additive separability tends to foster an abstract relation to our future selves. In a similar fashion, in an inter-generational optimization problem we tend to see other people as abstract individuals, as strangers, and it is hard to explain why we should therefore have an interest in their well-being or advantage.[14] Our relation to our own future selves, then, is as problematic[15] as it is to the lives of those in the future – as thinkers such as Hazlitt (1999) and Sidgwick (Gray, 2011) clearly understood.

Utilitarianism, then, weakens our sense of relationality with its focus on impersonal maximization. Since we only worry about maximizing the sum of abstract value we are not *inherently* concerned about the conservation of things which bear personal or particular values (Cohen, 2013). The problem remains that of the narcissist (Lasch, 1991): why should I *care* about the welfare of future generations when my relation to them that is at once asymmetrical and devoid of any genuine mutuality?[16] I can, it is argued, harm or benefit them but they cannot have a similar impact on me. Also, the *strength* of my concern for them is limited because my relation to them is sustained only by the imagination, degrees of altruism that become progressively weaker as I think about ever-more distant future generations, or by an abstract form of reason. 'The other' is an abstraction, and not the same as a 'thou', or my neighbour.

In reality, our obligations make more sense, and have greater weight, within the framework of a more limited and grounded perspective. The utilitarian perspective implies we take a stance 'from the point of view of the universe'. But given the beings we are, fragile and temporally bounded, it may be that a 'reasonable partiality' (Scheffler, 2010) offers a more realistic way of thinking about ethical behaviour.

Summarizing, we have seen that market societies may be making it more difficult for us to think about future generations. This is on the one hand a result of myopia and uncertainty and on the other because of a lack of continuity of interests and values across generations.

We have also seen that when it comes to climate change the understanding of time in economic theory (utilitarianism) isn't very helpful. Firstly, under utilitarianism (when the future is 'given') we may be myopic and discount the future too heavily. Secondly, our relation to people in the future is, as it is with regards our own future selves, too abstract. The lack of a sense of continuity between generations is unlikely to elicit a sense of care for their interests or welfare.

9.6 The end of temporality

If the world is fundamentally non-ergodic and relational it is questionable whether economic theory or modelling can capture these facts. But the problem of coming to grips with uncertainty is not simply a problem for economic theory. It may be true that human beings in general excel by using their imagination and reason to find patterns, intuit unity and posit a continuity of consciousness and time, but the looming environmental crisis opens up the new and radical question of how to deal with the possibility of the end of time. How do we live with the uncertainty that there might not even be a future?[17]

It could be that we are witnessing major changes in our contracts with time, the structure of temporality. Have we, in fact, reached the end of temporality, a time with no sequence or recurrence? Are we simply waiting to wind down time before the 'endgame' (Lear, 2008), enraptured by our momentary, bodily appetites?[18] Does thinking formed by "synchronic habits of zero-sum calculations" (Jameson, 2003, p. 705) entail the end of not just political/utopian thinking but of all forward-dreaming and story-telling as we embrace contingency and a present-centred perspective (Clark, 2012)?

As we've seen above, economic theory fails to deal with radical uncertainty since it usually thinks of the future as 'given'. Utilitarianism fares no better and is therefore not a useful approach to assess climate change, whose most salient feature may be uncertainty (Weitzman, 2011) – the possibility of a catastrophic end. How to determine, then, which particular ethical approach we should adopt in order to face the challenges of an uncertain future? And which institutions would give expression to that approach?

As stated in the previous chapter, I don't know if there is any easy way of thinking ourselves out of the possibility of a looming catastrophe. Perhaps we need to admit that we're *already* in a catastrophe and that it has come about because we've thought *too much* about the future (our utopian projects, fantasies of control, and economic imperative of fostering endless economic growth and infinite desires). Perhaps a more sympathetic and relational[19] approach might go some way to coming to terms with uncertainty. What kind of associations or institutions might embody such an approach remains to be fleshed out. But they won't be state-centred ones.

The idea that the state, as a 'deathless' body, might through its archival memory and future-oriented projects stand resolutely against a 'weightless' economy and a short-termism culture seems misplaced. As I have been arguing throughout this book, in the neoliberal era the state and the market are two sides of the same coin. Both rest on an impersonal view of the individual.

Let's return to one of the main objections to utilitarianism, namely that it encourages an impersonal and abstract relation to future generations. Is there an alternative view of time, one that is analogous to the idea of narrative unity of the individual? Avner-de-Shalit (2006) has written on the possibility of an inter-generational community with a shared background framework persisting over time. That framework is based on a shared culture (values, ideas, experiences and traditions), common political imaginaries, and moral similarity.

In a similar vein, Annette Baier (2012) has written on how we can fruitfully see ourselves as belonging to a 'continuous moral community' and how doing so can go some way to resolving the inter-generational environmental problem. It does so because in an inter-generational community our obligations are learned, sustained and developed in the small-scale and local associations of family, school, workplace and church (Burke's 'little platoons'). The goods and values they are aligned with are best seen as helping form a web of associations and interests between the generations (the dead, the living and the unborn).

Paradoxically, then, a view of ourselves as being both more limited and more dependent creatures could foster a sense of the 'inexhaustible', or at least a sense of value enduring over time. Under this view – which is inextricably linked with both cyclical time and a richer understanding of the household[20]– we have a greater degree of obligation to the maintenance, sustenance, nurturing and care of both other people as well as the environment (Mulgan, 2015). Nature is only really limited and 'exhaustible' when it is thought of as a scarce resource. In stark contrast to the cyclical view of time, the idea of limitless growth and the linear progression of time (which has been central to modernity and market economies) has gone hand-in-hand with an emphasis on a non-relational view of the individual. In linear time we count our losses and the remembrance of things past rises to the surface – if at all – by sheer coincidence.

In a similar vein to Avner de Shalit (2006), Scheffler (2016) maintains that at least part of what goes in to making us 'valuing creatures' is the sense that we want objects, ways of life and individual lives to continue to exist over time. The deep-rooted need for temporal extension may manifest itself in the high regard we give to remembrance, rituals and repetition on the one hand, and the importance of future-directed attitudes (intentions, expectations) and words on the other. A life without these features may "come to seem fractured and disjointed" (Scheffler, 2010, p. xcvii).

In a more relational approach it is incorrect to think that future generations cannot harm or benefit us – even after our own death. Many of the projects and objects we value – cancer research, aesthetic appreciation, intellectual, artistic and political activities – depend on future generations being around to complete, understand, maintain or further deepen them (O'Neill, 1993). Just as those presently alive can alter the past (Eliot, 1975) so, too, future generations can alter the meaning and purpose of our present endeavours. If we have obligations to future generations then it could also be said that we have them to previous generations as well since, as the late Seamus Heaney (2002) wrote, it is important to "keep the imagination's supply lines to the past open" (p. 78). A classic – in whatever aesthetic field – remains so because it is an "open work" (Eco, 1989), offering fresh insights in the light of new experience.[21]

That still leaves us with a problem discussed earlier in the chapter and it is this: if choice is a genuinely originating force and if human creativity and imagination mean anything, then human history is open-ended. If time cannot "pass without modifying knowledge" (Lachmann, 1977, p. 93) our theoretical approach needs to incorporate both a logical as well as a historical (open) notion of time.

However, if time is open-ended then we cannot be confident that there will in fact be a continuous moral community. The idea of an inter-generational community is not consistent with a commitment to simply ensuring that future generations have the formal, open-ended freedom to pursue whatever projects they wish. The strength of our obligations to future generations surely depends, at least to some degree, on the continuation of particular shared experiences, identities, memories and values over time.

9.7 Conclusion

In this chapter, I have suggested that either we erroneously believe that the future is not a problem (because things are on an upward and inevitable arc of progress), or we increasingly lack the capacity (and perhaps desire) to think seriously about the future. If climate change introduces the possibility of catastrophe in the near future then both these modes of thinking are problematic. And yet we cannot take the future for granted nor can we ignore[22] it.

Of course, we must try and avert catastrophe. But to do so depends, crucially, on us wanting a particular kind of future – one that is contiguous to our own history and values. If we only want *the* future to continue we are back to the abstract and implausible mode of thinking that characterizes utilitarianism, the kind of thinking that has been responsible for possibly bringing about the end of the future in the first place.

Perhaps this is too pessimistic a conclusion, for the record of human history reveals that at certain times people have had the capacity to continue living and thinking even after a catastrophe has struck, even after a way of life has come to an end. Lear (2008) calls that capacity 'radical hope', and it entails trusting – in the face of the most harrowing uncertainties – a commitment to the belief that the fundamental goodness of the world will continue. This holds even if one cannot picture the future in its details, and even if it lacks continuity with our own lives and our previous conceptions of a good life.

This capacity (or task) is similar to what Badiou (2012) calls *anabasis* – a return that "corresponds to no previous orientation" (p. 82). In fact, it could be argued that the modern age is co-existent with an acute awareness of the fragile and precarious nature of civilization (Jonas, 2001). Pocock (2009) and Kristeva (1992) inform us that we have had to make do without eternal and immutable models, a sense of transcendence, since the beginning of modernity. We may think that it is only we, the current generation, who sense that the future is radically uncertain or that our times are ridden by the pervasive sense of an ending, with no new beginnings in sight. An understanding of the past, however, indicates that human beings have always been living like this, or at least they have for some time now, for longer than we can perhaps remember. Contingency, uncertainty and finitude may not, after all, represent anything new under the sun.

Notes

1 Recent work by Calhoun (2012) shows that political thought does not have to always be 'progressive', forward-looking or utopian; radical thought can also be rooted in a sense of tradition and the past continuing into the future.

2 History might be deemed unimportant because, given the same parameters, countries will eventually converge to the same growth rate. Institutional economics hasn't really challenged this (see Acemoglu, Johnson and Robinson, 2005),

since there is little explicit modelling the interaction between institutions, culture, power and technology over time.

3 This seems implausible. The relation between utilities over time should take into account the possibility that there may be a difference between instant (present) utility and remembered utility. See Kahneman and Riis (2005).

4 The difficulty uncertainty poses to economic modelling has long been recognized (Hodgson, 2011). For Keynes, investment spending was subject to uncertainty, or what he called animal spirits. Knight (1997), emphasized the difference between radical uncertainty ('unknown unknowns') and risk (which involves a known probability distribution over events).

5 In addition we should make the distinction between 'ontological uncertainty' and 'epistemological uncertainty' (complexity). The latter arises from the unknowability (in practice, but not in principle) of probabilities in complex systems.

6 In a rapidly changing world the future is unformed and at least to some degree unknowable. The notion that the market tends to a pre-established, statically given equilibrium makes little sense under those circumstances.

7 Adam Smith also hinted that we may not always have stable and known preference and that we can learn over time (Gerschlager, 2008). In reality it is not uncommon to revise both our values and our judgements over time. However, human tragedy points us to the possibility that the mere passing of time does not confers on us greater knowledge or understanding. As technologies advance we may be heading to ever-greater levels of epistemological uncertainty.

8 This stands in stark contrast to the general view in economic theory that time is, as it were, laid out before us (or 'spatialized'). Regret, disappointment and systemic mistakes are hardly admissible under such a conception of time.

9 In section 4, I will argue that myopia is not simply a response to living in an uncertain world. Market societies encourage ceaseless change and endless growth, thus eroding the links between generations. Marketing, planned obsolescence and innovation all play a role in this (Streeck and Mitchell, 2009). If the future lacks any continuity with our present and our past it is not surprising that we tend to focus on the short-term present. This is, as we shall see, of crucial importance in discussions about climate change.

10 On 'intensification', see chapter 3.

11 On the disappearance of the individual, see chapter 4.

12 To the extent that our institutions and our self-conceptions are governed by ephemerality, spectacles and fleeting images (by what Marion, 2004 calls a 'televisual order') it is hard to imagine a long-term perspective taking root. It could be that our modern information societies (Crary, 2013) preclude the formation of a long-term framework from being established. In a 24/7 world we are bombarded by current information and 'live updates'.

13 As my research assistant, Ali Iftikhar points out, in a consumer society the overemphasis on our own current pleasures may prevent us from taking into account the harmful consequences of our actions on the welfare of future generations as well.

14 In the next section, I will tentatively argue that if community and sociality help us see our own lives as forming a continuous narrative they might also help foster a better understanding of our relation to future generations. That argument, however, rests on the continuation of common goods over time. The continuation of those goods is made less likely by the narrow conception of the individual in economic theory and by our being held captive, in modern capitalist societies, by the 'tyranny of the moment' (Eriksen, 2001).

15 How does the non-moral self we typically find in market economies shift gears and endorse a universalistic, impartial and temporally-neutral utilitarian position?

16 The problem is compounded by the fact that the identity and values of these future generations may be unknown or unrecognizable,

17 Inequality, debt, the decline of 'the public' and the eclipse of political/utopian thinking may already be locking some of us into a particular kind of temporality: a time in which there is only the present. This disappearance of the future is not, I think, unrelated to the disappearance of the individual (see chapter 4).
18 Arendt (1998) alerted us to the futility and 'worldlessness' of a consumer society nearly 60 years ago. On the idea that we are just our bodies, see chapter 4.
19 Morton (2018) writes, "Attunement is a living, dynamic relation with another being – it doesn't stop" (p. 139).
20 On the importance of household economics, see the following chapter.
21 Such attitudes to time are far removed from those that are consistent with the utilitarian approach.
22 We cannot stand, like Klee's *Angelus Novus*, with our backs to the future (Benjamin, 2013).

Bibliography

Acemoglu, D., Johnson, S., and Robinson, J. A. (2005). Institutions as the Fundamental Cause of Long-Run Growth. In P. Aghion and S. Durlauf (Eds.), *Handbook of Economic Growth*, 1A. Amsterdam: Elsevier North-Holland. Available at: https://doi.org/10.1016/S1574-0684(05)01006-3

Adam, B. (2003). When Time is Money: Contested Rationalities of Time in the Theory and Practice of Work. *Theoria: A Journal of Social and Political Theory*, *102*, 94–125. Retrieved from www.jstor.org/stable/41791393

Agamben, G. (1999). *The Man Without Content*. Stanford, CA: Stanford University Press.

Arendt, H. (1995). *Men in Dark Times*. San Diego, CA: Harcourt, Brace & Company.

Arendt, H. (1998). *The Human Condition*. Chicago, IL: University of Chicago Press.

Arendt, H. (2006). The Gap Between Past and Future. In *Between Past and Future: Eight Exercises in Political Thought*. New York, NY: Penguin Books.

Armitage, D., and Guldi, J. (2015). The Return of the Longue Durée: An Anglo-American Perspective. *Annales (English ed.)*, *70*(2), 219–247. doi:10.1017/s2398568200001126

Arrow, K. J. (1972). Gifts and Exchanges. *Philosophy & Public Affairs*, *1*(4), 343–362. Retrieved from www.jstor.org/stable/2265097

Arrow, K. J. (1996). *Discounting, Morality, and Gaming*. Working Paper, Department of Economics, Stanford University, Stanford, CA.

Badiou, A. (2012). *The Century*. Cambridge: Polity Press.

Baier, A. C. (2008). *Death and Character: Further Reflections on Hume*. Cambridge, MA: Harvard University Press.

Baier, A. C. (2012). *Reflections on How We Live*. Oxford: Oxford University Press.

Barton, D. (2011, March). Capitalism for the Long Term. *Harvard Business Review*. Retrieved from https://hbr.org/2011/03/capitalism-for-the-long-term

Bauman, Z. (2000). *Liquid Modernity*. Malden, MA: Polity Press.

Beckerman, W., and Hepburn, C. (2007). Ethics of the Discount Rate in the Stern Review on the Economics of Climate Change. *World Economics*, *8*(1), 187–210.

Bell, D. (1978). *The Cultural Contradictions of Capitalism*. New York, NY: Basic Books.

Benjamin, W. (2013). *Illuminations: Essays and Reflections* (H. Zohn, Trans.; H. Arendt, Ed.). New York, NY: Schocken Books.

Boland, L. (2005). Economics 'In Time' vs Time in Economics: Building Models So that Time Matters. *History of Economic Ideas, 13*(1), 121–132. Retrieved from www. jstor.org/stable/23723204

Bronk, R. (2009). *The Romantic Economist: Imagination in Economics.* Cambridge: Cambridge University Press.

Bronk, R. (2011). Uncertainty, Modelling Monocultures and the Financial Crisis. *Business Economist, 42*(2), 5–18.

Broome, J. (1999). *Ethics Out of Economics.* Cambridge: Cambridge University Press.

Broome, J. (2012). *Climate Matters: Ethics in a Warming World.* New York, NY: W.W. Norton & Company.

Brown, P. (1989). *The World of Late Antiquity: AD 150–750.* New York, NY: W.W. Norton & Company.

Calhoun, C. J. (2012). *The Roots of Radicalism: Tradition, the Public Sphere, and Early Nineteenth-Century Social Movements.* Chicago, IL: University of Chicago Press.

Camerer, C., Babcock, L., Loewenstein, G., and Thaler, R. (1997). Labor Supply of New York City Cabdrivers: One Day at a Time. *The Quarterly Journal of Economics, 112*(2), 407–441. doi:10.1162/003355397555244

Clark, T. J. (2012). For a Left With No Future. *New Left Review, 74.* Retrieved from https://newleftreview.org/II/74/t-j-clark-for-a-left-with-no-future

Cohen, G. A. (2013). Rescuing Conservatism: A Defense of Existing Value. In M. Otsuka (Ed.), *Finding Oneself in the Other.* Princeton, NJ: Princeton University Press.

Crary, J. (2013). *24/7: Late Capitalism and the Ends of Sleep.* London: Verso.

Crawford, M. B. (2015). *The World Beyond Your Head: On Becoming an Individual in an Age of Distraction.* London: Penguin Books.

Eco, U. (1989). *The Open Work.* London: Hutchinson Radius.

Eliot, T. S. (1975). *Selected Prose of T.S. Eliot.* New York, NY: Harcourt Brace Jovanovich.

Eriksen, T. H. (2001). *Tyranny of the Moment Fast and Slow Time in the Information Age.* London: Pluto Press.

Frydman, R., and Goldberg, M. D. (2008). Macroeconomic Theory for a World of Imperfect Knowledge. *Capitalism and Society, 3*(3). doi:10.2202/1932-0213.1046

Gerschlager, C. (2008). *Foolishness and Identity: Amartya Sen and Adam Smith.* DULBEA Working Papers, 3rd ed., Vol. 8, ULB, DULBEA. Retrieved from https://dipot.ulb.ac.be/dspace/bitstream/2013/13590/1/dul-0073.pdf

Gray, J. (2011). *The Immortalization Commission: Science and the Strange Quest to Cheat Death.* London: Allen Lane.

Haldane, A. (2015, February 17). *Growing, Fast and Slow.* Speech presented in University of East Anglia, Norwich.

Hart, O., Shleifer, A., and Vishny, R. W. (1997). The Proper Scope of Government: Theory and an Application to Prisons. *The Quarterly Journal of Economics, 112*(4), 1127–1161. doi:10.1162/003355300555448

Harvey, D. (1989). *The Condition of Postmodernity: An Enquiry Into the Origins of Cultural Change.* Cambridge, MA: Blackwell.

Hazlitt, W. (1999). *Selected Writings.* Oxford: Oxford University Press.

Heaney, S. (2002). *Finders Keepers: Selected Prose 1971–2001.* London: Faber and Faber.

Hodgson, G. M. (2011). The Eclipse of the Uncertainty Concept in Mainstream Economics. *Journal of Economic Issues, 45*(1), 159–176. doi:10.2753/jei0021-3624450109

IPCC. (2001). *Climate Change 2001: The Scientific Basis; Summary for Policymakers and Technical Summary of the Working Group I Report.* Cambridge: Cambridge University Press.

Jameson, F. (2003). The End of Temporality. *Critical Inquiry, 29*(4), 695–718. doi:10.1086/377726

Jameson, F. (2015). The Aesthetics of Singularity. *New Left Review, 92.* Retrieved from https://newleftreview.org/II/92/fredric-jameson-the-aesthetics-of-singularity

Jonas, H. (2001). *The Phenomenon of Life: Toward a Philosophical Biology.* Evanston, IL: Northwestern University Press.

Kahneman, D., and Riis, J. (2005). Living and Thinking About It: Two Perspectives on Life. In N. Baylis, F. A. Huppert, and B. Keverne (Eds.), *The Science of Well-Being.* New York, NY: Oxford University Press.

Kahneman, D., Wakker, P. P., and Sarin, R. (1997). Back to Bentham? Explorations of Experienced Utility. *The Quarterly Journal of Economics, 112*(2), 375–406. doi:10.1162/003355397555235

Keats, J. (2002). *Selected Letters of John Keats* (G. F. Scott, Ed.). Cambridge, MA: Harvard University Press.

Knight, F. H. (1997). *The Ethics of Competition.* Piscataway, NJ: Transaction.

Kristeva, J. (1992). *Black Sun: Depression and Melancholia* (L. S. Roudiez, Trans.). New York, NY: Columbia University Press.

Lachmann, L. M. (1977). Professor Shackle on The Economic Significance of Time. In *Capital, Expectations, and the Market Process.* Kansas City, MO: Sheed Andrews and McMeel.

Lasch, C. (1991). *The Culture of Narcissism: American Life in an Age of Diminishing Expectations.* New York, NY: W.W. Norton & Company.

Lear, J. (2008). *Radical Hope: Ethics in the Face of Cultural Devastation.* Cambridge, MA: Harvard University Press.

MacIntyre, A. C. (2003). *After Virtue: A Study in Moral Theory.* Notre Dame, IN: University of Notre Dame Press.

Marion, J. (2004). *The Crossing of the Visible.* Stanford, CA: Stanford University Press.

Marshall, A. (2009). *Principles of Economics* (8th edition). New York, NY: Cosimo Classics.

Morton, T. (2018). *Being Ecological.* UK: Pelican.

Mulgan, G. (2015). *The Locust and the Bee: Predators and Creators in Capitalism's Future.* Princeton, NJ: Princeton University Press.

Nelson, P. (1970). Information and Consumer Behavior. *Journal of Political Economy, 78*(2), 311–329. Retrieved from www.jstor.org/stable/1830691

Offer, A. (2006). *The Challenge of Affluence: Self-Control and Well-Being in the United States and Britain Since 1950.* New York, NY: Oxford University Press.

O'Neill, J. (1993). *Ecology, Policy and Politics: Human Well-Being and the Natural World.* London: Routledge.

Pocock, J. G. A. (2009). *The Machiavellian Moment Florentine Political Thought and the Atlantic Republican Tradition.* Princeton, NJ: Princeton University Press.

Runciman, D. (2014). *The Confidence Trap: A History of Democracy in Crisis From World War I to the Present.* Princeton, NJ: Princeton University Press.

Scheffler, S. (2010). *Equality and Tradition: Questions of Value in Moral and Political Theory.* New York, NY: Oxford University Press.

Scheffler, S. (2016). *Death and the Afterlife.* New York, NY: Oxford University Press.

Schelling, T. C. (1995). Intergenerational Discounting. *Energy Policy, 23*(4–5), 395–401. doi:10.1016/0301-4215(95)90164-3

Scruton, R. (2012). *Green Philosophy: How to Think Seriously About the Planet*. London: Atlantic.

Sennett, R. (2007). *The Culture of the New Capitalism*. New Haven, CT: Yale University Press.

Shalit, A. D. (2006). *Why Posterity Matters: Environmental Policies and Future Generations*. London: Routledge.

Simmel, G. (1961). *Metropolis and Mental Life*. Chicago, IL: University of Chicago Press.

Skidelsky, R. (2009). *Keynes: The Return of the Master*. New York, NY: Public Affairs.

Stern, N. (2014). Ethics, Equity and the Economics of Climate Change Paper 2: Economics and Politics. *Economics and Philosophy*, 30(3), 445–501. doi:10.1017/s0266267114000303

Streeck, W. (2015). Comment on 'On History and Policy: Time in the Age of Neoliberalism'. *Journal of the Philosophy of History*, 9(1), 33–40. doi:10.1163/18722636-12341289

Streeck, W., and Mitchell, S. (2009). *Complex, Historical, Self-reflexive: Expect the Unexpected!* Working Paper No. 09/15, Max Planck Institute for the Study of Societies.

Thompson, E. P. (1993). *Customs in Common*. London: Penguin Books.

Valéry, P. (1989). *The Outlook for Intelligence* (D. Folliot and J. Mathews, Trans.). Princeton, NJ: Princeton University Press.

Velleman, J. D. (1991). Well-Being and Time. *Pacific Philosophical Quarterly*, 72(1), 48–77. doi:10.1111/j.1468-0114.1991.tb00410.x

Wagner, R. E. (2013). *Mind, Society, and Human Action: Time and Knowledge in a Theory of Social Economy*. London: Routledge.

Weitzman, M. L. (2011). Fat-Tailed Uncertainty in the Economics of Catastrophic Climate Change. *Review of Environmental Economics and Policy*, 5(2), 275–292. Retrieved from https://scholar.harvard.edu/files/weitzman/files/fattaileduncertaintyeconomics.pdf

Zerzan, J. (2002). *Running on Emptiness: The Pathology of Civilization*. Los Angeles, CA: Feral House.

Zerzan, J. (2012). *Future Primitive Revisited*. Port Townsend, WA: Feral House.

10 Civil economy
Re-imagining an ethical economy[1]

A desperate flight from the specific; from all that used to be specific to the human species, rootedness, attachment, heritage, belonging, all now required to give way to the radiant sun of the intermediate, endlessly restless, flexible and detached ego.

(Juvin, 2010, p. 62)

There is nothing common in the capitalist endeavor.

(Fleming, 2015, p. 12)

Water is H2O, hydrogen two parts, oxygen one, but there is a third thing, that makes it water and nobody knows what it is.

(Lawrence, 2013, p. 6710)

10.0 Introduction

The main thesis of this book is that both market economies and economic theory are, in tandem, responsible for our current predicament: a number of convergent and inter-related problems and crises, ranging from the lack of meaning in work and inequality to the erosion of our common world and the possibility of an environmental catastrophe. They are responsible, it has been argued, because the picture of human beings that is represented by theory (rational, self-interested individuals), policies based on that picture and the functioning of actual real-world market economies have engendered a relational crisis.

Both market economies and economic theory have radically altered our understanding of ourselves and time, and distorted how we relate to other beings (human and non-human), places, objects of value and nature. Some of our most pressing socio-economic problems, therefore, can be seen through the prism of relationality: inequality, work and power relations, the decline of solidarity, social capital and the public sector ethos, the prevalence of loneliness and unhappiness[2] and the lack of concern for the future of our planet and its inhabitants.

Given these concerns, the main question this chapter poses is whether we can incorporate a more relational approach into economic theory. Since throughout the book I have been using the terms relationality, sociality and ethical interchangeably this amounts to asking if we can rethink the relation between ethics and economic theory. One possible answer, I suggest, is to draw upon the civil economy approach since it envisions both a more pluralistic account of human motivations and a more capacious notion of 'the good' than standard economic theory with its impoverished view of the individual and its narrow conception of the 'ends' of the economy ('the good').

Before doing so, however, I want to briefly trace, in outline, how we got to this impasse. In section 1 I introduce the notion of 'separation' and how the economy came to be established as a distinct 'realm'. I then note in section 2 how the economic paradigm, particularly from the 1970s onward, came to exert a growing influence on other, non-economic realms of social life. In particular this is an era which sees public policy debates increasingly being framed in economic terms and a growing focus on non-market sources of value (human, social, cultural and cognitive capital). In section 3, I suggest that the growing reach of the market economy and its supporting theory/ideology has led to a reduction of the importance given to political and moral values, as well as to a degradation in the quality of social life. The failure of late capitalism is really twofold: its inability to create wealth has led it to ever more desperate attempts to capture non-market social and ecological 'wealth' with often disastrous and counter-productive consequences; and its notion of abstract wealth is increasingly understood to be a pale shadow of 'the good' (Milbank and Pabst, 2016). In the final section I argue that since these problems stem, at least in part, from a particularly narrow characterization of both the purposes of 'the economy' and of individual economic agents (*homo economicus*), economic theory needs to take on board a more relational/ethical approach.

10.1 A separate science

One of the traditional tensions in modern thought is that between social cohesion, political freedom and wealth creation (Dahrendorf, 1996), or to put it another way, between morality, the polity and the economy – with the each realm having its own set of norms, values and distributive principles. In some sense each realm can be thought to define the limits of the others. For instance, we are quite accustomed to the view that the extent to which market interactions and principles should penetrate overall society is restricted by political and moral considerations. The boundaries between the realms – either in thought or in practice – are not, however, non-negotiable or ahistorically given. Therefore it remains the case, as with other border disputes, that the lines of demarcation are fiercely contested.

Central to this characterization of modernity is the notion of an autonomous, value-free[3] economic "sphere" (Walzer, 2010) and a corresponding 'thin' view of economic agents (who are assumed to be essentially non-relational rational, self-interested individuals).

When Lionel Robbins (1935) claimed that ethics and economics were not in any fundamental sense related to one another, he was summarizing a long line of thought stretching back to at least the 19th century.[4] It was becoming increasingly clear by then that economics could rightfully be considered a separate, albeit inexact science with little understanding of, or perhaps even interest in, normative issues (distribution or the final 'ends' of action).

The separation between ethics and economics in academia should, I think, be seen within the larger context of the separation[5] of ethics, politics and economics in liberal regimes. I think we are deeply ambivalent when it comes to the separation of ethics and economics. On the other hand, we are aware that the 'fragmentation of value' (Nagel, 2015) or a privatized morality (MacIntyre, 1998) is highly problematic. Alasdair Macintyre (1998) writes persuasively about how the lack of a common good in a liberal order prevents us from reflecting on central questions such as what is meant by a good life. This compartmentalization, which is mirrored in academia, means we have to work our way through a disconcerting array of norms, attitudes and roles in different spheres of life: from home to school, and from work to public life. For Macintyre (1998) "a compartmentalized society imposes a fragmented ethics" (p. 236) – and this makes it difficult for us to navigate our way through life.

On the other hand we recognize that a liberal political regime perhaps requires such distinctions or 'fragmentation', for without them looms the spectre of totalitarianism, the false unity of the collective. In fact, it is likely that the impetus behind the genesis of markets, contracts and a market ethos (a paradoxical 'community' of individuals, an asocial sociality) was partly a response to the tensions and conflicts that arise when social and economic exchanges are mediated by community identities. Such transactions might be hierarchical, limited or violent. In contrast, interactions in a market society, though based on a 'weak relational bond' (Bruni, 2012) would at least be formally egalitarian, inclusive and potentially universal.[6]

Of course, it is possible to stress the decline of ecclesiastical authority, the weakening of the moral economy tradition, changes in religious sensibilities[7] and later the Enlightenment (MacIntyre, 2003) as each contributing to the fragmentation. Foucault (2010) is probably correct to state that there is no single reason for this development but the extension of market activity itself must have helped pave the way for the breakdown of any consensus on what the common good might be. The market, as a supposedly natural mechanism, was from the outset held by some to be 'true' or efficient and not a site in which questions of justice or ethics could arise. Such a view has become commonplace today and is echoed by economists[8] and philosophers (Gauthier, 1986) alike. The market is a moral-free zone and the discipline of economics is value-neutral. Ethical considerations are subsequently either relegated to the private sphere (family, friends) or delegated to the state (care, redistribution).

For Foucault (2010) the emergence of *laissez faire* is to be thought of as an *internal* regulation of the police state, as part of the history of the state itself.[9] The market ethos, based on rationality, individuality, interests (or subjective desires), contracts and formal equality established, it was believed, a new and secure foundation to political and economic life.

From the mid-18th century onwards, then, the market comes to be seen as a principle of social organization and not simply as a place that is subject to regulation in the name of some 'higher' good. In this account there is the emergence of an idea, attributed to Adam Smith and one that is destined to gradually become orthodox in mainstream economics – that the amoral, self-interested interactions between individuals do not necessarily lead to anarchy but, instead, to order (Hirschman, 1982; Sahlins, 2008).

So, a market society is not only good because it efficiently allocates resources, maximizes growth and provides opportunities to individuals to satisfy their preferences. Charles Taylor (2007) is quite correct to say that markets are also deemed important because they form an essential component of modern society's social imaginary. The market serves as a metaphor for the peaceable resolution of differences in interests, a way of picturing our relations with one another as ordered, autonomous, peaceful, mutually beneficial[10] and productive. That is, market interactions are important because of the process freedoms they afford (Sen, 1993): the act of choice is itself something to be valued. This idea, too, can be traced back to Adam Smith since one of the points in favour of a market system was, he believed, that it allowed interactions between free and equal individuals. Equal exchange and contracts replace hierarchies/dependencies and status in the old feudal order. The ability to choose what to consume, where to work, and what to sell as an individual, not constrained by a political, moral or communal ordering of 'the good' is held to be both liberating and morally good. Seen in this light 'the economy' is, to paraphrase Charles Taylor (2007), not so much a threat to moral order but, rather, a reconfiguration of it.

10.2 Economic imperialism

In the previous section we saw how markets, with their emphasis on individualism, equality, rights and contracts were perceived to limit social hierarchies, religious dogmatism, and political dominance. The real problem, some would say, arises when market practices, rhetoric and mentalities come to dominate other areas of political and social life. In this section, we very briefly plot the course of this development.

From the late 1970s we have entered a period of neoliberal capitalism[11] or what is often called 'liquid modernity'. The extension of markets into the fabric of social and political life has gone hand in hand with the dominance of the neoclassical paradigm in economics departments. In academic and policy circles in this period, the belief that the neoclassical model is the best way to understand the market and its fluctuations becomes almost unchallenged. Moreover, it also comes to be believed that the model of economic behaviour can be applied to what were formerly considered disparate areas of social life. To use the metaphor of boundaries that we started off with: the discipline of economics becomes a colonizer.

This 'imperialism' is well documented by Lazear (2000), but how did we go from thinking of the market as one of way of conceptualizing our relations in society – one way amongst others – to it becoming a dominant principle? Have we forgotten, Rowan Williams (2010) asks us, that economic activity is only *one* thing amongst many that we do? After all, older economists had thought of political economy as necessarily being only a 'fragment of a greater whole' (Bronk, 2009). It is not clear, for example, that either Edgeworth or Adam Smith thought that economic motivations were applicable beyond a certain range of activities (exchange and trade) or, indeed, that they were the only ones required for a thriving market economy (Sen, 2010).

Given the tendency to abstraction, formalization and 'disembedding' or de-contextualization[12] in economic theory it is perhaps not surprising that the discipline would eventually have such a great influence on the other social sciences (such as political theory and sociology). It could be argued that, paradoxically, the very absence of formal content allows economic theory to be used to understand behaviour across a wide range of subjects, times and places.[13]

In fact, Marshall's 'austere conception' of the discipline was a forerunner of the ambitious contemporary claim that economics is a *universal* science (Collini, Winch and Burrow, 2010). We might profitably read Gary Becker as belonging to this lineage, with his belief that large swathes of human behaviour can be explained by economic theory – and the more recent 'law and economics' (Nussbaum, 1997) movement shares many similar tendencies.[14] Similarly, the advancement of institutional economics and a particular strain of economic history are also best seen in this light (Boldizzoni, 2011). Human behaviour, in any area of life, could therefore be described as 'economic' as long as it could be explained as arising from choices made by rational, self-interested individuals.[15]

It is, however, naive to believe that the domination of any theoretical perspective or discipline comes about solely as the result of its internal coherence or explanatory power.[16] More realistically, it is fair to say that the neoclassical paradigm received a great fillip from actual social, cultural[17] and political changes as privatization, the commodification and corporatization of everyday life, financialization and market ideology all reinforced one another. The very language of politics and ethics thus becomes displaced by the language of markets[18] (Judt, 2010) – at the cost of dissolving the idea of sociality and distorting our understanding of our relationship to people, the world and to time. Nature now becomes a resource or natural capital. Our relations to knowledge, other people and beauty now become human, social and cultural capital.

10.3 Why we need a relational theory

The central story of our times has been built around the belief that the principles enshrined in market economies are fundamental to the way in which we ought to organize society. However, it could be that this story is now unraveling – and for a number of distinct reasons. In the first place, it's not at all clear what is meant by a 'good life' or the 'good society'. As we saw in chapter 1, in earlier times political economists made the argument that markets promoted the 'wealth of nations' or overall utility (happiness). The fragmentation of value alluded to above has made it more difficult to agree on what is meant by 'the good' – both at the individual and the societal level. Economic growth for its own sake now seems increasingly futile[19] or at least unsustainable and there is little agreement on what is meant by happiness[20] or whether market economies in fact promote genuine human flourishing.

Secondly, since the financial crisis there has been intense speculation as to whether at the heart of the problem besetting modern societies there is not simply a failure of markets (Hutton and Schneider, 2008) but a deeper failure of values and judgement, a disregard for fairness and responsibility. Market societies, founded on the non-relational *homo economicus*, esteem competitiveness, contracts, private property, the pursuit of private interests, calculation and the reduction of values to the common denominator of money. This has a deleterious effect on values such as honesty, trust, respect, solidarity, sympathy,[21] accountability, a public spirit ethos and civic virtue.[22]

Thirdly, it should briefly be noted that market societies can often produce vast inequalities in income and assets. But it is hard to imagine a flourishing civil society and sociality amidst significantly large inequalities within a population. The ramifications of such developments are profound for it may be that greater economic equality and economic democracy are necessary for political equality, the very foundations of civil society (Dahl, 1990).

A fourth way in which a market culture and economy can be inimical to sociality is their restructuring our attitudes to time and place. Since E.P. Thompson's (1993) brilliant work on how capitalism alters our perception of time other social scientists have added to our understanding of the process by which this comes about (Adam, 2003). Bauman (2000) has argued that the culture of late capitalism has led to the "untying of the economy from its traditional political, ethical, and cultural entanglements" (p. 4). This, arguably, prevents the accumulation of experiences from being shaped into a narrative (Agamben, 1999; MacIntyre, 2003) and whittles away time for reflection on ultimate purposes; it also hinders the desire to pass on legacies to children, and to save for the future, with an excessive focus on 'me', hedonism and instant gratification (Offer, 2006).

In addition, the culture of late capitalism, with its emphasis on social mobility, unrestricted freedom of choice, individualism, zero-hours contracts and flexible labour may be both undermining our attachment to specific places as well as disrupting the web of relations that gives us a sense of continuity and duration.[23] The idea of relationality and common goods, based at least in part[24] on the commonality of language, history, as well as shared memories and culture (Rawls, 2001), have been eroded. Which means that the crucibles in which some of our civil attitudes -responsibility, solidarity and mutual reciprocity – are formed and fostered have been replaced by an abstract 'space of flows' and private notions of 'the good'.

Finally, any reconceptualization of how market economies and economic theory can incorporate a relational/ethical perspective will have to look at the attitudes and values tied to work. It has been persuasively that since the 1970s there has been an attempt to incorporate 'living labour' (*bios*) into the logic of productivity. Some of our fundamental human capacities and competencies are increasingly now seen as a source of innovation, creativity and profits to firms. Thinking, remembering and caring are, for example, now seen as important intellectual, affective and cultural capabilities that can potentially generate value[25] – if they can be 'enclosed' by the firm.

It is important to realize that these capacities are ultimately connected to our *social* character: they are made possible by a prior set of existing relations[26] and they are themselves relational in nature: we care for other people and non-human beings; we speak of and with other human beings; we trust strangers; and we can think together (see chapter 2). In other words, "Loving, like knowing, is something we do only with others" (O'Donovan, 2002, p. 19).

However, if the source of value is essentially social, part of what Peter Fleming (2015) calls 'the commons', then market economies are faced with an irreducible tension or contradiction (as Polanyi saw all those years ago). For the more pervasive biopower becomes, the more work extends into the lifeworld, the more genuine sociality and autonomy[27] are undermined. In other words, social capital is an oxymoron because the social is destroyed when it is manipulated to serve the purposes of capitalist enterprises (including the neoliberal university). Moreover, the idea that the individual is himself a micro-capitalist enterprise – an idea precipitated by human capital theory (Fleming, 2017) – is leading to stress, debt, insecurity, overwork[28] and uncertainty in the modern workplace. Since market economies in late capitalism are associated with global competition, short-termism, rapidly evolving skills, the decline of trade unions, and the threat of automation they are leading to social isolation and the hollowing out of the idea of a coherent self – and to what Richard Sennett (2007) calls the "specter of uselessness"? Well, might our era be one of superfluous – and therefore alienated, angry and frustrated – men and women (Monbiot, 2017).

Putting life (*bios*) to work is equally problematic for economic theory. Despite the proliferation of metrics and the development of an audit culture in knowledge and service industries since the 1980s, the problem remains that relationality cannot be measured, or represented in either commodity or monetary form; nor can it be theorized in a paradigm whose core outlook is fundamentally shaped by methodological individualism.

10.4   The civil economy

Given that some of the problems associated with market economies described above stem from an overly restrictive and unrealistic non-relational theoretical view of economic relations, and from an impoverished concept of 'the good', is there a way of incorporating a relational/ethical approach into our theorization of economic[29] interactions? The parsimonious nature of the foundational assumptions of neoclassical economics (Hirschman, 1985) is now well known. In recent times criticism of the paradigm's narrowness has been added to by behavioural economists. My aim, however, is to highlight other strands of criticism, drawing on what might be called a 'moral economy' tradition – illuminated by Amartya Sen (2013) – and a civil economy tradition.

In a moral economy approach economic behaviour is not exclusively driven by asocial self-interested individuals and welfare is not the only goal. Instead, market participants can be influenced by a whole set of motivational factors, ranging from moral/social norms and strong reciprocity[30] to altruism, obligations and commitment (Sen, 1977). Individuals can be – and often are – concerned about fairness in the economy (and equality and solidarity within society). As economists we should not, therefore, necessarily think of the maximization of an individual's free choice[31] or his individual welfare as the only considerations worthy of our attention.

To enter into a genuine relation, then, requires a degree of openness to the world and to other people, a relation that is not characterized by possession or confrontation. It may also require of us an acknowledgement that there is no stable 'I' prior to our relations and that to connect with others can involve a relinquishing of something of agency (Ingold, 2016).

If we move away from the self-interest assumption, however, and include 'other-regarding' preferences in our analysis we do so at the cost of assuming that there is an element of 'bestowal' (O'Donovan, 2016) involved such that agents can only express these 'social preferences' by sacrificing some resources (goods or utility). For example, this is the standard way in which economics conceptualizes altruism, gratuity, 'strong reciprocity' and commitment.

The difficulty, then, is to picture an arrangement of mutually beneficial exchange having social and moral content. Bruni and Sugden (2008) maintain that such an orientation is indeed possible if we draw on a civil economy tradition. Under this approach individuals are neither exclusively self-regarding nor 'other-regarding'. Instead, individuals are motivated by a sense of fellow-feeling, or fraternity, which means that they enter a transaction with the express motivation that it will be mutually beneficial.

In Zamagni's (2012) analysis fraternity and the common good are at the heart of the civil economy approach. Those features are intimately related since the person – rather than the isolated individual – is by definition or nature a relational subject who is interested in common goods (and the common good). As Rowan Williams (2012) has acutely remarked, a perspective that lays emphasis on 'the person' implies a commitment to both dependence and independence. In fact, it may be that at least some forms of dependence are necessary if we are to flourish as persons.[32] And just as our own selfhood is inextricably bound with our relationship to other people and our habitat, similarly we are not be able to conceive of our own good without taking into account the common good. Common goods are, therefore, produced, enjoyed and reflexively understood *as good*, by relational subjects (Donati, 2014).

The idea of the common good deviates from the standard economic perspective in which the pursuit by each individual of her private good that leads to the public good. Charles Taylor (1997) is right to point out that this notion of the public good is still individualist in nature and more akin to a convergence of private interests and private goods. This is a distinct notion from the common good, as understood in the medieval tradition and which can succinctly be summarized as 'the good of each and all' which is achieved together. The common good, therefore, embodies both a substantive notion of 'the good' – integral human development (Schindler, 2010) – and the idea of inclusivity ('for all').

One concept that can help us make sense of this perspective is 'the household'.[33] It should be noted that the original meaning of the word 'economy' was house-hold management. Despite the obvious negative connotations associated with 'the household' (hierarchical, exclusionary, privative, etc.) there are some features of the concept that make it quite appealing, namely: a life lived in common, a level of stability that allows each member to flourish over time and a place where the vulnerable are cared for.

The question arises, however, as to whether this model of our relations with one another can accommodate values that we take for granted and that are in some sense may seem at odds with the classical definition of 'the household'; values such as openness, dynamism, equality, autonomy, pluralism and innovativeness. How do we reconcile, for example, freedom of choice with relationality when the latter may entail a curtailment of our *individual* freedoms? (Zamagni, 2008).

Economic theory and market economies have simultaneously lead to an eclipse of the idea of 'the common good'. The dominant idea of 'the good' in market economies is preference satisfaction and this makes thinking about the common good difficult. It is not only that our desires are less likely to converge with other people's desires, or that individual preference satisfaction is a poor substitute for a determinate or objective notion of the individual good. The problem is, rather, that the notion of the *common* good is undermined for it requires that individuals work together towards the 'good of all' and that each person both understands and enjoys their engagement in promoting the things they commonly value (Skidelsky, 2008).

Similarly, because markets and economic theory focus on autonomous and self-interested individuals they are inimical to the idea of the person. Just as the common good cannot be reduced to the summation of individual goods (since an aggregation implies trade-offs) a community is something over and beyond a collectivity of individuals. And the two concepts – 'the person' and 'the common good' – are themselves related for as Maritain (1966) writes, "The common good is common because it is received in persons . . . a good received and communicated" (p. 49). Or, to put it another way, community is defined by the sharing of 'goods' since a 'we' is constituted and sustained over time in relation to common goods. The quality of *our* attachments is the quality of *our* understanding.

10.5   Conclusion

Without a shared culture to provide a common background of language, prac-tices, institutions, lifestyle and understandings how, it is often asked, can we form the notion of the common good. And yet the recovery of the concept is a vital task today given that some of the major problems we face today are inextricably linked with our lack of a common perspective: the erosion of our cultural, social and natural commons (Žižek, 2009). The continued enclosure or the 'privatization' of the commons is a process that continues to haunt us, even after the demise of Communism.

It is still possible to realize, however, that the common meal (Hirschman, 1996) or the image of us sitting around a table (Arendt, 1998) serve as important and powerful metaphors for how to think about how we should organize our societies. Both images incorporate the idea of plurality and individuality, dependence and independence; and both suggest a common purpose.

The civil economy approach I have outlined here (like the idea of team reasoning, Etzioni's (1990) 'I-We' perspective and the notion of sympathy) can help us imagine a more relational economy since it entails us thinking of, with and for the other. Politically, it offers a 'third way' that breaks free from the old dichotomies of a narrow, atomistic, disembedded individualism on the one hand, and an all-subsuming, rigidly defined and hierarchical collectivity on the other.[34]

Much work still needs to be done to get an idea of what kind of institutions can support civility, sociability and our profoundly human desire for conviviality. Our only hope is that despite all of our differences and conflicts we may now finally be beginning to realize that our shared ground experiences (Nussbaum, 1988) and our ability to understand and empathize with people from very different cultures warrants some form of optimistic thinking. If we reject the assumptions underpinning *homo economicus* and accept that we are by nature social beings, then we can still work to solve our common problems together.

Notes

1 This chapter draws upon (Mir, 2015).
2 See Bruni (2008) for the importance of genuine sociality.
3 As we saw in chapter 1, it is not immediately clear whether (or to what extent) the maximal wealth or overall utility generated by the economy is the same thing as 'the good'. Moreover, since at least the 1930s economics has prided itself on being a positive, and therefore value-free, science. It is not surprising, therefore, that there's been a disappearance of welfare economics from textbooks and research work (Atkinson, 2001).
4 Another illustrious economist from an earlier generation, Alfred Marshall, could write of the need to take into account 'ethical forces' but for practical purposes these were not central to his economic analysis.
5 In fact, we're quite accustomed to a whole range of binaries: public/private, scared/profane, culture/nature and work/leisure. On the importance of Adam Smith's dualistic perspective for the founding of modern political economy see the insightful work of Pabst (2011).
6 For economists like Greif (2000) it is the transition from community based systems to generalized trust, individualistic cultures and formal institutions that explains why some countries developed and others did not.
7 For the latter see Tawney (1926) and Bruni (2012).
8 Hayek's influential views are discussed in Finn (2006).
9 This point is echoed by Hirschman (1978) in his discussion of the relation between capital flight and governance.
10 Mutually beneficial even though there is mutual indifference and no intention to benefit any other transacting party.
11 I do not draw a distinction between a market economy and capitalism even though some have argued it is an important one. The former, it is claimed, is actually well represented by economic theory since it is the domain of interaction between

small-scale, perfectly competitive firms under conditions of certainty and perfect information. And on the demand side we still tend to think of transactions through the prism of exchange theory, as if there were complete and enforceable contracts between the relatively equal, good willed and well-informed 'brewer and baker' of Adam Smith. Capitalism, on the other hand, is exploitative and not overly concerned about perfect competition, equality or even the production of value as long as profits are there to be made (Boltanski and Chiapello, 2007). Real-world industrial and post-industrial economies, however, have rarely conformed to the theoretical picture in which debt, power, time and uncertainty play little role. Crucially, *homo economicus* (a rational, self-interested individual) is central to both the theoretical representation of market economies and to capitalism (real-world market economies).

12 It is interesting to note that Rawls's influential work continues with the assumption that individuals are self-interested; the thought experiment from which he derives his principles of justice depends on an abstract notion of individuality since under the 'veil of ignorance' personal identities are irrelevant. See Rawls (1985).

13 The removal of psychology and ethics from the discipline (Bruni and Sugden, 2007) cannot be discounted, a point hinted at by Sen (2013) who acutely notes that modern utility theory is remarkably shorn of content, thus allowing it to be utilized in explaining a wide range of social behaviour. This shift is reflected in economic theory as economics textbooks increasingly discuss 'the market' (in formal, ahistorical terms) rather than specific markets with their own cultural and institutional features. See Rodgers (2011).

14 The proliferation of economic analyses of the law and the emergence and dominance of rational expectations from the 1970s onwards has arguably resulted in a "narrowing down of institutional society into world-pictures of isolated individuals" (Rodgers, 2011, p. 73).

15 Public policy in this period is dominated by a cynical view of human nature, a restatement of the older public choice theory of economists like Buchanan: economic agents – public servants, managers, policy makers, politicians and 'consumers' – are all at heart 'knaves', self-interested rational maximizers (Le Grand, 2013).

16 On the influence key thinkers and think tanks have had in promoting market fundamentalism see Mirowski (2014) and Klein (2015).

17 By the 1990s, it is argued, contemporary culture was devoid of a common ground and had taken on a "decentered, fragmentary, surface-obsessed, patchwork character" (Rodgers, 2011, pp. 157–158). The lack of a stable identity in late capitalism is mirrored in economic theory since we typically only consider abstract individuals. When identity does play a role it is a mere choice or preference. That is, social identity may enhance our 'identity utility' but it still does so in the context of being a mere argument in an *individual's* utility function.

18 On the importance of the idea of freedom to the neoliberal turn see Harvey (2011).

19 The futility of a laboring activity that is only related to bodily survival and consumption, rather than to the making of durable objects ('work') was recognized by Adam Smith (see Arendt, 1998).

20 Even on the narrow interpretation that equates happiness with subjective utility it is not clear that affluent societies are getting any happier (Layard, 2006). In the happiness literature this is known as the 'Easterlin paradox' (Skidelsky and Skidelsky, 2012). Economic theory doesn't offer much help either since utility is not related to a substantive notion of 'the good' (Broome, 1999). Since theory pays scant attention to welfare economics and typically avoids questions of distribution (inequality, for example), it offers little guidance on what the social good is. Even

when it does, it usually retains its individualistic bias and therefore has little to say about genuine sociality or relationality.

21 Market economies can seriously incapacitate our imaginative lives – how we imagine, and empathize with, the lives of others (Williams, 2012).

22 The argument here is that both market economies and economic theory promote a non-relational understanding of the individual and 'the good' with negative consequences for the fabric of social life and the existence of common goods. This in itself is bad but it also ultimately undermines the possibility of capitalism reproducing itself.

23 John Berger writes about duration with great profundity. He writes, "No social value any longer underwrites the time of consciousness" (Berger, 1984, p. 12).

24 In the next section I will argue that commonality is best not thought of as simply the possession of shared characteristics, as in a natural community. But it's also not political as commonly understood. For the coming community commonality is not the unity of a people (represented by the Leviathan) that arises as a response to fear (Virno, 2004). It is the movement to a common understanding, and care of, an attentiveness to the common objects of love.

25 It is no wonder that in this period economic theory has increasingly emphasized the importance of immaterial labour, human, social and cultural capital to economic growth.

26 On the link between reasoning and a 'given' language, community or relationality, see MacIntyre (2002). As Sandburg (1970) says, "Something began me and it had no beginning" (p. 589).

27 We do not have to completely agree with the idea that the pre-modern person actually had a richer individuality (Vodolazkin, 2017; Maritain, 1938) than us. It does appear, however, that the kind of freedom fostered by market societies is either morphing into compulsive behaviours or is only made possible by greater bureaucratic oversight (Graeber, 2015). The lack of autonomy in modern societies was one of the main themes of Ivan Illich's (1978) work.

28 This *qualitative* notion of 'overwork' is intimately related to growing sense of work being pointless (Fleming, 2017) and to our earlier discussion of scarcity (chapter 1).

29 I say 'economic' rather than 'market' because the latter hardly seems to be possible without private property, contracts and the pursuit of profit. 'Oeconomy', on the other hand, is a more capacious concept and can plausibly accommodate the commons, pacts and gift exchanges, as well as the pursuit of goals other than pecuniary returns. I do not, however, elaborate upon the precise organizational forms in which a relational view might be sustained beyond saying that it will of necessity involve intermediate institutions (Pabst, 2015).

30 Strong reciprocity indicates that people are willing to help others who have helped them even if this entails a cost to themselves (i.e. even if it goes against the dictates of rational self-interest). For an extensive survey, see Gintis, Bowles, Boyd and Fehr (2005).

31 Keat (2012) has noted that markets may not necessarily be moral-free zones because they involve voluntary transactions between free and equal agents. Within a liberal approach, freedom is itself a substantive good. In addition, Marshall and Bottomore (1992) argue that market economies have fostered social integration and civil life by enhancing the spread of material enjoyment and the social right to it.

32 MacIntyre (2002) writes, "We cannot have a practically adequate understanding of our own good, of our own flourishing, apart from and independently of that whole set of social relationships in which we have found our place" (pp. 107–108).

33 On the history of the idea, see Booth (1994), Swedberg (2011) and Dupré (1993).

34 Since both the market and the state are impersonal, they weaken the sense of attachment to specific people, places and common goods, which is at the root of our notion of relationality and the social.

Bibliography

Adam, B. (2003). When Time Is Money: Contested Rationalities of Time in the Theory and Practice of Work. *Theoria: A Journal of Social and Political Theory, 102,* 94–125. Retrieved from www.jstor.org/stable/41791393

Agamben, G. (1999). *The Man Without Content.* Stanford, CA: Stanford University Press.

Arendt, H. (1998). *The Human Condition.* Chicago, IL: University of Chicago Press.

Atkinson, A. B. (2001). The Strange Disappearance of Welfare Economics. *Kyklos, 54*(2 and 3), 193–206. doi:10.1111/1467-6435.00148

Bauman, Z. (2000). *Liquid Modernity.* Malden, MA: Polity Press.

Berger, J. (1984). *And Our Faces, My Heart, Brief as Photos.* New York, NY: Vintage International.

Boldizzoni, F. (2011). *The Poverty of Clio: Resurrecting Economic History.* Princeton, NJ: Princeton University Press.

Boltanski, L., and Chiapello, E. (2007). *The New Spirit of Capitalism.* London: Verso.

Booth, W. (1994). Household and Market: On the Origins of Moral Economic Philosophy. *The Review of Politics, 56*(2), 207–235. Retrieved from www.jstor.org/stable/1407816

Bronk, R. (2009). *The Romantic Economist: Imagination in Economics.* Cambridge: Cambridge University Press.

Broome, J. (1999). *Ethics Out of Economics.* Cambridge: Cambridge University Press.

Bruni, L. (2008). *Capabilities and Happiness* (F. Comim and M. Pugno, Eds.). Oxford: Oxford University Press.

Bruni, L. (2012). *The Wound and the Blessing: Economics, Relationships, and Happiness.* Hyde Park, NY: New City Press.

Bruni, L., and Sugden, R. (2007). The Road Not Taken: How Psychology was Removed From Economics, and How It Might Be Brought Back. *The Economic Journal, 117*(516), 146–173. doi:10.1111/j.1468-0297.2007.02005.x

Bruni, L., and Sugden, R. (2008). Fraternity: Why the Market Need Not Be a Morally Free Zone. *Economics and Philosophy, 24*(1), 35–64. doi:10.1017/s0266267108001661

Collini, S., Winch, D., and Burrow, J. (2010). *That Noble Science of Politics: A Study in Nineteenth-Century Intellectual History.* Cambridge: Cambridge University Press.

Dahl, R. A. (1990). *A Preface to Economic Democracy.* Berkeley, CA: University of California Press.

Dahrendorf, R. (1996). Economic Opportunity, Civil Society and Political Liberty. *Development and Change, 27*(2), 229–249. doi:10.1111/j.1467-7660.1996.tb00587.x

Donati, P. (2014). Relational Goods and Their Subjects: The Ferment of a New Civil Society and Civil Democracy. *Recerca. Revista de pensament i anàlisi., 14,* 19–46. doi:10.6035/recerca14.2

Dupré, L. (1993). The Common Good and the Open Society. *The Review of Politics, 55*(4), 687–712. Retrieved from www.jstor.org/stable/1407612

Etzioni, A. (1990). *Moral Dimension: Toward a New Economics.* New York, NY: Free Press.

Finn, D. (2006). *The Moral Ecology of Markets: Assessing Claims About Markets and Justice*. New York, NY: Cambridge University Press.

Fleming, P. (2015). *Resisting Work: The Corporatization of Life and Its Discontents*. Philadelphia, PA: Temple University Press.

Fleming, P. (2017). *The Death of Homo Economicus: Work, Debt and the Myth of Endless Accumulation*. London: Pluto Press.

Foucault, M. (2010). *The Birth of Biopolitics: Lectures at the Collège de France, 1978–1979* (G. Burchell, Trans.; A. I. Davidson, Ed.). Basingstoke: Palgrave Macmillan.

Gauthier, D. P. (1986). *Morals By Agreement*. Oxford: Clarendon Press.

Gintis, H., Bowles, S., Boyd, R., and Fehr, E. (2005). Moral Sentiments and Material Interests: Origins, Evidence, and Consequences. In H. Gintis, S. Bowles, R. Boyd, and E. Fehr (Eds.), *Moral Sentiments and Material Interests: The Foundations of Cooperation in Economic Life* (pp. 3–40). Cambridge, MA: MIT Press.

Graeber, D. (2015). *The Utopia of Rules: On Technology, Stupidity, and the Secret Joys of Bureaucracy*. Brooklyn, NY: Melville House.

Greif, A. (2000). Impersonal Exchange and the Origin of Markets: From the Community Responsibility System to Individual Legal Responsibility in Pre-modern Europe. In M. Aoki and Y. Hayami (Eds.), *Communities and Markets in Economic Development* (pp. 3–41). New York, NY: Oxford University Press.

Harvey, D. (2011). *A Brief History of Neoliberalism*. Oxford: Oxford University Press.

Hirschman, A. O. (1978). Exit, Voice, and the State. *World Politics, 31*(1), 90–107. doi:10.2307/2009968

Hirschman, A. O. (1982). Rival Interpretations of Market Society: Civilizing, Destructive, or Feeble? *Journal of Economic Literature, 20*(4), 1463–1484. Retrieved from www.jstor.org/stable/2724829

Hirschman, A. O. (1985). Against Parsimony: Three Easy Ways of Complicating Some Categories of Economic Discourse. *Economics and Philosophy, 1*(01), 7–21. doi:10.1017/s0266267100001863

Hirschman, A. O. (1996). Melding the Public and Private Spheres: Taking Commensality Seriously. *Critical Review: A Journal of Politics and Society, 10*(4), 533–550. doi:10.1080/08913819608443437

Hutton, W., and Schneider, P. (2008). *The Failure of Market Failure Towards a 21st Century Keynesianism*. Provocation 08, Working Paper, NESTA.

Illich, I. (1978). *Toward a History of Needs*. New York, NY: Pantheon Books.

Ingold, T. (2016). On Human Correspondence. *Journal of the Royal Anthropological Institute, 23*(1), 9–27. doi:10.1111/1467-9655.12541

Judt, T. (2010). *Ill Fares the Land*. New York, NY: Penguin Books.

Juvin, H. (2010). *The Coming of the Body*. London: Verso.

Keat, R. (2012). *Market Economies as Moral Economies: The Ethical Character of Market Institutions*. Report, University of Edinburgh.

Klein, N. (2015). *This Changes Everything: Capitalism vs. The Climate*. New York, NY: Simon & Schuster.

Lawrence, D. H. (2013). *Delphi Complete Works of D. H. Lawrence (Illustrated)*. Hastings: Delphi Classics.

Layard, R. (2006). *Happiness: Lessons From a New Science*. London: Penguin Books.

Lazear, E. P. (2000). Economic Imperialism. *The Quarterly Journal of Economics, 115*(1), 99–146. doi:10.1162/003355300554683

Le Grand, J. (2013). *Motivation, Agency, and Public Policy: Of Knights and Knaves, Pawns and Queens*. Oxford: Oxford University Press.

MacIntyre, A. C. (1998). *The MacIntyre Reader* (K. Knight, Ed.). Notre Dame, IN: University of Notre Dame Press.

MacIntyre, A. C. (2002). *Dependent Rational Animals: Why Human Beings Need the Virtues*. Chicago, IL: Open Court.

MacIntyre, A. C. (2003). *After Virtue: A Study in Moral Theory*. Notre Dame, IN: University of Notre Dame Press.

Maritain, J. (1938). *True Humanism*. New York, NY: C. Scribner's Sons.

Maritain, J. (1966). *The Person and the Common Good*. Notre Dame, IN: University of Notre Dame Press.

Marshall, T., and Bottomore, T. (1992). *Citizenship and Social Class*. London: Pluto Press. doi:10.2307/j.ctt18mvns1

Milbank, J., and Pabst, A. (2016). *The Politics of Virtue: Post-Liberalism and the Human Future*. London: Rowman & Littlefield International.

Mir, K. (2015). Civil Economy: Re-imagining an Ethical Economy and the Implications for Citizenship. In H. Bashir and P. W. Gray (Eds.), *Deconstructing Global Citizenship: Political, Cultural, and Ethical Perspectives*. Lanham, MD: Lexington Books.

Mirowski, P. (2014). *Never Let a Serious Crisis Go to Waste: How Neoliberalism Survived the Financial Meltdown*. London: Verso.

Monbiot, G. (2017). *Out of the Wreckage: A New Politics in the Age of Crisis*. London: Verso.

Nagel, T. (2015). The Fragmentation of Values. In *Mortal Questions*. Cambridge: Cambridge University Press.

Nussbaum, M. C. (1988). Non-Relative Virtues: An Aristotelian Approach. *Midwest Studies in Philosophy, 13*(1), 32–53. doi:10.1111/j.1475-4975.1988.tb00111.x

Nussbaum, M. C. (1997). Flawed Foundations: The Philosophical Critique of (A Particular Type of) Economics. *The University of Chicago Law Review, 64*(4), 1197–1214.

O'Donovan, O. (2002). *Common Objects of Love: Moral Reflection and the Shaping of Community*. Grand Rapids, MI: W.B. Eerdmans.

O'Donovan, O. (2016, December 6). Communicating the Good: The Politics and Ethics of 'The Common Good'. *ABC Religion and Ethics*. Retrieved from www.abc.net.au/religion/articles/2016/12/06/4587889.htm

Offer, A. (2006). *The Challenge of Affluence: Self-Control and Well-Being in the United States and Britain Since 1950*. New York, NY: Oxford University Press.

Pabst, A. (2011). From Civil to Political Economy: Adam Smith's Theological Debt. In P. Oslington (Ed.), *Adam Smith as Theologian*. New York, NY: Routledge.

Pabst, A. (2015). Prosperity and Justice for All: Why Solidarity and Fraternity Are Key to an Efficient, Ethical Economy. In A. Q. Curzio and G. Marseguerra (Eds.), *Solidarity as a "Social Value" Paradigms for a Good Society*. Città del Vaticano: Libreria Editrice Vaticana.

Rawls, J. (1985). Justice as Fairness: Political Not Metaphysical. *Philosophy & Public Affairs, 14*(3), 223–251. Retrieved from www.jstor.org/stable/2265349

Rawls, J. (2001). *The Law of Peoples With The Idea of Public Reason Revisited*. Cambridge, MA: Harvard University Press.

Robbins, L. (1935). *An Essay on the Nature and Significance of Economic Science*. London: MacMillan and Company.

Rodgers, D. T. (2011). *Age of Fracture*. Cambridge, MA: Belknap Press of Harvard University Press.

Sahlins, M. D. (2008). *The Western Illusion of Human Nature.* Chicago, IL: Prickly Paradigm Press.

Sandburg, C. (1970). *The Complete Poems of Carl Sandburg* (revised and expanded ed.). London: Harcourt Inc.

Schindler, D. L. (2010). The Anthropological Vision of Caritas in Veritae in Light of Economic and Cultural. *Communio: International Catholic Review, 37*(4).

Sen, A. K. (1977). Rational Fools: A Critique of the Behavioral Foundations of Economic Theory. *Philosophy & Public Affairs, 6*(4), 317–344. Retrieved from www.jstor.org/stable/2264946

Sen, A. K. (1993). Markets and Freedoms: Achievements and Limitations of the Market Mechanism in Promoting Individual Freedoms. *Oxford Economic Papers, 45*(4), New Series, 519–541. Retrieved from www.jstor.org/stable/2663703

Sen, A. K. (2010). Adam Smith and the Contemporary World. *Erasmus Journal for Philosophy and Economics, 3*(1), 50–67. doi:10.23941/ejpe.v3i1.39

Sen, A. K. (2013). *On Ethics and Economics.* Malden, MA: Blackwell.

Sennett, R. (2007). *The Culture of the New Capitalism.* New Haven, CT: Yale University Press.

Skidelsky, E. (2008, September 28). The Return of Goodness. *Prospect Magazine.* Retrieved from www.prospectmagazine.co.uk/magazine/revival-of-virtue-ethics

Skidelsky, R., and Skidelsky, E. (2012). *How Much Is Enough?: Money and the Good Life.* New York, NY: Other Press.

Swedberg, R. (2011). *The Household Economy: A Complement or Alternative to the Market Economy?* Working Paper No. 58, Center for the Study of Economy and Society, pp. 1–39.

Tawney, R. H. (1926). *Religion and the Rise of Capitalism.* New York, NY: Harcourt, Brace & Company.

Taylor, C. (1997). *Philosophical Arguments.* Cambridge, MA: Harvard University Press.

Taylor, C. (2007). *Modern Social Imaginaries.* Durham, NC: Duke University Press.

Thompson, E. P. (1993). *Customs in Common.* London: Penguin Books.

Virno, P. (2004). *A Grammar of the Multitude: For an Analysis of Contemporary Forms of Life.* Cambridge, MA: MIT Press.

Vodolazkin, E. (2017, June). The Age of Concentration. *First Things.* Retrieved from www.firstthings.com/article/2017/06/the-age-of-concentration

Walzer, M. (2010). *Spheres of Justice: A Defense of Pluralism and Equality.* New York, NY: Basic Books.

Williams, R. (2010). Theology and Economics: Two Different Worlds? *Anglican Theological Review, 92*(4), 607–615.

Williams, R. (2012, October 1). *The Person and the Individual: Human Dignity, Human Relationships and Human Limits.* Lecture presented at The Fifth Theos Lecture in Methodist Central Hall, Westminster.

Zamagni, S. (2008). Reciprocity, Civil Economy, Common Good. In M. S. Archer and P. Donati (Eds.), *Pursuing the Common Good: How Solidarity and Subsidiarity Can Work Together.* Vatican City: Pontifical Academy of Social Sciences.

Zamagni, S. (2012, February 20). *Imagining a Civil Economy.* Lecture presented in The Margaret Beaufort Institute of Theology, Cambridge.

Žižek, S. (2009). How to Begin From the Beginning. *New Left Review, 57*, 43–55. Retrieved from https://newleftreview.org/II/57/slavoj-zizek-how-to-begin-from-the-beginning

Index